Beyond the Cheers

SUNY series on Sport, Culture, and Social Relations

Cheryl L. Cole and Michael A. Messner, Editors

Beyond the Cheers

Race as Spectacle in College Sport

C. Richard King
and
Charles Fruehling Springwood

State University of New York Press

Published by
State University of New York Press, Albany

For information, address State University of New York Press,
State University Plaza, Albany, N.Y., 12246

Production by Michael Haggett
Marketing by Patrick Durocher

Library of Congress Cataloging-in-Publication Data

King, C. Richard, 1968–
    Beyond the cheers : race as spectacle in college sport / C. Richard King
and Charles Fruehling Springwood.
        p. cm.—(SUNY series on sport, culture, and social relations)
    Includes bibliographical references and index.
    ISBN 0-7914-5005-8 (alk. paper)—ISBN 0-7914-5006-6 (pkb. : alk. paper)
    1. Discrimination in sports—United States.   2. College sports—United
States.   I. Springwood, Chalres Fruehling.   II. Title.   III. Series.

GV706.32.K52 2001
796.04'3'08900973—dc21   00-054797

10 9 8 7 6 5 4 3 2 1

We dedicate this book to our children,
Abigail and Ellory Gilliland-King
and Jacob and Josua Springwood,
with the hope that their future will be
more just, equitable, and enlightened.

Contents

Acknowledgments

It is too easy to forget the many people and relations who make scholarship possible. Here we want to pause briefly to remind ourselves and our readership of the countless individuals who gave their time, ideas, and expertise. We express our deep gratitude to our families, friends, colleagues, and students for their contributions and sacrifices.

We have been lucky throughout the writing of this book to work with talented editors. The enthusiasm of Cheryl Cole and Michael Messner, the series editors, was critical in pushing this project toward its completion. And we are grateful also for the patience and guidance of one-time SUNY Press acquisitions editor Dale Cotton, and SUNY production editor Michael Haggett.

We owe much to numerous individuals, whose unique efforts greatly improved *Race as Spectacle in College Sport*. Although we cannot reconstruct the full list, we wish to thank the following people for their advice, encouragement, and ideas: Shari Addonizio, Teddy Amoloza, Jim Anderson, Marsha Brofka, Edward Bruner, Paul Bushnell, Karen Conner, Catherine Davids, Norman K. Denzin, Gerald Ensley, Irv Epstein, Robert Eurich, Brenda Farnell, Allan Hanson, Suzan Shown Harjo, Patti Hartman, Ginna Husting, Ishgooda, Alisa Ittner, Abby Jahiel, Kevin Karpiak, Bill Kelleher, Harvey Klevar, Lyle Lockwood, Tom Lutze, Shana Marie Basmarion Miller, Patra Noonan, Mwenda Ntarngai, Anthony Paredes, Chris Prendergast, David Prochaska, Debbie Reese, Bob Rinehart, George Rundblad, Joseph Schneider, April Schultz, Jim Sikora, David Sansing, Jim Stanlaw, Rose Stremlau, Lori Stanley, Ellen Staurowsky, Synthia Sydnor, Sally Thomason, and Mike Weis.

We have benefited from generous institutional support as well. The Mellon Center at Illinois Wesleyan University awarded Charles

Springwood an Artistic and Scholarly Development Grant, and the Humanities Center at Drake University provided financial assistance for this volume. The librarians at both universities, particularly Sue Stroyan, Kris Vogel, and Bruce Chamberlin, were invaluable. And editorial assistant Andrea Wyant offered key support in the preparation of this manuscript.

The authors are grateful to SUNY Press and Cheryl Cole, Michael Messner, and John Loy for permission to print our chapter, "Kill the Indians, Save the Chief": Native American Mascots and Imperial Identities. This chapter was originally accepted for publication in *Exercising Power: The Making and Re-making of the Body*, C. Cole, M. Messner, and J. Loy (eds.). This SUNY collection is forthcoming.

The authors are grateful to the University of Nebraska Press for permission to reprint our chapter, "Sammy Seminole, Jim Crow, and Osceola: Playing Indian and Racial Hierarchy at Florida State University." This chapter originally appeared with the title, "The Best Offense: Dissociation, Desire, and the Defense of the Florida State University Seminoles," in *Team Spirits: The Native American Mascots Controversy*, C. Richard King and Charles Fruehling Springwood, editors (2001). Lincoln: University of Nebraska Press.

C. Richard King acknowledges those who have uniquely imprinted his scholarship. Most importantly, he expresses his deepest gratitude to his family—his partner, Marcie Gilliland ("the best thing that ever happened to me") and his daughters, Abigail and Ellory Gilliland-King—rare jewels, all—who continually inspire and enlighten him; his parents and brothers, who provided useful suggestions and enduring encouragement and, finally, Charles Fruehling Springwood, for his support, critical perspective, and friendship.

Foremost, Charles Fruehling Springwood wishes to thank C. Richard King, from whom he learned the intellectual pleasures of co-authorship. He also is grateful for the enduring support of his family—in particular, his loving friend and partner, Cheryl Springwood, and his sons, Jacob and Josua. Far too often during the preparation of this book, afternoons and evenings were spent at the office rather than at home.

1

Posting Up:
Introductory Notes on Race,
Sports, and Post–America

American sports, we argue in what follows, in common with the broader national context shaping them, always have been rendered in the overly simplistic racial terms—red, white, and black. In our minds, the ritualization and representation of racial difference associated with intercollegiate athletics, from mascots and half-time shows to media coverage and popular narratives, have long offered the clearest illustrations of this pattern. Importantly, we contend, as the articulations of signifying practices, political ideologies, and social conditions have changed, described variously as post–civil rights, postmodern, or postcolonial, the complex, contentious, and ultimately conflicted interplay of redness, blackness, and whiteness in college sports has become increasingly significant.

   We begin with impossibilities, structures, and sentiments no longer conceivable to capture the centrality of racial spectacle to college sports. We do not introduce these episodes to erect a screen onto which to project a progressive tale about the unenlightened evils of previous formulations of race in sports. Rather, we want to caution readers against trivializing, if not evading, the fundamental importance of the interpenetration of redness, whiteness, and blackness. We dwell on these moments, then, to activate the critical faculties of our audience, to alert them to the political economy of racial signs in college sports.

1

In 1891, Yale University and Princeton University renewed their rivalry on the gridiron. The *New York Times* not only covered the game but attended to the symbolic struggle between students as well. Fans from Yale paraded their established icon, a bulldog, across the field. Not to be outdone, supporters of Princeton, shortly thereafter, invented an impromptu mascot, designed to match the school colors of orange and black (quoted in Oriard, 1993, pp. 229–230):

> Princeton was not going to be outdone in that way . . . pretty soon came out old Nassau's mascot, and the boys of the blue had to confess that they of the orange had scored a point. Princeton's mascot was a comely young colored girl. She was dressed in a flaming orange dress, with an orange bonnet and an orange parasol. She walked around the field eating an orange and apparently entirely unconscious of the tremendous sensation she created.

Euro-American fans crafted themselves and their teams not simply by displaying racialized bodies but by playing, enacting, or otherwise mimicking them as well. In the first decade of this century, students at Simpson College, a private, Methodist school in central Iowa, adopted "The Scalp Song" to cheer their Redmen. The victory chant made reference to the ferocity and bellicosity of the Simpson football team through allusions to cannibalism and combat (see Springwood & King, 2000). Elsewhere, drawing on the myth of the frontier, popular stereotypes about American Indians, Wild West shows, and a longing to escape modern life, students, coaches, administrators, and journalists facilitated the invention of Native American mascots (Davis, 1993; King & Springwood, 2000; King & Springwood, 2001; Staurowsky, 1998). Throughout the first third of the twentieth century, but especially during the 1920s, at schools as diverse as Dartmouth College, Eastern Michigan University, Juniata College, Mississippi College, Stanford University, the University of Illinois, and William and Mary College, they elaborated rich traditions of "playing Indian" (Deloria, 1998; Green, 1988; Huhndorf, 1997; Mechling, 1980).

Ironically, at precisely the moment Euro-Americans began to imagine themselves as invented Indians, embodied Indians rose to prominence on the gridiron (Churchill, Hill, & Barlow, 1979; Deloria, 1996; Oxendine, 1995). At boarding schools designed to educate and even "civilize" Native Americans, most famously at the Carlisle Indian Industrial School, football became an important tool of assimilation. Playing football promised to make disciplined, modern subjects of Native American boys, promoting dominant Euro-American values of fairness, responsibility, and autonomy (Pratt, 1964). The students at Carlisle eagerly embraced and by all measures excelled at the sport, producing a number of all-Americans, most notably Jim Thorpe, during the first decade of the twentieth century. In spectacles attended by thousands, in some cases more than 15,000, Carlisle competed against and often defeated the elite teams of the day. These games frequently were read as racial contests. Media coverage was commonly racist, stressing the savagery, physicality, and innate differences of the Indian players (see Oriard, 1993). Importantly, the mass appeal of these games, combined with the success of Carlisle, may have challenged stereotypes (Gems, 1998), while leaving white supremacy intact (King & Springwood, 1999).

In spite of the celebrity enjoyed by Native American collegiate athletes during the first quarter of the twentieth century, Jim Crow haunted college athletics and American society more generally. Many white Americans endorsed and enjoyed the privileges associated with the structural separation of blacks and whites. In sports, teams and institutions often were entitled to refuse to play interracial games. On occasions when "this gentleman's agreement" was invoked, black players were held out of the competition. For instance, before agreeing to play in the 1939 Cotton Bowl, Clemson University insisted, and its opponent Boston College agreed, not to play its star black running back, Lou Montgomery. Rarely did fans, coaches, athletes, journalists, or administrators question the tradition of Jim Crow in college sports. One notable exception occurred at New York University (NYU) in 1940. The Violets were scheduled to play the University of Missouri Tigers, an all-white team, which objected to competing against a black player. They requested that NYU leave its fullback, Leonard Bates, at home. NYU agreed, a decision that sparked intense student protests at the institution, calling for the end of Jim Crow in sports, while prompting lively debates at many other Eastern universities (Spivey, 1988).

In retrospect, the scopic pleasures, the fears and desires, the fragile, fabricated identities, and the rigid social asymmetries embedded within such racial spectacles rose to the surface. Indeed, the briefest glance at previous regimes of signification and classification makes plain, if not palpable, the power at work in the play of difference—the power to adopt the visage of the other, to define, to name, to educate, to civilize the vanquished, to exclude. Moreover, reread today, these historical events and all that they imply unsettle, evoke dis-ease, and even disgust. The easy reading and evocative force of such incidents turn on the deep contrast between previous and present configurations of racial signs and sports spectacles: that is, the regimes and representations typifying the postmodern, postcolonial, post–desegregation present invert those peculiar to the modern, imperial, segregated past. Whereas Native Americans, once celebrated as embodied athletes, now operate largely as empty images, African Americans, formerly excluded from the spectacular economy of college sport, are currently energized as star players and troubled delinquents. Largely invisible but pervasive throughout, Euro-Americans remain constant as spectators, coaches, administrators, journalists, and athletes; they perform and police frequently unmarked as racial subjects.

These shifts, as well as their causes and consequences, suggest something more. As in the past, the provocative tensions between presence and absence highlight the flows and fault lines of racial signs in college sports. They direct attention, on the one hand, to the practice of "playing Indian at halftime," the use of stereotypical images of Native Americans as mascots, and, on the other hand, to the "pleasures" of gazing at black bodies at play. By an overwhelming margin, the most prevalent of "human" mascots characterize Native American peoples and histories, yet, Native Americans play a seemingly insignificant role—as athletes, spectators, coaches, and owners. The conspicuous presence of Indian signs and symbols, underscored by their relative absence on the field of play, is contrasted in a curious fashion with the overwhelming presence of African-American athletes, albeit characterized by a virtual absence of black mascots. The way in which Indian mascots have emerged as being central to the identity of sports teams, and the way in which black American participation

in sport has grown, suggests that contemporary athletics stage—
perhaps unwittingly—particular, often stereotypical images of race
and racial difference. The cultural and racial differences embodied
within these images serve to communicate something about the
identities of the people who created them in the first instance—
European Americans.

In what follows, we offer a history, an ethnography, and a social critique of racial spectacles in intercollegiate athletics. Focusing on the spectacles associated with contemporary intercollegiate
athletics, including halftime performances, commercialized stagings, media coverage, public panics, and political protests, we outline the constellation of overlapping techniques through which
individuals and institutions have (re)constructed, contained, and
challenged racialized images, imaginaries, identities, and imagined
communities during the last twenty years. Restricting our gaze to
revenue sports, football, and basketball, we explore the political
economy of racial signs structuring and structured by intercollegiate sports. We simultaneously address formulations of redness,
whiteness, and blackness, endeavoring to locate the larger system
of racializing signifying practices at the heart of collegiate sport.
Drawing upon a rich corpus of semiotic scholarship that recog-
nizes how social relations and social identities are inseparable
from performance, history, and power, we examine the way in
which collegiate sporting signs and spectacles produce multiple
(overlapping and contradictory) systems of knowledge *of*, *for*,
and *about* others. We seek to move beyond more commonplace
studies of campus, sport, and race (Adler & Adler, 1990; V. Andrews, 1996; Brooks & Althouse, 1993; Hawkins, 1995/1996;
Lapchick, 1991, 1995; Shropshire, 1996, Smith, 1993; Wonsek,
1992)—which typically have displayed a preoccupation with nar-
rowly defined or statistical notions of stratification, racism, and
structural roles—to interrogate the ways in which racial difference
is practiced within the imaginaries of university athletics. Indeed,
we aim not simply to document *why* race matters but to make
sense of *how* it matters.

Linking whiteness, redness, blackness, and racial difference,
we foreground the ironies, articulations, and contradictions of
the racial sign systems structuring and structured by intercollegiate athletics. It is inappropriate to consider signs in isolation,

as independent bodies. Signs work in relation to one another within a necessarily open, historically positioned system. In addressing racial difference within college sport, then, we must understand how the formation of racial icons and identities is mutually constructed across time and space. We understand signifying practices to be fundamental to such constructions. Indeed, everyday actions and interpretations (both personal and institutional) constitute meaning, power, agency, and resistance. In our interpretations of these racial signs and their convergence within institutions of higher learning, we take culture to be a messy, even contradictory, process, characterized by contestation and change.

This nuanced understanding of culture affords a complex rendering of the intersections of race and college sports. It permits us to interrogate specifically the ways in which the university has become a staging ground for many aspiring athletes to showcase their talents in hopes of getting a professional sports contract, revealing the entanglements of the distribution of financial resources, recruitment, stereotypes, post–secondary educational goals, and the exploitation of students. We argue that the contemporary system of collegiate sport is experienced by students, student athletes, professors, and the broader public through a vast array of public spectacles (Debord, 1970/1967), such as halftime shows characterized by Native American mascots and Confederate flags, or glossy media portrayals of the black college athletes, or the racialized social narratives of angst over which college athletes will or will not "go pro." Indeed, collegiate sport and its close relative professional sport are produced as a spectacle imbued with a range of contradictory meanings and narratives. In the post–civil rights era (see Frankenberg & Mani, 1993; King, 2000; Stratton, 2000), we are convinced that Americans have come to know and think of themselves as a freer, more racially harmonious society largely through sport and discourses that boast of an integrated sporting world. And yet, sport, as a social field characterized by a series of (mass) mediated spectacles (Rinehart, 1998), unpacks and celebrates racial difference, often from the point of view of the Euro-American spectator. Such spectacles are best viewed as cultural practices that locate, structure, and perform race and racial identity in America.

Importantly, by situating racial constructions of redness, whiteness, and blackness at the center of this analysis, we do not pretend that either the United States or the American university can be reduced to three racial poles. At all levels, the university is comprised of numerous individuals beyond the population of Native Americans, Anglo-Americans, and African Americans. Furthermore, in locating the prevailing system of power that structures the university and its sporting spectacles within a matrix of historically fashioned white practices, we do not also assume that American colleges are controlled exclusively by white interests, or even that there could be such a monolithic thing as white interests, or for that matter, minority interests. We intend, however, to read how exhibitions of these predominant signs of racial difference have been practiced under the influence of particular, uneven regimes of power.

As should be apparent by this point, this is not simply a book about sport and race. It is not merely about mascots or the predominance and exploitation of the black athlete. It is not a sociological book about graduation rates, achievement levels, or the success or failure of interracial relationships. It is neither an apology for, nor a critique of, attempts to explain the success of the black athlete in terms of genetics. It is not a formal, institutional critique of collegiate athletics and its legal apparatuses. It is not a comprehensive survey, but a partial interpretation that aims to illuminate the technologies employed in the narratives, performances, and stagings of intercollegiate athletics to reconfigure, even to reanimate, racial difference. We endeavor to craft an account of race and sport that, in the words of Lawrence Grossberg (1992, p. 64), "describes how practices, effects, and vectors are woven together, where the boundaries are located and where the fault lines lie. This structured assemblage is a force-field encompassing different forms of objects, facts, practices, events, whatever can be found along the way." Thus *Race as Spectacle in College Sport* offers a cartography of racial spectacles in contemporary collegiate sports, mapping how the processes underlying them change over time. It traces the means and meanings of materializing race in college sports, exploring the linkages connecting signifying practices and social structures, binding images, ideologies, and identities in disparate contexts.

STRUCTURES AND SPECTACLES

Race continues to imprint intercollegiate athletics, as well as the idioms, identities, and imaginaries animated by it. In fact, as we argue throughout, sports has become an increasingly important space in which individuals and institutions struggle over the significance of race. It simultaneously facilitates efforts to reproduce, resist, and recuperate naturalized or taken-for-granted accounts of difference, culture and history. Too often, fans, media, coaches, and players fail to recognize the significance of sports stories. Indeed, scholars and spectators frequently think of sport as a fun diversion, a pleasurable release, a cultural time-out that is mere entertainment. The celebration of sports as the ideal, if not the only, instance of racial harmony in post–integration America exacerbates the difficulties of thinking about representations of race in association with sports. These views, in our opinion, (dis)miss the centrality of athletics to popular interpretations of race and race relations, formulations of identity and difference, and efforts to create public culture. Moreover, they neglect the vitality of racialization in college sports, inhibiting critical accounts of its force.

In *Race as Spectacle*, we work against the trivialization of race and sports. We interpret moments in which individuals and institutions activate, enjoy, ignore, contest, and refuse racial difference. We highlight competing means and meanings of making race matter. On the one hand, we linger on the ease with which whiteness, blackness, and redness materialize within sport spectacles, while on the other hand, we direct attention to the myriad efforts to challenge such enactments, making them uneasy. We gather together disparate incidents to interrogate the practices and precepts energizing the production and consumption of racialized ideologies and identities. We seek to understand the significance of fleeting feelings and enduring sentiments such as the following.

At the University of Illinois at Urbana-Champaign, one Saturday afternoon in the Fall of 1995, a handful of students protested the school's Native American mascot, Chief Illiniwek, and related misappropriations of Indianness. Carrying anti-Chief signs, they marched outside the football stadium. Although not expecting a warm welcome from supporters of the mascot, they were shocked by a large sign posted on a Winnebego RV that read "Save the Chief, Kill the Indians!"

After a loss in 1994, Keith Dambrot, the white basketball coach at Central Michigan University—the Chippewas—informed his players, "We need to have more niggers on this team." (quoted in Chideya, 1995, p. 162)

Bobby Bowden, the white football coach at Florida State University—the Seminoles—signs autographs for fans with the identifying phrase, "Scalp'em."

In the early 1980s, whenever Oklahoma State University played football or basketball against its in-state rival, the University of Oklahoma, the campus radio station would stage fictitious interviews with black athletes. The following dialogue, according to Funk (1991, p. 43), exemplifies these racial dramas.

> **Interviewer:** Well, Mr. Tisdale, what are your thoughts on the upcoming game?
>
> **Tisdale:** Ugah bugah hoogaloo ugh ugh.
>
> **Interviewer:** Really—would you share your thoughts on your coach, Billy Tubbs?
>
> **Tisdale:** I be, yo be, we be, yo' mama!

These incidents underscore a simple truth animating this study: American colleges and universities, intercollegiate athletics, and sporting spectacles structure and are structured by an insidious, if largely invisible, white supremacy. We engage this complex system knitting together structures, symbols, sentiments, and subjectivities through the political economy of racial signs.

Even the briefest glance at contemporary intercollegiate athletics reveals significant racial differences. Although African Americans receive less than 25 percent of athletic scholarships at National

Collegiate Athletic Association (NCAA) institutions, they dominate
the revenue sports, particularly basketball.[1] Of the 844 men's scholarship athletes in basketball in 1997, 532 were black (Haworth,
1998). That is, 63 percent of those who play college basketball are
African American. In football, roughly 40 percent of the players are
black. The presence of African Americans becomes even more disparate, even problematic, when one considers that they represent
only a fraction of the total student body at predominantly white institutions, often less than 5 percent. Importantly, sports does not enhance social mobility for most participants (see Riess, 1990). Fewer
than 45 percent of all African-American scholarship athletes and 37
percent of male basketball players—compared to 62 percent and 47
percent for Euro-Americans—graduate from college, and only a
few will ever become professional athletes.

✦ Coaching and administrative positions show a similar racial
asymmetry. Indeed, in spite of their importance as players, African
Americans do not hold positions of authority. A recent study of
football coaches at NCAA institutions found that while roughly 50
percent of players are black, only 18 percent of coaches are African
American, with an additional 1.6 percent representing other minority groups (Suggs, 1999, p. A49). In fact, of 112 Division I-A
schools, only five have African American head coaches, and for all
three divisions, less 8 percent of head coaching positions are held
by blacks. Although slightly better, the distribution in basketball
mirrors that in football: 10.6 percent of head coaches in men's
basketball (7.8 percent for women's basketball) were African
American (Suggs, 1999, p. A50). Even fewer athletic directors are
African American; only 1 percent of assistant, associate, or chief
athletic directors are black.

Beyond the numbers, race matters, because popular concep-
tions of the difference it makes—particularly in terms of perceptions of physiological features (such as speed) and their presumed
organic linkages to psychological qualities (such as intellect)—
shape the positions coaches assign to individual players. In the
1970s, sports sociologists noted this pattern, which they termed
"stacking," or the segregation of players by position (Lewis,
1995; Smith & Harrison, 1998; Yetman & Berghorn, 1993). "In
football," to take just one example, Stanley Eitzen (1999, p. 19)
observes that Euro-Americans "are more likely to play at the

thinking and leadership positions that more often determine the game's outcome. African Americans overwhelmingly play on defense and at positions that require physical characteristics such as size, strength, speed, and quickness." Such stereotypes also mold media coverage and popular appreciation of intercollegiate athletics. Here again, whereas African Americans tend to be praised for their physical talents, European Americans are celebrated for their mental gifts. In a brief, albeit informal, study of five NCAA basketball games, Derek Jackson observed that 63 percent of comments about intelligence referred to white players, while 77 percent of remarks about physicality described black players. What is more, over 80 percent of the stupid plays were associated with African-American athletes.

The prevailing theoretical concept that inspires this study is "spectacle," a highly layered, nuanced term developed by Guy Debord (1970/1967, p. 10), which "unifies and explains a great diversity of apparent phenomena." Debord was concerned with the practices and ideologies that animated the contemporary media and consumer society. In particular, images, commodities, and spectacles form the structuring structures (Bourdieu, 1990/1980) of this televisual world. "Spectacles are those phenomena of media, culture, and society that embody the society's basic values, serve to enculturate individuals into this way of life, and dramatize the society's conflicts and modes of conflict resolution" (Kellner, 1996, p. 458). Here we bring into focus those spectacles that transform the university space into a broader field of public culture where race is, quite literally, practiced as an allegory of play and performance. People do attend these games and rituals, merging with those who perform them, in such a way that, "Experience and everyday life is . . . mediated by the spectacles of media and culture that dramatizes our conflicts, celebrates our values, and projects our deepest hopes and fears" (ibid.).

Using an approach informed by Foucauldian genealogical history (1979, 1981, 1987), an appreciation for an affective, postmodern political economy of meaning and signification (Baudrillard, 1983; Kellner, 1995; Giroux, 1992), and a neo-Gramscian reading of power and hegemony (Comaroff & Comaroff, 1991; Gramsci, 1971; Hall, 1980, 1981, 1985), we consider history and power inseparable and practice and agency contingent upon positionality and an array of continually emerging social fields. David Palumbo-Liu (1997, p. 4) asks, "How is cultural hegemony refused, diffused, absorbed, reproduced, and reconfigured, given the particularites of its interpolation into multiple contexts and under different pretexts by various agents?" This project, by tracing the intersections of red, white, and black as practices of racial signification, seeks to throw light on possible answers to Palumbo-Liu's question by engaging the everyday complexities of university athletics through critical ethnography, historical analysis, and semiotic deconstruction. This set of orientations permits us to speak of the forms of power, the fields of discourses, and the conditions of possibility that, through sport and play, construct "America."

RACIAL PEDAGOGIES

Critical cultural studies have begun to grasp how racial difference animates much of the popular aesthetics of sport. Understandably, to date, much of this scholarship has focused on professional athletics, notably the National Basketball Association (NBA) and Michael Jordan (Andrews, 1996; Cole & Andrews, 1996; Denzin, 1996; Dyson, 1993; Kellner, 1996). Here we shift the frame. The university, as we elaborate, is a particularly useful site for critically unpacking the racialized social relations of sport. "Recognizing that whiteness is produced differently within a variety of public spaces as well as across the diverse categories of class, gender, sexuality, and ethnicity" (Giroux, 1997, p. 381), we consider the 1990s' social field of collegiate sport predominant in terms of economic, political, and popular capital, and thus analytically ideal for unpacking the complexities of race and American history. Indeed, the articulation of sport and the university in many ways has always turned on the play of racial signs and the production of "racial pedagogies" (ibid.).

The so-called revenue sports of college athletics (football and basketball) are wholly interwoven with the larger world of professional sport, and the political economy of this relationship needs to be critically examined in the context of the university's historical role as a site of public symbols and meanings. The university has commonly been idealized as a liberal place that champions social equality and justice while encouraging social innovation. Campuses will always be remembered as spectacular spaces of the 1960s' student political protests, when the struggle for civil rights articulated with antiwar and antigovernment movements. Thus it is here—where lecture halls and libraries have become linked to a multibillion dollar sporting world—that the discursive ruptures of a utopic, postintegration mythos are perhaps most contradictory and conspicuous.

To offer one example, in February 1995, at Rutgers University, President Francis L. Lawrence, reportedly after reading *The Bell Curve*, commented at a faculty meeting that Africans Americans were "a disadvantaged population that doesn't have the genetic heredity background" to succeed in higher education. Once made public, his repugnant remarks sparked a national controversy. At the local level, black students responded to Lawrence not in letters to the editor nor through an occupation of the administration building; instead, they interrupted a men's basketball game between Rutgers University and the University of Massachusetts on the evening of February 7. The audience assembled to watch the mostly black teams compete, rather than applaud the actions of the protesters, insisted that the game resume and yelled "Niggers and spics . . . go back to Africa."

As at Rutgers, these racial spectacles frequently highlight, or play off of, the homosocial (white, middle-class) nature of many college campuses, in such a way that these "performances of difference" constitute racial identities. In the idealized space of equality, university culture remains silent about the racially (and otherwise) stratified nature of its student bodies, where participation in revenue sports (and thus, nonrevenue sports) is strongly racialized. In many medium-sized colleges, for example, nearly the entire basketball team is black, while the swimming team is largely white, but the meaning behind this stratification is not engaged, critically or reflexively, by students, professors, and administrators. In what follows, we initiate such a project in the hope of encouraging dialogues about race, power, and representation on college campuses and throughout public culture. To clarify the form and force of racial spectacles in collegiate athletics, we fix our interpretive gaze on the construction and contestation of red-ness, blackness, and whiteness.

PLAY BY PLAY

As authors, we write from particular positions and relate to our project with certain personal and social histories. Both European American, we were raised in the Midwestern United States during the 1960s and 1970s. We both enjoyed sports as well as school. We participated in games of "Cowboys and Indians," and we played with action figures depicting fictious characters, such as Custer or Geronimo, to reimagine the past. Playing Little League baseball and youth basketball, we were affected by games bringing white children and black children into proximity for the first time. C. Richard King attended the University of Kansas (Big Eight) as an undergraduate, while Charles Springwood studied at Purdue University (Big Ten). Each institution exposed us to the intense spectacle of collegiate sport and its position within a tremendously powerful political economy. We both matriculated to the University of Illinois to complete our doctorates in anthropology. There we reacted to the mascot, Chief Illiniwek, with similar horror. We closely observed the practices of the athletic department, sports teams and their student athletes, and the community, more gener-ally. In fact, many University of Illinois athletes, from both "rev-enue" sports and "nonrevenue" sports, attended the classes we taught as teaching assistants. While we each continue to watch athletic contests—both collegiate and professional—we now do so more skeptically. Throughout this book, then, our past entangle-ments with and ongoing enjoyment of intercollegiate athletics en-courage us to offer a "contaminated critique" of the place of race in these spectacles.

In the next chapter, we map out the complex, often contradic-tory stagings of race in American intercollegiate athletics as the twentieth century drew to a close. We focus explicitly on tech-niques of erasure, on the narrative, media, and exhibitionary per-formances that dematerialize race. In this chapter, we work against commonsense notions of integration within popular, commercial, and official representations of race, history, and sports after desegregation. The prevailing understanding has long been that America has been integrated and racially united through sport. By examining popular accounts of desegregation and public exhibition of sports history, we argue that racial spectacles often operate by excising the significance of race.

In Chapters 3 and 4, we turn our attention to Native American mascots. We present detailed interpretations of the means and meanings of playing Indian at halftime at the University of Illinois and Florida State University. We examine the manner in which the invented Indians associated with these universities have circulated, marking identities and shaping lives while grounding imagined communities, new social movements, and uneasy alliances. We focus here on the mobility of mascots, on the continuous, seemingly countless ways in which their significance has been made (up) in motion, in processes of (dis)placement, and on the multiple receptions evoked by their stagings. Throughout our analyses, we develop a complex conceptualization of hegemony, multivocality, and consent to apprehend, on the one hand, the creation of coalitions between Native American communities and universities with Native American mascots and, on the other hand, the articulations between redness, whiteness, and blackness.

Against this background, in Chapter 5 we discuss the use of exaggeration to materialize race, particularly blackness, in public discourses about intercollegiate athletics. We work through the manner in which the black athlete has become a racial spectacle. We explore the ways in which race energizes discourses about race, suggesting that the media has remade blackness in such a way that prevailing (white) notions of criminality, respectability, and responsibility work to racially mark individuals and populations, as well as their styles, habits, and cultivations of self (see Cole, 1996; Cole & Andrews 1996; Cole & Denny 1995). In particular, we focus on two recent public panics: (1) the contradictions and uneven portrayals of the predicaments of Lawrence Phillips, a University of Nebraska football star who was suspended and nearly expelled from his team for his arrests for domestic violence; and (2) popular concerns about athletes "turning pro," leaving school early to pursue careers in professional athletics. To contextualize our interpretations, we locate the emergence of the aesthetization of the black athlete as a spectacle within this earlier history of the black-face performances—representations such as Aunt Jemima and Uncle Ben—and mythologies of black cannibals.

In Chapter 6, we turn our attention to whiteness and its defense. Focusing on the University of Mississippi with Notre Dame University, we detail the diverse, even competing, formulations of whiteness at play in college sports. At the former institution, "Colonel Reb," who resembles the stereotypical portrayal of a nineteenth-century plantation owner (see "Ole Miss . . . ," 1997/1998)—a mascot contrasting with the ubiquitous Native American mascot— along with the presence of the Confederate flag and the song "Dixie," affords students, fans, and alumni the opportunity to rehabilitate white identities through nostalgic restagings of the Confederacy. In recent years, concerns voiced within the university community have curtailed the official use of such symbols, challenging the ideological core of this neo-Confederate whiteness. We contrast Ole Miss with Notre Dame. Supporters of the Fighting Irish frequently celebrate its emblematic whiteness. To establish the significance of this unmarked whiteness, we connect the current popularity, reputation, and affection of the renowned institution and its mascot to the historical processes through which the Irish became white. Whiteness is both embattled and applauded, mutable and multiplied, a privilege and a position in process.

Having mapped the erasures, inflations, and elaborations of redness, whiteness, and blackness in the preceding chapters, in our final chapter we again turn our attention to impossibilities, to the emergent desires, policies, and practices that begin to undo reigning racial spectacles. Concerned with efforts to refuse and reinvent dominant ideologies and identities, we ask difficult questions: Has whiteness as conventionally formulated become unbearable? Has a more critical or progressive understanding of Indianness begun to take shape in the wake of activism directed at mascots? Is there hope that interventions and innovations will reconfigure blackness? We begin with an analysis of current policies that prohibit colleges and universities from playing against schools with Native American mascots, and then we reflect on related attacks of white supremacy. We then speculate on the possible reformations of university life and policy that might reconcile various discursive and representational contradictions identified throughout this book.

2

White Out:
Erasures of Race
in Collegiate Athletics

In 1988, Iowa State University rededicated its football stadium to the memory of Jack Trice. Neither a wealthy alumnus nor a former administrator, he played in only one football game during his brief matriculation at the central Iowa land-grant institution. For all of its brevity, Trice's career was remarkable. He was one of the first African Americans to play college football at Iowa State University, and he understood the persistent significance of racial difference. In 1923, three schools had refused games with Iowa State University because they had a black player. The discrimination he faced coupled with the opportunity at Iowa State University profoundly impacted his sense of self, society, and sport. The night before his initial appearance in a Cyclone uniform he penned a note to himself and carried it onto the field the following day (quoted in Spivey, 1988, p. 290, emphasis original): "The honor of my race, family, and self is at stake. Everyone is expecting me to do big things. *I will!* My whole body and soul are to be thrown recklessly about the field tomorrow. Every time the ball is snapped, I *will* be trying to do more than my part. On all defensive plays I must break through the opponents' line and stop the play in their territory." Tragically, he died from injuries sustained during his premiere appearance against the University of Minnesota. Although the intentions and motivations of the Minnesota players were less than clear, some charged that they sought to hurt and sideline Trice

17

because he was black (Ashe, 1988, vol. II, p. 93; Spivey, 1988, p. 290). As shocking as his life and death appear in retrospect, they were atypical more for their extremity than for their occurrence.

Perhaps more surprising was Iowa State University's decision to rename its stadium after Trice. To be sure, colleges and universities secure public memory through naming, memorializing the sacrifice of individuals, as in the countless memorial stadiums built after World War I, more commonly enshrining wealthy benefactors, prestigious alumni, and accomplished coaches. Naming the stadium after Trice paid tribute to the qualities he displayed in his brief career. What sets apart the selection of Trice is that it underscores not simply the historical struggles endured by black athletes but foregrounds the asymmetrical, painful, and even tragic race relations structuring college athletics during the interwar period. In pairing glory and tragedy, it demands that the race not be forgotten. Consequently, Jack Trice Stadium does something extremely rare in college sports spectacles. It reminds fans, students, alumnus, and players of the centrality of race. In contrast, as we explore in this chapter, more often than not the ideologies and enactments associated with intercollegiate athletics erase race, displacing and deferring it, even as they rely upon it.

By all accounts, sporting spectacles make it easy to forget. They distract the masses from their troubles and struggles in everyday life as the play of bodies and signs absorbs them into a libidinal economy of excess. Beyond the individual subject, spectacles also hide the relations that make them possible. Under conditions variously described as "the end of history," postmodern, hyperreal, and the society of spectacle, according to Genevieve Rail (1998), current stagings of sport dehistoricize, disconnect, and displace. In agreement with numerous theorists, she suggests that the increasing commodification and mass mediation of social production and consumption have profoundly altered public memory, evacuating historical consciousness. Fredric Jameson (1991) has lamented over the effacement of history and the rise of nostalgia, and Jean-Francois Lyotard (1984/1979) has pronounced the collapse of master narratives. Guy Debord (1970/1967, p. 114) has diagnosed the "social organization of a paralyzed history, a paralyzed memory," and Michael Rogin (1993, p. 507) has concluded that the "superficial and sensately intensified . . . short lived and repeatable" qualities of spectacles give rise to historical amnesia. Although we are sympathetic with these interpretations of spectacles, particularly Rail's concerns about the changing contours of sports at the turn of the millennium, we neither endorse their pessimistic tone nor embrace their simplistic terms. These renderings, as brilliant as they are, often are as detached and flat as the social contexts that they purport to apprehend. To our minds, it is not that time has stopped, engulfed by space, eradicated by the play of signs, or otherwise liquidated by changing social conditions; instead, individuals and institutions continue to make history.

College sports spectacles hinge on recollection. Big games, championship seasons, storied rivalries, and memorable moments—a last second shot or a 99-yard touchdown run—impact on the lives of those who watch, cover, and participate in them. Players, coaches, fans, and even casual spectators, often create and recreate themselves and the world through remembrance of spectacles past. They recall in personal and collective ways—video montages, mementos, and so on—where they were, who they were, and what their society was like when their team won (or lost) the championship; they tell stories about great games and superstar athletes who they once watched; they account for the present state of social relations through past events and transcendent processes. Thus we are concerned not so much with the end of history but with the ends to which people put various reconstructions of the past, precisely because we do not find that spectacles make people forgetful as much as they encourage them to remember particular events from specific standpoints. Indeed, "The media, along with other public and private entities (including churches, schools, families, and civic organizations, among others) constantly make available particular narratives and not others. In turn, such consistently reinforced presences reproduce the world in particular ways" (Lubiano, 1992, pp. 329–330). Clearly then, sports spectacles, rather than refusing the past, rework it, edit it, and reconstruct it. To make present and to materialize particular (racialized) histories, they make absent and dematerialize specific (racial) struggles and structures.

In this chapter, we explore the ways in which the production and reception of collegiate sports spectacles erase race. We are concerned with a set of technologies that effects a "white-out," what

Eileen M. Jackson (1993, p. 376) has termed "whiting-out":
"Whiting-out is a metaphor . . . a back-formation from White-
Out, opaque fluid used to paint over errors on a typewritten page
. . . whiting-out is a process of eliminating some approaches in
favor of others. . . . Whiting-out is a routine activity . . . and thus
remains largely invisible." In what follows we make visible the un-
seen operations and effects of whiting-out race from sports history.
Focusing on historical narratives, we argue that although racial
difference is central to collegiate athletics, it remains intangible,
seemingly insignificant, precisely because representational tech-
niques dematerialize it, excise it, and otherwise dismiss its continued significance. Central to these refusals of racial difference are
celebratory discourses of achievement and greatness that excise
tragedy, conflict, and stratification. We attend to popular and official renderings of sports that absorb, defer, or exclude race. We
elaborate our argument in three contexts. To begin, we analyze the
NCAA Hall of Champions and the National College Football Hall
of Fame, exploring the place of race in official accounts presenting
the history of college sports. Against this background, we discuss
narratives about integration in the domain of college athletics, detailing the exclusions central to these progressive accounts. Finally,
we probe (auto)biographical accounts told by and about athletes,
interrogating the ideological force of the American Dream.

EXHIBITIONARY EXCLUSIONS

Even in a social context increasingly saturated by media and capital, institutions (colleges, universities, and not-for-profit organizations, namely, the NCAA) shape public memory of college sports.
These institutional histories, similar to those told in other social
fields, more often than not are instrumental histories. They offer
official accounts, sanctioned, partial, and highly constructed, if not
finely crafted, versions of the past. They fashion positive historical
narratives, cleaning, editing, and literally manipulating individuals,
events, and epochs. In the process of formulating celebratory stories, their interpretations twist, elide, and otherwise exclude uncomfortable elements. Almost invariably, institutional histories of
college sports exclude race. They do not discuss it, refusing both to

present historical asymmetries or to interpret their reconfigurations. Instead, they erase it. This propensity is most marked in museums, halls of fame, and other exhibitionary spaces dedicated to the history of college sports. To clarify the erasure of race from institutional histories of intercollegiate athletics here we tour the NCAA Hall of Champions and the College Football Hall of Fame.

Amid the glittering office complexes in suburban Kansas City, the NCAA Hall of Champions offers, what a promotional brochure terms, "A one-of-a-kind tribute to intercollegiate athletics . . . a photographic and video salute to all of the NCAA's 21 sports" ("NCAA Hall of Champions," no date). A 96-foot mural devoted to the history of the NCAA greets visitors as they enter the museum. To the right and left stand galleries, each containing exhibits of varying sizes on all sports governed by the NCAA. A movie theater joins the galleries at the rear of the museum. Throughout the Hall of Champions, visuality eclipses textuality. Countless images adorn the walls, moving visitors and stories through, between, and beyond the exhibit halls. Entire walls are given over to photographs of great coaches or all-Americans, for instance. Much like the administrative body, the categories of sport (such as football, swimming, lacrosse, or volleyball), gender, and division (I, II, or III) organize the Hall of Champions. Not surprisingly, it gives precedence to the dominant elements in each of these categories—the revenue sports of football and men's basketball, men's sports, and Division I athletics. Within these subdivisions, it literally revolves around the exploits of champions. It weaves together singular events and exceptional individuals to elaborate the meaning of college sports. In images and videos, it enshrines individuals who excelled as coaches and players and teams that for one shining moment or throughout their careers achieved greatness; it celebrates great men (and women), great teams, and great games.

The Hall of Champions does not present a single history of college sports. Rather, it uses several techniques to capture the spirit and significance of intercollegiate athletics. In its obsession with championships, it offers a series of time lines, fixing memory on chronological succession and the accomplishments of particular teams and individuals. On occasion, it actually narrates a standard history, as in its lengthy exhibit devoted to the evolution of basketball. Here decades and developments, along with dynasties and personalities, dominate. Throughout, it presents the past as a pastiche of legendary individuals and memorable moments, and its visual economy encourages intimate or personal memory—"I remember that game! He was so great! Woody Hayes was what all coaches should be!"—detached from the social relations enabling them. Together, these historiographies displace more critical, reflexive accounts of the past, literally writing over them happier, more positive renderings in terms of athletic glory.

Race has no place in the NCAA Hall of Champions. Its celebratory displays and discourses cannot accommodate it. It engages neither the asymmetries of segregation nor the dynamics of integration. Even its account of the history of basketball fails to work in the rise and fall of Jim Crow. Rather than present a full account of sport as a social field, structured by and structuring racial politics, it situates intercollegiate athletics in a realm beyond the social. Instead of presenting both the greatness of Jim Brown and the discrimination he struggled against, it reduces him to a shallow icon; instead of considering the way biases segregated basketball programs, such as the great University of Kentucky teams coached by Adolph Rupp, it refuses race, hoping to rehabilitate, even sanitize, sports, now as then, in its absence. It does not discuss racial difference and power, because such discussions call into question many of the fond memories that the Hall of Champions celebrates in its exhibits. Undoubtedly, it ejects race, moreover, because the subject makes spectators, particularly Euro-American spectators, uncomfortable, if not defensive and hostile. Finally, the Hall of Champions excludes race because of the NCAA's culpability in historic and current racist practices.

Although the College Football Hall of Fame, located in South Bend, Indiana, combines a narrower focus, devoted exclusively to the history of a single sport, with a much larger, more sophisticated exhibitionary space, it too fails to engage race. Through objects, images, videos, narratives, and interactive exhibits in some twenty-four galleries, it encodes the meaning of college football. Underwritten by a number of multinational corporations, including Coca-Cola and Burger King, the College Football Hall of Fame encourages visitors not only to appreciate the game—from coaching and media coverage to memorable moments and bowl games—but to get them into the game as well. Several exhibits afford the opportunity to test one's knowledge, strategic aptitude, athletic abilities (passing, running, and kicking skills), and physicality (flexibility, strength, agility, and balance). Still, as a hall of fame, greatness centers the College Football Hall of Fame, which devotes exhibitions to legendary players, great rivalries, and renowned coaches, as well as the greatest upsets (presented by Alka Seltzer) and the national champions. The Hall of Honor enshrines the "outstanding accomplishments, great sacrifices and contributions that are recognized" ("Everybody Plays," no date, p. 8). On the mezzanine level, one can view portraits of all Heisman Award winners. Kiosks with touch screens present "unforgettable games and plays" (ibid.). As at the NCAA Hall of Champions, celebrations of singularity deter engagements with social process within the College Football Hall of Fame.

Not surprisingly, nostalgia saturates the College Football Hall of Fame. Like other displays of sports history (see Springwood, 1996), it turns on the longing for a social context imagined to be safer and simpler, a desire to recover the moral goodness and clarity of social relations and categories. The College Football Hall of Fame stages the history of college football in rather simple terms, removing it from the commercial, political, and social context in which it has taken shape. Throughout, the narratives and images celebrating the greatness of the past events and individuals evoke a sense of the qualitative superiority of sport before it became a mass-mediated entertainment industry. Amongst other figures, the scholar athlete anchors these longings. To arrive at the exhibits and galleries, visitors must descend a spiral ramp that circles a large diorama entitled "Pursuit of a Dream," which includes a statue of two football players celebrating with a high five in front of a game scoreboard. But the majority of the display is dedicated to the stereotypical student university experience. Laundry supplies, clothes, a large globe, and other items of daily living surround a tower—approximately two stories high—that consists of a stack of ice coolers and oversized academic textbooks. Visitors can read off such generic books titles as Ethics, Medicine, Science, Algebra, and Finance while they walk down the ramp. This display represents a larger effort by the Hall of Fame to continually foreground the nostalgic link between college football and academic scholarship. One of the authors overheard a father and son as they circled around the diorama. The father asked the young boy, "What's under those coolers? Do you see? *Books!* You can't play college football without reading books!"

The nostalgic and celebratory contours of the College Football Hall of Fame obscure the tensions and controversies characterizing the relationship between scholastic pursuits and collegiate athletics. Of course, celebratory museums such as sports halls of fame rarely adopt a critical self-reflexivity. But, in South Bend, the College Football Hall of Fame's silence regarding a variety of issues, from academics to the de facto professional aura surrounding Division I sports, is conspicuous. Moreover, the museum makes no attempt to clarify the significance of race. It does not engage the prominence of Native American athletes, nor the conditions under which they excelled in and later all but disappeared from intercollegiate athletics. It instead avoids the subject. More noteworthy, given its centrality to sports, media, and politics in American culture, it fails to discuss the African-American experience in intercollegiate athletics, especially the dramatic rise in the number of African-American players over the past half-century. The chronological arrangement of the topical galleries gives the impression that race has impacted on sports only recently. Up through the 1950s, one sees virtually no African-American players featured. Indeed, one might conclude that up until that point, the sport was essentially a white game. But as the presence of African-American players emerges decisively in the displays of more recent decades, the museum does not provide any historical context or even explanation of any kind for what appears visually to have been a progressive integration of nonwhite players in college football. For example, one might anticipate that one or more noteworthy moments of integration at particular universities would be detailed, or perhaps the trials of integration faced by some black players mentioned. Yet these instances have no place in the discourses of greatness, celebrity, and nostalgia circulating in the College Football Hall of Fame.

The College Football Hall of Fame also refuses to engage in current discussions of the articulation of race and sports. Most notably, it completely bypasses any mention of the numerous Native American mascots or Confederate mascots of some Southern schools. Its exhibit on mascots centers on actual-size photographs of several familiar characters. The accompanying narrative exclaims:

WHAT A CHARACTER!

Mascots are part of almost every school's history and tradition. When live animal mascots and their handlers lead the team's charge onto the field, the crowd roars in anticipation of the action ahead. Animated and creative character mascots have a contagious charm that spreads school spirit in a special way.

Feel the magic by posing with the life-size mascots.

The exhibit revels in the frivolity of mascots, avoiding any mention of current controversies. Visitors are encouraged not simply to revere tradition and laugh at wacky icons but to insert themselves in the spectacle. Fun trumps politics, as pleasure elides race.

The refusal of race shapes the solitary occasion on which the College Football Hall of Fame explicitly discusses racial difference. It presents one small display on the "centennial of black college football." Under a photograph featuring pre-game ceremonies for a game on October 17, 1992, between Johnson C. Smith University and Livingstone College to commemorate the centennial, the museum copy informs:

In 1992, college football celebrated a century of play at historically black colleges and universities. The rich tradition began on 27 December 1892, with the first game between Biddle (now Johnson C. Smith) and Livingstone in Salisbury, North Carolina. Biddle won 4–0. Most historically black colleges rose from the ashes of the Civil War, founded on an inclusive philosophy. "Come One Come all. Come Learn."

As the schools began to develop facilities and funding, football teams were formed that by the 1940s were the backbone of varsity sports programs. One hundred years after the Biddle–Livingstone game, 43 historically black colleges and universities were fielding teams within the NCAA—the enduring legacy of legendary African-American coaches, athletes, and institutions.

It is not the enduring legacies of segregation worthy of note, but the perseverance and talent of African Americans. Jim Crow laws and virulent racism did not prompt the creation of historically black colleges and universities. Rather, it was "an inclusive philosophy" among African Americans. Their individual greatness, not the conditions in which they became great, merits recollection. As such, this display and the College Football Hall of Fame as a whole evade the details of historical struggle, terror, and frustration that surely characterized the experiences of African-American students who began playing on previously all-white teams. Further undermining the significance of this presence is its placement in the College Football Hall of Fame. It is not central but marginal; it is not an integral, integrated feature of football but an element set aside, literally segregated from the color-blind, more mainstream athletics. As a consequence, even when race merits attention, the representational strategies of the College Football Hall of Fame trivialize it.

In both the NCAA Hall of Champions and the College Football Hall of Fame, as our brief ethnographic snapshots underscore, race is ever-present, yet absent and intangible. Their celebratory and even nostalgic histories literally erase race. Cultivating pleasure and enshrining greatness, their exhibits displace the dis-ease of taking race seriously, repressing the political consequences of watching and playing college sports.

POPULAR PROJECTIONS

Despite the silences and exclusions of official exhibitions, the historical articulations of race and college sport enter into the popular consciousness. More often than not, desegregation centers on personal and collective accounts of the racialized past. The changes associated with desegregation have facilitated reinterpretations of race, power, and history. Accounts of the desegregation of college sports are pervasive, precisely because over the past half-century, college sports, as a field of social relations, has occupied a fundamental place in its efforts to become integrated into American society. Significantly, as we argue below, desegregation has prompted stories that simultaneously materialize and dematerialize race. Although these narratives discuss race relations, they tend to trivialize the continued significance of race. These interpretations invariably are progressive, stressing change, opportunity, and equality; they permit fans, sports writers, players, and administrators to work through past inequities, while explaining away the asymmetries of the present. Informed by a progressive impulse, then, media coverage, vernacular narratives, and life histories elide race.

To ground and complicate our discussion of popular readings of desegregation, we pause briefly to highlight the extended struggles, false starts, and unrealized ideals that characterize this most hopeful, conflicted, and traumatic reconfiguration of racial relations. We foreground three moments or scenes to tease out the tense rearticulations of race encoded and erased in accounts of desegregation.

Scene 1

Two years after *Brown v. Topeka Board of Education*, North Texas State College desegregated its football team in 1956, a process which by all accounts was rather smooth and supportive (Marcello, 1996). That same year, segregationists throughout the South protested school integration; Southern colleges withdrew from sports tournaments because opposing teams had black players; and the state legislature of Louisiana passed a law prohibiting interracial athletic competitions (ibid.).

Scene 2

Against the backdrop of church bombings, police violence against peaceful civil rights demonstrators, and continued efforts to maintain segregation at the University of Alabama, the Crimson Tide was crowned the 1964 National Champions in football. This institution, like many Southern schools, had a racially segregated team and refused to schedule games against schools with integrated squads. Many balked at honoring Alabama with the championship. Jim Murray, sports columnist for the *Los Angeles Times*, interrogated the propriety of such distinction: "So Alabama is the 'National Champion,' is it? Hah! 'National' Champion of what? The Confederacy?" (quoted in Doyle, 1996, pp. 80–81).

Scene 3

In 1969, amidst a series of revolts by black athletes (see Edwards, 1969; Wiggins, 1997), fourteen black players on the University of Wyoming football team requested, or demanded, depending on who recounts the incident, to wear black armbands during an upcoming game against Brigham Young University. The athletes wanted to protest the Mormon institution's treatment of blacks. The coach refused and removed the players from the team. During the ensuing struggle over the legitimacy of the expulsion, fans remarked, "We can go all the way even without our niggers," and "Gettin' rid of them will turn out to be a blessin" (quoted in Michener, 1976, p. 159).

Amid the hype (and hope) of March Madness in 1999, Tarvener Johnson, the men's head basketball coach at Murray State University, suggested that race is no longer an issue in sports. He offered his remarks during a brief profile of him and his team included in a corporate-sponsored pre-game show introducing the second round of the annual NCAA Basketball Tournament. Johnson, who formerly coached high school basketball in Mississippi before integration, gave voice to a pervasive understanding of race in American culture: race, conceived of exclusively in terms of black and white, used to be a problem; however, attitudinal and institutional changes, perhaps most noticeably and effectively in the domain of athletics, (happily) have nullified its significance. Although not pushed to explain his statement, we believe it speaks to the popular assessment of race and sports in three ways. First, through his own achievements, becoming the head coach of a major collegiate basketball program; second, integration and (a more) equal opportunity have replaced the explicit segregation of sports, education, and society; and third, once marginalized African-American athletes not only play with their Euro-American peers without evoking discomfort, debate, or public dissension, but they have even come to dominate many of the sports in which they compete. Race does not matter, is not an issue in sports, then, because it promotes individual opportunity and achievement without regard to race, while encouraging racial interaction, if not racial harmony.

Johnson is not alone in his progressive reading of race and sport. In fact, the power of athletics to break down hierarchies, reverse prejudices, and improve race relations is a fundamental feature of contemporary American common sense, and it structures a popular historiography of race as well. Often individuals emplot a teleological account of the racial past. In a recent article discussing the disappearance of the white athlete, S.L. Price (1997, p. 33) exemplifies this technique of erasure.

> [Jackie] Robinson ushered American sports into an era of significance beyond the playing field. During the next two generations, the once monochromatic world of team sports became a paradigm of, and sometimes a spur to, racial equality. One milestone followed another: Larry Dobey broke into the American League several months after Robinson's debut; the NBA and the NFL were completely integrated; a Texas Western basketball team with an all-black starting lineup beat Adolph Rupp's all-white Kentucky squad in the 1966 NCAA final; the same year the Boston Celtics' was named the first black head coach of a major professional team; the Washington Redskins' Doug Williams in 1988 became the first black quarterback to win a Super Bowl. Management was still firmly white— and, regrettably remains so today—but one could argue that the playing field has become the nation's common ground, the one highly visible stage on which blacks and whites acted out the process of learning to live, play, and fight together as peers.

For Price and countless others, (college) sports has played an active role in realizing American ideals of opportunity, solidarity, and parity. It has brought people who were formerly separated together, fostering racial equality more notable for its sense of coevality than its structural symmetry. The broad strokes of this account present a rather tidy, even seamless, image of the changing state of race relations in the United States. It acknowledges the processible dimensions of historical change, only to jettison the power, conflict, and resistance animating such processes. Consequently, it offers a safe, superficial rendering of the past, attentive to the overcoming and undoing of race in American life.

The singular event or defining moment performs similar cultural work. Price references the 1966 NCAA Championship game between Texas Western University and Kentucky University. This game has become an archetype in popular perceptions of race and intercollegiate athletics. On several occasions during every NCAA men's basketball tournament, commentators invoke it. The game pitted the all-white perennial powerhouse, Kentucky, coached by the legendary Adolph Rupp, against the virtually unknown Texas Western team, coached by Don Haskin, with an all-black starting lineup. In brief asides, feature stories, and reminiscences, media personalities discuss the game as the turning point in college athletics, the singular moment after which the sport and public culture would never be the same. As David Israel describes, "It was the *Brown v. Board of Education* of college basketball ("The Final Four," 1989). Not unlike a Supreme Court decision, it literally mandated change, fostering (or so the story goes) unprecedented equality and opportunity. The selection of this game as the hallmark of integration is, of course, ironic, given that it pitted an all-black starting team against an all-white team—and thus may be more about segregation than its unraveling. In popular reflections on the contest and its significance, the event eclipsed historical processes. Desegregation was simple and easy, devoid of struggle, tensions, or refusals. Integration and equality, as these accounts like to conceive of the state of race relations in college sports, have been achieved; race is not a social problem; enjoy the game, they seem to say, and do not worry about discrimination or prejudice—these issues were solved long ago.

Read against our brief episodic history the significance of these three forms of public memory—subjective assessment, the progressive epic, and the singular event—becomes plain. They simplify, flatten, and reduce social process and historical change. They excise conflict and contestation, obscuring revolutionary and reactionary response to the shifting significance of race. They impose order and insist on an ending, thus offering closure. Importantly, they suggest that race, especially in the domain of college sports, is a historical artifact. They distance fans, coaches, players, and the media from the uneasy relations and inhumane asymmetries associated with racial stratification in the United States. They resolve the tensions and contradictions emergent in American race relations, reassuring participants and spectators that race does not matter. More often than not, postintegration celebration of sports and race veils the very real inequities central to intercollegiate athletics, described by renowned sport sociologist Harry Edwards (1984, p. 13):

> Thus since Jackie Robinson's debut, blacks have made vir-
> tually no progress beyond the athlete role in major Ameri-
> can sports. And, even as athletes in these sports, blacks
> often enjoy far less than total equality of opportunity. The
> evidence suggests, then, that in sport, America has "pro-
> gressed" from a "Jim Crow" pre-Jackie Robinson era to a
> post–Robinson era characterized by what I would term
> "Mr. James Crow, Esquire"—a system whereby the tradi-
> tional inequities of interracial relationships are camou-
> flaged and sustained through more subtle, sophisticated,
> exploitative and—for the sports establishment—highly
> profitable means.

Progressive interpretations of the desegregation of college sports exaggerate its effects, imposing a happy ending on ongoing strug-gles. They invoke race only to (dis)miss its continued significance.

AMERICAN DREAMING

Although great men and championship teams displace difference and progressive historiographies revise social processes, the indi-vidual remains central to the erasure of race. In particular, the commonsense notions of the self-made man and the American dream work against personal and collective engagements with the materiality of racial difference. Individualism, effort, application, and ability congeal to obscure the conditions and effects of racial hierarchy. Sandell (1995, p. 71) nicely encapuslates these asymmetrical structures:

> Statistically speaking, and compared with all young men in the United States, young black men are twice as likely to be unemployed, three times more likely to have been arrested, and six times more likely to have served time in prison. Nearly half of all black youths live in families below the poverty line, and one in five black youths aged 18 to 21 lack the basic certificate of education needed for most entry-level jobs. The most shocking statistic, however, is that homicide is the leading cause of death for most black teenagers and young adults. . . . These figures suggest that while race may be a social and ideological construct, it carries very real material effects.

In this highly stratified context saturated with ideologies of openness, mobility, freedom, and industry, the (auto)biographical instances told by and about athletes frequently overcome race. Tarvener Johnson's comment discussed above hints at this pattern. More revealing are the crystallization and recollection of dreams about "going pro," for these popular desires perpetuate myths that sports is a way of amassing great wealth, securing social position, and achieving individual happiness (see Hoberman, 1997; Riess, 1990). College is not an end in itself but a stage—both a phase to pass through and a staging ground to develop and demonstrate one's discipline, talent, and character.

In this section, we explore such narratives in two contexts, a recent Nike ad campaign and the celebrated documentary *Hoop Dreams*. In both instances, we find, these accounts foreground race not to seriously examine it but to transcend it. Indeed, a "rhetoric of transcendence," to borrow a phrase from Cheryl Cole's (1996, p. 387) elegant analysis of Michael Jordan, Nike, and the recoding of race and deviance, obscures racial difference. Exceptional abilities and exploits literally liberate athletes such as Jordan—regularly celebrated as the greatest to play the game—from race. "For example, Nike public relations director Liz Dolan argues that Nike does

not think of Jordan in racial terms. In her words 'We don't think of
our athletes as black and white. We think of Mike Jordan as the
best basketball player in the world' " (quoted in Cole, 1996). Chicago Bulls owner Jerry Reinsdorf even queried once, "Is Michael
Jordan black? . . . Michael has no color" (quoted in Kornbluth,
1995, p. 26). These comments and constructs, as Cole (1996,
p. 387) argues, "distance Jordan [and other extraordinary black
athletes] from the semiotic field that locates and positions other
African-American men/players. Additionally, the repetition of transcendence masks the power/knowledge grid through which Jordan
is made intelligible and through which American identities are constructed." The rhetoric of transcendence and its effects, as the following examples clarify, is not limited to professional athletics but
rather shapes the lives and life histories of college athletes as well.

Two Nike advertising spots that ran in 1995 expose the work-
ings of these life histories: the first a success story, entitled "Work,"
narrated by then-professional basketball superstar Penny Hardaway, and the second a tale of regret and missed opportunities offered by streetball legend Peewee Kirkland (quoted in Goldman &
Popson, 1998, p. 98).

> Nah! I wasn't born with a basketball in my cradle.
> For some believe we come out dunking once we are
>   conceived.
> Superstar? I got it made, right?
> I went from nothing to something overnight.
> Well, don't believe the hype.
> I had to work to get where I'm at and that's a fact.
> Mom and Grandma raised me to be proud
> and they instilled their philosophy in me
> knowing that no one could take that from me.
> Nah! I had to work to get here.
> At the Boys and Girls club. At Memphis State.
> I had to work to be great.
> Just do it.
>
> My Name is Peewee Kirkland.
> I'm the guy who could have made it, but walked away.

I'm the guy who got drafted by the Chicago Bulls.
I'm the guy who scored 135 points in one game.
In the beginning I lived every kid's biggest dream.
In the end I lived every kid's worst nightmare.
The streets, the life of crime, takes lives and that needs to
  be remembered.

These life histories map out opposite itineraries, success, super-stardom, and the American Dream juxtaposed with failure, obscurity, and a societal nightmare. The individual, they assert, makes his or her fortune based on his or her effort and ability. The system is open, fostering upward mobility for individuals with talent, character, and discipline. Indeed, as Goldman and Popson (1998, p. 110) suggest in their discussion of these narratives, "Though these ads allude to questions of social structure, Nike prefers to highlight an individualism that privileges the role of proper values, personal choices, and the willpower not to give in to the lure of easy pleasures. Lose your discipline and you can lose everything. Such morality tales are redolent of traditional middle-class accounts of individual success in a capitalist society."

Significantly, these morality tales about sports and mobility turn on and turn away race. Racial difference, embedded in urban poverty, saturates these advertisements, but it is not part of them. Hardaway does pause at the outset of his autobiography to highlight and quickly refute a popular racist stereotype, but then he turns his attention to the development of his character and work, both of which enabled him to become a superstar. It is he as an individual who achieves, with the assistance of his mother and grandmother. He works not against racial and class stratification but to realize his potential. Race is not mentioned in Kirkland's life history. Rather, the problems often associated with urban life paint an image of a personal failure, of promise and opportunity lost in the streets where they began. The focus here, as in Hardaway's account, is on the individual, not on social relations and historical conditions. In both ads, the individual eviscerates the significance of race. It is not race that makes a difference but character, industry, and talent.

Hoop Dreams, the critically applauded, surprisingly popular documentary, centers on the American Dream. It simultaneously celebrates and critiques the interpenetration of mobility, discipline, and character. The synopsis released with the video describes the film in the following terms (quoted in Sandell, 1995, p. 60).

> They have nothing—expect talent and a dream—and in this tough Chicago neighborhood, dreams are all they can count on. *Hoop Dreams* is the critically acclaimed true-life story of Arthur Agee and William Gates and the unforgettable five-year experience that turns them into men. You will come to know them and root for them as if they were your friends, your family, as against all odds, these boys prove with faith, talent, and a little luck anyone can achieve the American Dream.

Or, as bell hooks (1995, p. 22) asserts, "The lure of *Hoop Dreams* is that it affirms that those on the bottom can ascend this society, even as it is critical of the manner in which they rise. This film tells the world how the American Dream works." In exploring the operations and effects of this ideological construct, the film and accompanying speaking tour promoting it overcome race.

We agree with Cheryl Cole and Samantha King (1998, p. 71), who wrote, "There are a number of ways in which *Hoop Dreams* indicts and fails to indict the economies of sport. We contend that while Hoop Dreams gestures toward criticizing the exploitative treatment and commodification of William, Arthur, and other urban African-American youths . . . criticism is ultimately directed to and displaced onto the bodies of particular social agents who are visualized as virtuous or vicious." Or, as Jillan Sandell (1995, p. 71) phrases it, "The story focuses only on individuals, not on the systematic nature of race and class oppression." For example, St. Joseph's basketball coach, Gene Pingatore, is seen as one who values the young men exclusively for their basketball talents and is less supportive when either expectations for performance are not met or when his black players are confronted with various personal and familial difficulties (see Robbins, 1997). In the United States, the predominant reaction to the film seems to have been celebratory, as the glossy images of NBA stars and coaches, Gates' and Agee's dreams of "going pro," and the drama of the basketball games in which they starred generate within audiences a pleasurable response. Viewers are likely to pick up on the narrative of exploitation. They ultimately find comfort in the ways in which various individuals in the film show compassion for these students, and in the ways in which the families of these young men persevere in the face of adversity. Audiences may indeed experience a collective sense of ethical concern for the plight of Gates and Agee, while excusing themselves from a more critical examination of the broader social contexts that create these spaces of exploitation (see Cole & King, 1998). For example, neither *Hoop Dreams* nor the popular readings of the film question the overwhelming degree of emotional and material investment of these students and their families into the desire to play collegiate and, later, professional basketball. Certainly the ways in which such social agendas are informed by racial identities and experiences are never addressed (see Smith, 1995).

For example, in one of the opening scenes of the film, Gates is watching the NBA All-Star game on television, along with family members. Following the game, viewers hear him speak about his aspirations:

> Right now, I want, you know, to play in the NBA like anybody else would want to be. That's who, tha's, tha's somethin I dream-think about all the time, you know, playing in the NBA. [Cut to . . . a slow motion image of William dunking on the netless rim, now accompanied by the cheers . . . heard earlier (during the All-Star game). Then, to an extreme close-up of William's mother:] He's just doing somethin' that he loves so much. He jus love it so much, you know, I'm just happy for him. (dialogue quoted in Cole & King, 1998, p. 58)

In spite of a severe knee injury and subsequent surgery during high school, Gates was recruited by a number of colleges to play basketball and decided to attend Marquette University on a basketball scholarship. He never achieved on the court what both he and others anticipated years earlier, but he graduated with a degree in communications.

William's older brother Curtis was not as fortunate. Working as a security guard, he too once had hoop dreams, but in his words, "I ain't amounted to nothin'." Like his brother, he was an outstanding high school basketball player, receiving a scholarship to the University of Central Florida. Following difficulties with the coach, he withdrew from school. He and his mother agree that he never realized his promise, nor his dreams, because of his choices.

Read against one another, the operations of the American Dream become apparent, as do their consequences for critical understandings of race and class. Individual character and choices and personal discipline and drive, not social conditions, determine what one becomes—a failure who made a bad choice or a success who pursued his dreams. In neither case is race invoked or explored either by the film or its subjects.

Individualism and the American Dream expunge race from the promotional speaking tour associated with the film. During the spring 1996 semester, William Gates gave a presentation at Luther College in Decorah, Iowa, as part of a speaking tour sponsored by the film company promoting *Hoop Dreams*. He spoke to an auditorium filled with Luther College students and a few faculty, a largely white, Christian, Midwestern audience. The agenda for his talk was vague at best and could be characterized as a set of spontaneous remarks about, variously, the experience of having been the focus of this popular documentary, of being heavily recruited to play "big-time" high school and college basketball, and of life and philosophy in general.

Dressed in a tan suit and necktie, Gates appeared poised for an interview. He stood alone on a stage, and with the audience he watched a brief clip that featured audience and media reactions to the film. Afterward, Gates began to speak, admitting to being a "bit nervous" but quickly establishing a relaxed presence, even a charming sort of irreverence, as though talking with friends about school, family, and the "system." He boasted that *Hoop Dreams* had become the best-selling documentary ever, and then he proceeded to offer the audience an update on the lives of key figures in the film.

"Arthur's [Agee] Dad got into some real trouble with drugs. I am happy to report that he has been drug-free now for 4½ years. And Arthur's mom is now an R.N." The audience responds with applause. Gates then notes that he has been married for two and a half years to his sweetheart, whom he dated since the seventh grade. "She sells Mary Kay!" he adds. "We have a seven-year-old daughter Alicia, and a one-year-old son—he's a 'Little Hoopster'." Again, individuals, not social categories or circumstances, are the center of the discussion. Moreover, these individuals have made something of themselves. They have renounced easy pleasures; and better, they have applied themselves to improving their lives through education and enterprise.

Gates then begins to address the issue of drug usage more broadly, articulating what will be one of the key messages he hopes to convey. "I never felt pressured to do drugs. I knew what I wanted and I stayed focused. I didn't let peer pressure get to me, and believe me, there was a lot of pressure to do drugs." Then he contrasts his experience to Shannon's, a friend of Arthur's, who "never made it out of the 'hood" because of drugs. He adopts a tone of admonishment in urging students not to do drugs. At another point, he pauses, looks out at the audience, and tells the males to be very careful and sensitive to their partners, "because date rape is horrible." Again, loud applause. He returns then to the topic of his marriage and children, the oldest of which he fathered as a high school student. "I encourage you not to have kids at your age. It is very, very difficult." Oddly, from this disorganized platform, he fashions himself as a cultural and social critic, whose voice seems to lack authority. Still, Gates' message cannot be missed: he succeeds through a combination of discipline and character, and he implores others to emulate him.

What failed to materialize during his remarks was an explicit discussion of race. The erasure was conspicuous. Here was a black graduate of Marquette, speaking to Luther College students about a documentary that had made him famous. The film, even by the most conservative commentators, urged audiences to think about the problems of power, race, and exploitation that pervade basketball recruitment and coaching. Yet Gates did not mention race even once before it was ultimately brought up by members of the audience during the question-answer period. But Gates was in a space in which he was doomed to fail, in terms of what his presence was designed to do. Here was one of the film's featured "stars" who was jettisoned in various ways by an uncaring system, who perhaps remained—at this point in his life—unfocused, jaded, and insecure, being positioned as a seasoned, much wiser, insightful critic of American youth culture.

Undoubtedly, Gates may have been wiser, but he had just graduated—no mean accomplishment for anybody—and now he had to design a life and career without basketball, the very essence of his earlier visions of the future. Further, if he were indeed emotionally poised and articulate enough to voice a mature critique of the system that *Hoop Dreams* itself indicts only partially, the platform from which he spoke would not allow it, for the film was received in many ways as a celebration of the high school athlete and the social investments in transforming eighth graders into NBA stars.

CONCLUSIONS

Celebratory sporting discourses, whether exhibits playing tribute to greatness, stories of social progress, or accounts of individual achievement, erase race. They literally white it out. Excising, deferring, or repressing race, they obscure the social structures, inequities, and conditions of possibility animating intercollegiate athletics. They clear a space (without or beyond race) to fashion self and society in terms of progress, equality, and mobility. As such, they fit into a broader social field nicely encapsulated by Robyn Wiegman (1995, pp. 40–41).

> The processes of subjection we now live within . . . too often feature integration without equality, representation without power, presence without the confirming possibility of emancipation. Ours is a white supremacist system, asymmetrical in its economic and political allotments, triumphant in its ability to mask deep disparity on the one hand, and yet thoroughly rigid in its maintenance of naive individualism and rhetorical democracy on the other.

The deeply imbricated erasures discussed in this chapter then must be understood as manifestations of white supremacy. They trivialize race, perpetuating the commonsense conviction that race does not matter. They encourage individuals and institutions to accept that race is not an issue, that it is a historical evil, defeated on the playing field, and/or that individual effort and talent, regardless of race, not social structures, make a difference. Moreover, these ideologies and effects make whiteness invisible, they secure white privilege. Against this backdrop, for the remainder of the text, we turn our attention to explicit materializations of race, excavating the elaborations, articulations, and contestations of racial difference in red, black, and white.

3

"Kill the Indians, Save the Chief":
Native American Mascots
and Imperial Identities

On a Friday night in October 1989, several University of Illinois undergraduate students gathered in a small, upstairs room of the TKE fraternity house. These students "partied" into the night, typical of a weekend college celebration, and their reverie was punctuated the next day when the university football team, the "Fighting Illini," played its fourth game of the season. The group, a mix of young white men and women, was situated around a rectangular table in the dimly lit, smoke-filled quarter, as the loud but not deafening stereo speakers boomed with the music of Pink Floyd.

In preparation for the drinking game they would play, mugs and glasses were filled with either beer or Jack Daniels whiskey. One of the participants used a shot glass decorated with the image of the University's mascot, Chief Illiniwek, to hold his whiskey. The image was a colorful, modernist interpretation, in impressionist style, of a painted Indian face adorned with a feathered headdress. The same image was emblazoned on the front of a sweatshirt worn by one of the women. The shot glass was a strikingly appropriate tool, for the game that would soon commence was called "Indian." This drinking game shares the common goal of other such games—ultimately to get drunk—but it allows its participants to play at "being Indian" in highly caricatured ways as they pursue their aim.

41

The action began with everybody forming a circle and gently tapping their mugs or glasses on the table in a steady rhythmic fashion, ostensibly mimicking the sound of Indian drumming. Each player was then given an "Indian" name reflecting some real aspect of his or her personality, such as "Dances with Marijuana" or "Nintendo Red Hawk." Then the leader asked, "What's the name of the game?" and the others responded in unison, "Indian!" Then, "What's the purpose?" was met with "To get fucked-up!" Each player then chose an arbitrary hand "sign" or signal as his or her own for the duration of the game, such as sticking out his or her tongue or imitating the chopping motion of a tomahawk. The game proceeded as everybody took a turn at calling out one of the Indian names. As a name was called, its "owner" had to respond by appropriately performing the correct sign. Anyone who committed a verbal or physical mistake was forced to drink.

The game is not unique to the Champaign–Urbana campus of the University of Illinois; it is undoubtedly played by college students across the land. But its existence at Illinois assumes an unusually striking emblematic value. The game is one of those interactional moments of cultural practice that shape and inform subjectivity, in this instance, a subjectivity bearing the imprint of neocolonial histories and relations of power. On this campus, however, the game unfolds in a discursive space especially well marked and motivated by layers upon layers of structured symbolic violence (see Bourdieu & Passeron, 1977, p. 4), which victimizes the sensibilities and sense of well-being of many Native Americans, including those few who actually attend the university.

At the center of this sociohistorical formation is Chief Illiniwek, the proud symbol of the university, which becomes an embodied reality as the mascot (person/object) of the athletic teams. Present, in particular, at the games of the "revenue" sports teams (football and basketball), Chief Illiniwek performs a series of Indian dances as the spiritual cheerleader of the "Fighting Illini." Indeed, he would perform this variety of amusement at halftime during the football game attended by those students, hungover, who—the previous night—had practiced their own version of Indian fun, using Chief Illiniwek shot glasses purchased from the university book store for $4.95. The tools, toys, and games of these students can best be interpreted by considering their circulation within this political and affective economy of Indian exhibition. Perhaps only on this campus, then, does a recreational activity in which young white Americans can caricature Native Americans in a seemingly harmless, playful drinking ritual fully realize the complete force of neocolonial hegemony (see King & Springwood, 2000, 2001; Prochaska, 2001; Rosenstein, 2001; Spindel, 1997).

In this chapter, we explore the history of this dancing Indian, a fully mature representation of alterity, beginning with its formal invention in 1926 and focusing in particular on the University of Illinois' shifting colonial strategies of Native American displacement/misplacement/replacement and the erasure and resuscitation of Indian voices. Analytically, this institutional technology of mimesis and alterity can best be read as a highly produced form of "playing Indian" that enacts a Manifest Destiny narrative of Indian conquest, sacrifice, and domination, all in the sustained interests of the empire. The performance literally as well as ritually inscribes the relations of imperial power directly onto the Native American body—represented by a white male student painted as an Indian—and, in Foucauldian parlance, then, is a technology of bodily discipline. In particular, we argue that the exhibitionary and narrative practices that endow Chief Illiniwek with significance reproduce images and imaginaries of the colonial past in the postcolonial present. These practices freeze Native Americans, reducing them to rigid, flat renderings of their diverse cultures and histories. At the same time, and this is perhaps the most significant aspect of "Playing Indian," they are primarily moments of writing and rewriting a Euro-American identity in terms of conquest, hierarchy, and domination.

Finally, a significant portion of this reading focuses upon the recent episodes of protest against the Chief and the sustained efforts to have the embodied icon retired. The prime movers behind this protest are a small group of Native American students and staff at the university, whose efforts are perhaps best situated in the broader context of a nationwide series of protests against native American mascots that began in earnest in the 1980s. However, the protest against Chief Illiniwek, who enjoys broad popular support in the community, seems to have cut right to the core of Euro-American subjectivity, as it has led to highly impassioned defenses of the mascot, discussed in greater detail below.

Through an examination of the local struggle of these students and their supporters as well as the university's battle of position against them, the complicated, often opaque, process of imperial hegemony and the political construction and reconstruction of particular voices emerge with greater clarity. Ultimately, the story of the University of Illinois' invigorated defense of its traditional symbol becomes an ironic one of resurrecting the voice of the Illini Indians— once vanished, thrice displaced, yet ostensibly still in existence—by positioning them as owners of the only legitimate opinion on the issue of whether or not Chief Illiniwek should be retired.

INVENTING CHIEF ILLINIWEK

This account of how Chief Illiniwek came to be begins appropriately with one of the many endings imposed upon the indigenous peoples of Illinois. In 1916, Truman Michelson conducted three weeks of fieldwork on the Confederated Peoria Tribe, a sociopolitical unit incorporating the native nations once referred to collectively as the Illinois. In his brief ethnographic report to the Illinois Centennial Commission, he made observations about Peoria folklore, linguistics, social organization, demography, and dance. Importantly, his anthropological observations informed the writing of the multivolume, centennial history of the state of Illinois (Alvord, 1920). The articulation of anthropological and historical technologies once again fixed, flattened, and literally froze the peoples and practices of native North America, imprinting images of them as prehistoric and primitive peoples caught within the flows of Euro-American history and civilization.

Based upon Michelson's (1916, p. 1) examination of these accepted elements of "authentic" and "traditional" culture, including language, mythology, and ritual, he concluded that the Peoria had "practically lost their ethnology," forgetting distinctive features and central "truths" of their culture and history. Michelson's findings would surprise neither the anthropological community nor the general public. Native Americans were understood to be on the verge of extinction; or to borrow from the title of Joseph Dixon's (1972/1913) book, originally published three years before Michelson went into the field, they were "The Vanishing Race."

Not only did his conclusions echo comments made by Donaldson thirty years earlier—"No Peoria of pure blood is (probably) now living" (1886, p. 141)—but they emerged in a sociohistorical context in which policy makers, academics, and citizens anticipated that Native Americans would either be assimilated or would expire (see Dippie, 1982; Hoxie, 1979).

Within a decade of Michelson's fieldwork, the native nations of Illinois were "reborn," entering popular culture through static categories borrowed from the fields of anthropology and history. Building on one of the earliest, most conspicuous forms of Indian mimesis—the nineteenth-century practice of American universities securing a Native American image or name with which to identify themselves (Banks, 1993; Churchill, 1994; Coombe, 1999; Davis, 1993; Frazier, 1997; King & Springwood, 2000, 2001; Pewewardy, 1994; Slowikowski, 1993; Springwood & King, 2000; Staurowsky, 1998; Wenner, 1993)—the University of Illinois became known as the Fighting Illini in the early 1920s. The one-time campus football hero Robert Zuppke located the spirit of his university—a land-grant state institution of national renown—in the historic/mythic space of the Native Americans who once lived in central Illinois. At a pep rally, he informed, "Illini is the name of a tribe of Indians and the word 'Illiniwek' means the complete Indian man, the physical man, the intellectual man, and the spiritual man" ("Chief Illiniwek Tradition," undated document). Seeking to transform the University of Illinois' proud tradition of honoring the Illini Indians into something more tangible, Lester Leutwiler—whose infatuation with Native Americans was nurtured by his Urbana Boy Scout Troop 6—put together an Indian outfit and prepared a series of dances in order to bring the otherwise extinct Illini back to life in the form of Chief Illiniwek. Under the guidance of marching band director Ray Dvorak, Leutwiler—who had once organized a powwow for his senior project at Urbana High School—recreated "Redskin heritage" during halftime at the 1926 University of Illinois–University of Pennsylvania football game. An anonymous document in the University of Illinois archives described the moment:

> Just as the Illinois Football Band (so named in those days) was about to march into the formation PENN, Chief Illiniwek ran from his hiding place just north of the Illinois

stands and took over the leadership of the band with a genuine lively Indian dance. Halted in the center of the field,
the band played "Hail Pennsylvania," Pennsylvania's alma
mater song. As Chief Illiniwek saluted the Pennsylvania
rooters, William Penn (impersonated by George Adams,
U of I drum major in appropriate Quaker dress), came for-
ward and accepted the gesture of friendship offered by the
Indian chief and joined him in smoking the peace pipe. At
the close of the halftime ceremony, William Penn and Chief
Illiniwek walked arm in arm across to the Illinois side of
the field to a deafening ovation. (Undated, untitled document, University of Illinois Library Archives)

Although clearly not high-brow political drama, this enactment—
which at a variety of levels is encoded to be read and must be read as
a *rendering* of past events—is emblematic of dramatic practices that
reproduce the historical process as unmarked by violence or oppression. Of course, William Penn, the Quaker founder of the State of
Pennsylvania, probably never met a chief of an Illinois tribe, not to
mention one named Chief Illiniwek. Nevertheless, the event staged
on the athletic turf served to effectively and *ritually* resolve the historical conflicts between the Indian and the Euro-American, while
confirming the dominance of the latter. In retrospect, then, it was a
moment of colonial kitsch theater; but in the eyes of Leutwiler and
the supporters of Chief Illiniwek, it was pious drama.

Importantly, Leutwiler had not recreated the Illinois by piecing
together aspects of their material culture or elements of their performative repertoire. Instead, he fashioned Chief Illiniwek from
the manner of dress associated with the native nations of the Plains
and an amalgam of movements identified as "Indian." Four years
after the invention of Chief Illiniwek, efforts were made to more
systematically authenticate the mascot and its performances. Once
again, those involved turned away from the presumably (ethno-
logically) extinct Confederated Peoria Tribe, previously studied by
Michelson, locating the appropriate fashions and proper image for
Chief Illiniwek on the Northern Plains. Webber Borchers, also a
former Boy Scout who succeeded Leutwiler and portrayed the
mascot during the 1929 and 1930 football seasons, insisted that a
new and "authentic" costume made by "traditional" Native Americans was needed to enhance the value and significance of his per-

formances. Initially, he attempted to secure funding for the new costume from the student body, but he raised only thirty dollars (Borchers, 1959, p. 2). Indeed, as he recalled in a letter nearly thirty years later (ibid., p. 1): "He visited nearly every Sorority and Fraternity on the campus, but without much success due to the fact that the houses had heavy mortgages, and the depression was in full sway." On the advice of Robert Drake, Borchers approached local businessman and Illini supporter Isaac Kuhn, who agreed to finance the fabrication of a new costume if Borchers "would personally see to the proper authenticity of the regalia" (ibid., p. 2). After securing the funding in the summer of 1930, he hitchhiked to South Dakota, arriving at the Pine Ridge Reservation in August. Through the agent and local traders, he located an elderly Oglala woman, who Borchers claimed "as a girl she had helped mutilate the dead of Custer after the battle [sic] of Little Bighorn" (ibid.). She agreed to supervise the manufacture of the outfit by three younger women. Borchers paid $500 for the costume, overseeing the process until forced to return to Urbana–Champaign for the fall term. A press release described the impressive ensemble upon its completion three months later: "It is all white calfskin. The breastplate is made of deer bones and porcupine quills and the war bonnet has real eagle feathers. The shirt has beaded insignia over the shoulders and so do the trousers, which are made in white man's style because of the activity involved in the Illiniwek dance" ("An Illinois Illustrated Newsfeature," c. 1930). On November 8, 1930, the authentic "Indian" attire debuted in a parade down Fifth Avenue prior to a football game against Army. In subsequent years, Borchers added a horse to his performance. A member of the Reserve Officer Training Corps (ROTC) cavalry on campus, he trained a horse named Pinto in order to ride bareback onto the field and then leap off to begin his dances. This tradition was short-lived because of damage to the football field.

Euro-American commentators applauded the resurrection of the Illinois through the ritual reenactments of Chief Illiniwek. Indeed, twenty-six years after the invention of the athletic mascot, Burford (1952, p. 407) underscored its significance:

It was, and is, appropriate that Chief Illiniwek, the embodiment of the Red Men who had vanished before the overwhelming waves of White Men, should return to the land of their fathers. It was fitting that he should revisit the Illinois campus. In the name of his tribe and in memory of his fore-fathers and of the warriors who had struggled and died both in prehistoric and historic Illinois, it was both proper and pleasing that the Chief should strut his stuff and perform his ancient ritualistic dances, in the lovely days of Indian Sum-mer, while the Marching Band played weird [*sic*] incanta-tions before the packed Stadium of contemporary Palefaces.

Chief Illiniwek's presence continued through the years, and when one chief impersonator graduated, another male student was selected as a replacement. The tradition remained closely allied with the University Marching Band, which organized the perfor-mances and the selection of Chief Illiniwek. The Indian dances have always been juxtaposed or interspersed with the band's per-formances. Customarily, the band plays a song or two, and then Chief Illiniwek, face streaked with paint, makes his entrance into the football stadium or onto the basketball court and dances to the accompaniment of the band. On the football field, the band seems to shift in formation to "make a hole" or a framed space for Chief Illiniwek to enter. His "background music" is largely percussive, with a series of Hollywood-style rhythmic beats signifying "Indian music." Such performances seem to inspire a state of impassioned reverence in stadium audiences.

Documentation detailing how Chief Illiniwek's actual perfor-mances were "choreographed" is sparse, although since the tradi-tion began, improvisation has been paramount. The parameters and guidelines for Chief tryouts provided by the Department of Bands in 1993 included these requirements:

- The entrance is from under the goalposts at the north end of the stadium.
- The downfield dance begins at approximately the 35–50 yard line and moves to the end zone.
- The solo dance is done on the 50-yard line facing the east stands at the very center of the field.
- The only required movements in the performance are the three split-jumps.

These guidelines advise that, "The steps used in the dance are entirely left up to you, but you will be judged by the following criteria . . ." and then follow with a list noting qualities such as rhythm and timing, grace and agility, and, finally, creativity and imagination. Contemporary performances do not vary widely, however, and they always include some set of leg kicks and postured spins with folded arms held high in front of the chest.

Today, Chief Illiniwek's impersonator wears a feathered headdress weighing approximately twenty-five pounds. In order to accomplish his routine, he must be in excellent physical condition. Running onto the field in bare feet, before he is finished, Chief Illiniwek typically completes three running split-jumps, wherein the feet are brought up to shoulder level, a number of double-steps in time to the music, a couple of long running sprints across the field, and then three consecutive high kicks.

The public also may reimagine itself as part of the "Indian community" by purchasing a share in artificially created "sodalities" in joining the "Fighting Illini Scholarship Fund." Donations are invited according to a hierarchical scale, so that for $100, one becomes a member of the Tomahawk Club; for $250, the Brave Club; for $500, the Warrior Club; for $1,000, the Chief Club; and for $3,000, the Tribal Council. In summary thus far, the production of Chief Illiniwek is best read as a multlilayered construction: a set of racist stereotypes about Native Americans, a magical talisman of identification and imagination for students, alumni, and fans, and an allegorical site for restaging and countering domination.

REMAPPING HISTORY
ONTO THE BODY OF AN INDIAN

The Chief Illiniwek tradition can be characterized as a ritual drama serving to reconcile a dominant pattern of violence that marks the history of white America in its relations with Native Americans. In the most general terms, rituals are considered repetitive social practices with patterned sequences that are intended to effect an "evocative presentational style" (Moore & Myerhoff, 1977, p. 7). Further, they have a collective dimension in that they are practices of signification that convey meaning—but such meaning must always be understood as a commentary about relations of power. That is, rituals are best considered articulations of myth and history, sometimes playful, sometimes serious.

The performances of Chief Illiniwek are social rituals grounded in a long tradition of colonial mimicry of the colonized Other. In this case, the one indispensable material instrument needed to practice the ritual is the body—one that mimics/signifies "Indianness" as this category extends from Euro-American subjectivity. Of course, it is not the body of a "real Indian" but rather the social body of all Native Americans, enacted by a young white student. The individual members of the audiences of these dramas, largely non-Indian people, are able to participate in a ludic encounter with history. In fact, using this invented Indian body as a ritual map, they are able to participate in remaking the colonial past in the post-colonial present by unwittingly imagining a new version of Manifest Destiny.

Manifest Destiny was an important ideological tool in the nation-building project of white America. Rooted largely in seventeenth-century Puritan theology, this was the set of colonizing beliefs and practices grounded in the doctrine of a divine prophecy insisting that white Europeans were destined to discover, conquer, spiritually liberate, and otherwise give order and structure to the New World and its peoples (Segal & Stineback, 1977). In other words, America was God's country and Europeans were God's chosen people, and the conquest of New World territory—which was to include the sacrifice of large numbers of Indian people—was to unfold as a sacred drama. This historical process was driven by a "romantic racial nationalism" (Horsman, 1981) based upon a hierarchy of humankind with Anglo-Saxons at the top and Indians several rungs lower. Manifest Destiny articulated biblical support for the often violent and messy practice of Empire building, which in the United States included slavery and the forging of two blood-stained paths of diaspora, a trans-Atlantic one and a domestic one that crisscrossed the Continental United States.

The supporters of Chief Illiniwek insist that they are keeping alive the memory of the Illinois as well as Native Americans more generally (see King & Springwood, 2000). They claim that the exhibitionary practice of Chief Illiniwek "honors" Indian people.

According to a report by a previous member of the Illini Marching Band (Hofer, 1994, p. 17, emphasis added), other band members intoned such comments as, "The chief is not your typical mascot. He is *sanctified* and represents U of I as an institution of higher-level thinking people. It would be beneath the U of I to have a Hawkeye, and all of the typical 'hey, rah, rah stuff.' " Similar opinions are voiced regularly by members of the local community and by students of the university. Clearly then, representing the athletic mascot is considered a very serious matter and a grand responsibility.

These meanings inscribed onto Chief Illiniwek's performance—and literally, his body—arise from the "romance" implicit in the mythology of Empire that turns on the social ambivalence of colonial subjectivity and colonial terror. An odd mix of adventure, promise, guilt, and sorrow structures this subjectivity, often giving rise to representational forms of "imperial nostalgia," an idea fully developed by Renato Rosaldo (1989, p. 70; see also, Slowikowski, 1993):

> [It] occurs alongside a peculiar sense of mission, "the white man's burden," where civilized nations stand duty-bound to uplift so-called savage ones. In this ideologically constructed world of ongoing progressive change, putatively static savage societies become a stable reference point for defining (the felicitous progress of) civilized identity. [Colonizers] valorize innovation, and then yearn for more stable worlds, whether these reside in our own past, in other cultures, or in the conflation of the two. . . . When the so-called civilizing process destabilizes forms of life, the agents of change experience transformations of other cultures as if they were personal losses.

Just as the project of Anglo-Saxon providence turned the corner—having effectively subdued any potential of Native American military resistance—this imperialist nostalgia began to emerge everywhere in spaces of representation.

As King (1998) has effectively demonstrated, the nineteenth century was dominated by practices of inscription and exhibition, framed especially as forms of ethnological science, which constructed Indians as an either vanished or vanishing race of people. From the rise to dominance of the Smithsonian Institution as the authorial narrator of American Indian history and culture to the theater of Buffalo Bill's *Wild West Show* to such prominent figures as Teddy Roosevelt (see Kaplan, 1993), who embodied this imperial frontier image, the late 1800s put the final touches on the subjectivity of the white oppressor. At this point, the sign value of the Indian effectively superseded and displaced the human existence of Native Americans as interactional reality. In fact, the Indian was appropriated to serve as the central object of fascination and longing in the development of a white, masculine, character-building movement whose emergence bridged the fin de siècle.

Specifically, this movement—whose agenda was articulated in a popular series of youth novels, health manuals, speeches, and the literature of the Boy Scouts of America—encouraged young boys to embrace certain elements of Indian life as a way of instilling in them discipline, courage, and an intimate knowledge of nature, health, and moral character. Essentially, the aim was to teach white children Indian ways (Mechling, 1980, p. 19), but what constituted "Indian ways" was a set of highly idealized stereotypes of Indians as scouts, hunters, and craftspeople. Ernest Thompson Seton was perhaps foremost in consolidating this set of principles into a coherent package and then communicating this message through his popular series of Woodcraft books. "Woodcraft" was the name Seton gave to the general notion of using the child's natural instincts to build character (ibid.). A brief sampling of the titles of his volumes is revealing. In 1903 he published *Two Little Savages: Being the Adventures of Two Boys Who Lived as Indians, and What They Learned*, followed by *Red Book: Or, How to Play Indian* (1904). Seton's defining moment came in 1912 with *The Book of Woodcraft and Indian Lore*, where in a later installment in this series he summarized the significance of the Indian to the people of the United States:

> America owes much to the Redman. When the struggle for freedom came on, it was between men of the same blood and bone, equal in brains and in strength. . . . The great advantage of the American was that he was trained

in Woodcraft, and this training which gave him the victory, he got from the Redman. . . . But the Redman can
do a greater service now and in the future. He can teach
us the ways of outdoor life, the nobility of courage, the
joy of beauty, the blessedness of enough, the glory of service, the power of kindness. . . . For these were the things
the Redman stood for; these were the sum of his faith.
(Seton, 1926, p. 8)

In addition to locating nearly all positive qualities of human nature
in Native American "culture," Seton actually claims that the Indians lost to the colonizers because of what the latter learned from
them. Further, he effectively articulates the discursive formation
through which Chief Illiniwek would emerge.

Indeed, when in the 1920s football legend Zuppke decided to
anchor his university's spirit and purpose in the legacy of the Illinois Indians, he was merely working within this same formation.
Chief Illiniwek was born in a spatial and historical moment,
structured by residual practices of frontier ideology and imperialist nostalgia. For example, the university's marching band,
which inspired and shaped his development, is both a real and
symbolic extension of military formations as celebrated bodies of
conquest and expansion. In fact, until as recently as the 1940s,
students attending land-grant state universities were required to
participate in either the ROTC or the marching band. Further,
the Indian mascot was linked, from the start, to college athletics
and to the Olympian spirit of masculine character and healthful
morality.

As such, it is fitting that Leutwiler was a Boy Scout, where he
was directly exposed to Seton's Woodcraft manuals. Traditionally
requiring Chief Illiniwek's impersonator to be an Eagle Scout reflects this ideology. Participation in the Boy Scouts of America is a
Euro-American suburban practice that can be read at multiple levels as a ritualized neocolonial extension of frontier ideology. In
Champaign–Urbana, this practice, in articulation with an emergent patriotism on the Illinois campus marked by a nationally famous marching band and athletic program, served to construct a
social field upon which the image and history of the American Indian could be ritually disciplined.

Chief Illiniwek's appearances have since their inception staged a mythical narrative of the historical relationship between Anglo-Saxon pioneers and Native Americans. It is a narrative of ambivalence that includes contact, friendship, and subsequent submission. It is a sensual narrative that turns on wildness, sexuality, and savagery, and it is a nostalgic narrative mourning the loss of these once-great warriors and their glorious society. To be sure, the performance "honors" the Indian, but it does so through unconscious forms by allowing white America to simultaneously enact its grief for and to consecrate the memory of the Indian. It is a celebration of the Indian sacrifice in the name of imperial progress according to the divine plan of Manifest Destiny. It is a celebration of imperial power, then, that ritually incorporates the tragic figure of the Indian into the "imagined community," in Benedict Anderson's (1983) words, of the United States of America. It allows white America to primitively reimagine itself as a partial embodiment of Indianness, and in the process, it attempts to psychically and sympathetically join with the Indian in the formation of a "shared" American consciousness.

But it is not in any simple way a liberating ritual, for it remains comfortably informed by oblique relations of power. Chief Illiniwek's continued performances, especially in the face of Native American protests, are testimony to (neo)colonial power as the power to represent and recontextualize. The broader landscape of this Saturday afternoon ritual—the frame within which the Chief performs his rehearsed movements with such ritual piety—must be interrogated. The football stadium, which at the University of Illinois holds over 65,000 people, can be viewed as a panopticon turned inside out. "Instead of the one in the center monitoring the bodies and the behavior of hundreds around the perimeter, the thousands around the perimeter monitor the behavior of the few in the center" (Fiske, 1993, p. 82). In this instance, however, only *one* Indian body is monitored and disciplined.

The ultimate site of power, especially of colonial power, is the body, where technologies of imperializing knowledge and discipline tend to accumulate. Dancing in the stadium, Chief Illiniwek becomes the symbolic body of the American Indian, onto which is ritually mapped all of the white readings of the significance of the Indian to the history of America. Discipline, or control, relies upon the technology of enclosure, and Chief Illiniwek is physically enclosed not only by the circular stadium but also by the Illini Marching Band, which tends to mold itself around the performing body as it enters the center of the field. Upon the completion of these dances and kicks, the band sweeps back across the field in formation, literally whisking the barefooted, paint-smudged Chief away, leaving the audience standing, cheering, and awestruck. Chief Illiniwek—the American Indian—is disciplined by colonial fascination, colonial libido, and colonial angst.

Indeed, efforts to locate within the native social body, a constellation of sexualized wildness and savagery, have long been central to the colonial narrative. This trope of the erotic native articulates the hidden possibilities of what may genuinely and more accurately reside within the heart and mind of the colonizer. A confusing mix of power and askew passion frequently imbues the subjectivity and discourse of colonial violence (see Root, 1996, pp. 34–41).

Finally, the suggestive parallel of this performative setting to the caging of an animal is conveyed by the actions that unfold on the field. In fact, Chief Illiniwek, and therefore the general category of the Indian, is ritually merged with the conceptual realm of the nonhuman animal, in part based upon the historical momentum that has always informed the practice of athletic mascots more generally. The overwhelming majority of athletic mascots are animals—usually large, potentially dangerous carnivores such as lions, bears, and tigers, or large majestic birds such as eagles or hawks. This practice clearly suggests the cultural tradition of totemism and totemic folk classification, wherein kin-based lineages locate a mythical ancestor from whom all members trace their descent. This ancestor is frequently a wild animal whose "power" the clan seeks to symbolically appropriate (Lévi-Strauss, 1963).

At many levels, the use of animals as mascots for athletic teams should be read as a symbolic survival of more ancient systems of totemism. Such systems offer conceptual statements about the organization of the universe and the relationship of human beings to their natural and material surroundings. After animals, by far the next most popular athletic mascots are Native American people, followed by an odd collection of roles and occupations, such as Boilermakers, Cowboys, and Patriots. The preponderance of Native American sports mascots reproduces a discursive alignment of Others with animals, a practice deeply rooted in the Western tradition of colonialism. When one of the authors pointed out to a Chief supporter that enjoying Native Americans as sports mascots was, in essence, symbolically categorizing them as animals, he heartily agreed. "That's the point! That is precisely why the Chief and other mascots honor Indians. If we didn't like them, or feel strongly about their courage and bravery, we wouldn't want to tap into the power of their symbols." These practices of mimicry, wherein the colonized subject is seized as an object that the colonizer may use as a model for his or her own playful, psychic, yet temporary transformation, affirm something crucial about colonial relations of power. Michael Taussig (1993, p. 19), in a phantasmagoric account of what he calls the mimetic faculty, concludes that, "The ability to mime, and mime well . . . is the ability to Other." Indeed, imperial forms of power often rely on staging the colonized Other as exotic and different, and the commonsense knowledge of these differences informs a colonial subjectivity.

RACIST NOTIONS AND
ROMANTIC SENTIMENTS

In 1884, Carlos Montezuma, a member of the Yavapai Tribe, graduated from the University of Illinois at Urbana–Champaign, writing his senior thesis in chemistry on "The Valuation of Opiums and Their Products." In many respects, his life before and after his college years was more eventful (see Arnold, 1951; Iverson, 1982). Prior to attending the university, he was kidnapped as a child by three Pima raiders, and later was sold to a photographer, Carlos Gentile, for thirty dollars, residing with him for brief periods in Chicago, Galesburg, and Brooklyn. After leaving Urbana–Champaign, Montezuma received his medical degree, working first as a physician in the Indian Service and then in private practice; he then became an influential Native American leader, a prominent proponent of assimilation, and a harsh critic of the Bureau of Indian Affairs.

We linger briefly on the career of Montezuma here as a way of revealing how institutions such as the University of Illinois can—by developing practices such as Chief Illiniwek and supporting the political economies in which he has thrived—perpetuate colonial discourses and imperial, ahistoric images that effectively obscure and fail even to remember or account for the hybrid identities and experiences of those Native Americans who as real, historical actors moved through and impacted them. A presentation of Montezuma's life and experiences creates a space that challenges the Indian who is inscribed through the production of Chief Illiniwek.

Moving to Urbana–Champaign, Illinois, in 1879, Montezuma lived with a local preacher and his family. Following his baptism and two years of preparatory study, he entered the University of Illinois, taking a variety of courses, including German, physiology, physics, chemistry, mineralogy, and zoology. Throughout this period, Montezuma participated in extracurricular activities, and apparently he was quite popular with his peers. In an unpublished autobiography, written shortly after he graduated, Montezuma (1888, p. 14) recalled, "During my four years in college, I was not treated as a curiosity nor patronized by the Whites, with whom I associated on terms of perfect equality." In fact, his classmates elected him class president in 1883 and a year later president of the Aldelphic Debate Society. This should not, of course, be read to indicate that racial prejudice did not inform Montezuma's experience at the university and its environs. Indeed, he remarked elsewhere about how prevailing perceptions of race structured his everyday life.[1]

Over a century after Montezuma graduated, the few Native American students currently attending the University of Illinois do not feel the equality he described. Instead they speak of discrimination, marginalization, and alienation from the campus community. Why is it then that Montezuma felt equal and achieved such a prominent position within the university as the United States was expanding its imperial projects beyond the confines of North America, while in post–civil rights, post–red power America, Native Americans feel harassed and discriminated against at the same university? Chief Illiniwek's invention, which occurred some forty-two years after Montezuma graduated (and just two years after Native Americans were granted constitutional citizenship by the

1924 Indian Citizenship Act), and the momentum that this icon
has gained have provided space for a more conspicuous eviscera-
tion of Native American sensibilities and histories.

Chief Illiniwek is clearly a stereotypical representation of Native American cultures and histories informed by racist notions and
romantic sentiments, operating as a double-coded icon that simultaneously illustrates the prevailing uses and understandings of the
indigenous inhabitants of Illinois and the broader category of
"Indianness." Although Chief Illiniwek purports to represent
inhabitants of the present State of Illinois, the mascot does not incorporate material or expressive aspects of their sociocultural formations, including dress, ritual adornment, dance, or music.
Instead, the images and performances associated with the mascot
utilize the popular conception of the indigenous peoples of the
Plains, particularly the clothing and accoutrements associated with
them. Although produced in a particular sociocultural context, the
university, the performers, and the audience do not employ the
buckskin outfit and accompanying headdress, not to mention
the war paint and breastplate, to refer to one nation. In fact, they
tend to assert that Chief Illiniwek portrays all Native Americans,
signifying generic "Indianness." This sentiment undoubtedly derives from the cinematic and literary images of Native Americans
most familiar to Euro-Americans.

On film, according to Bataille and Silet (1980, p. xvi), "The Indian—no tribe, no identity, almost always male—was either noble
. . . or bloodthirsty and viscous. There were certainly variations on
the stereotype—the drunken Indian, the heathen, the lazy native—
but still it was a picture of a creature less than human." The mascot Chief Illiniwek, then, not unlike its cinematic and literary kin,
depends upon the dominant tendency to reduce all Native Americans to hegemonic, dehumanizing representations. Importantly, the
enacted images of Chief Illiniwek have derived from the slippage
between the indigenous cultures of the Plains at the end of the
nineteenth century and the category "Indian" (Ewers, 1965). Thus
these performances enact a symbolic elision wherein images and
objects of Plains tribes are taken as a synecdochical sign sub-
stitutions for all forms of "Indianness," and Chief Illiniwek, an
icon that supposedly represents and reveres the Illinois, actually
imagines them not as they were (imagined by Euro-American con-

temporaries) or as they would image themselves but as Euro-Americans have imagined Native Americans—as romantic, even resistant warriors and nomads of the Plains, caught in a historical struggle that they ultimately will lose to the superior force and advancing civilization of the United States.

The latter idiom of armed resistance and cross-cultural conflict emplotted through the prevailing uses and understandings of Chief Illiniwek conforms to a historical pattern that constructs Native Americans as being hostile and violent. It is significant that Chief Illiniwek functions largely in the context of athletics and that the university teams are, collectively, the "Fighting Illini." The accepted interpretation of this nomenclature, as reiterated by university archivist Maynard Brichford, indicates that "Fighting" refers to "a trait esteemed in athletic competition" (November 30, 1995). Those who have invested in the athletic mascot fail to acknowledge the ways in which racist stereotypes have constituted the teams represented by Chief Illiniwek. Numerous other attributes would evoke qualities esteemed on the playing field, but instead it is violence, competition, and force, which are invested in the school symbol. When read against past and present representations of Native Americans within American popular culture, this association becomes clear: it draws upon the Euro-American knowledge of Native American cultures, misconceptions that paint them as savage warriors removed from the mores of civilization and constantly eager for combat.

In our opinion, to characterize the indigenous peoples of Illinois or of any other native nation of North America as warlike or bellicose dehumanizes and demonizes them. More importantly, it disregards both their culture and history. It reduces them to a single aspect of life, namely war, ignoring the numerous other experiences and activities more valued than war. The name "Illini" refers historically to a group of Algonkian–speaking Native American tribes, which included the Peoria, Kaskaskia, Michigamea, Cahokia, and Tamaoroa, who inhabited a region covering southern Wisconsin and northern and central Illinois. Although diverse, these tribes shared a political history as well as similarities in social structure, modes of production, and language. Ultimately, the experiences of these peoples converged further in Diaspora, as they collectively became the Confederated Peoria Tribe, along with the

Pea and Miami nations, in 1854. In the traditional parlance of ethnographic culture area categories, the Illinois tribes are identified as Woodlands Indians, which indicates, among other things, that they combined fishing and hunting with farming and pottery and lived in small, circular villages (see Bauxar, 1978; Callender, 1978; Prochaska, 2001).

But both the image of the Indian-as-Warrior and the orthodox scholarly depiction of the "Illini" as "Woodlands Indians" neglect the lived, military history of the Illinois, especially the changing nature of Illinois military action following European colonization. According to Hauser (1973, pp. 309-355), their conception and practice of war shifted radically: individual agendas became orchestrated tribal concerns, as something akin to organized "armies" replaced smaller war parties; political and economic motivations displaced the previous socioreligious foundations of conflict; and overkill scenarios undermined the previous emphasis on capture-oriented skirmishes. But then perhaps this pattern of neglect and reduction is precisely the point, to imagine an Other, who is at once militaristic, hostile, and savage, not simply to denigrate the Illinois or Native Americans more generally but to encapsulate and legitimate Euro-American history and identity. Chief Illiniwek confirms imperial recollection about (Native) American history: "they" were savage, uncivilized, and bellicose; "we" had an obligation to civilize, conquer, and settle North America; "we" did not want to kill "them" but "they" resisted "us." Undoubtedly, neither students nor citizens consciously recite such stories, but they enact these narratives daily and, when pushed to articulate the significance of symbols such as Chief Illiniwek, often they will revert to some version of this invented history. J. Bradford Churchill, a graduate student, epitomized this pattern. Native American cultures, he contended, "were not complex or sophisticated enough to endure the influences of the Europeans. Their passing," he continued, must not burden "our culture with guilt over its own success." Chief Illiniwek thus condenses popular stories and sentiments about the conquest of North America, justifying the subjugation, removal, and genocide of Native Americans by glossing "Indianness" in terms of violence, warfare, and conflict.

However, authentic "Indianness," as the invention and reproduction of Chief Illiniwek more generally indicates, is not about historical accuracy or ethnographic validity but rather derives from a reductive logic that suggests that all Native Americans are alike, sharing a universal culture and history. It entails a series of erasures. Having produced Chief Illiniwek in this fashion, the University of Illinois is merely reproducing a long, historical tradition—well over 100 years—of appropriating the Plains Indian as the quintessential symbol of the American Indian; in so doing, the university's dancing Indian indeed effaces the very Illini it pretends to portray. The performative and visual reproduction of the athletic mascot expunges the Illinois confederacy, the collection of native nations it supposedly celebrates. At the same time, the icon effaces the existing experiences and identities of the Confederated Peoria Tribe, the remnants of the Illinois Confederacy joined with the Miami and Pea nations, as well as their present practices and precepts. Its mis/appropriations of "Indianness" silence particular indigenous histories, the policies, personalities, and events that transformed the Illinois Confederacy into the Confederated Peoria Tribe. It displaces their removal from the territory of Illinois and their resettlement on a series of reservations, first in Kansas territory, then in Indian Country proper (present-day Oklahoma). It discounts the death and despair of these processes, the arrival of European emissaries, diseases, and ideologies, the bloody conflicts with neighboring nations provoked by European trade networks, and the international relations and alliances forged as the English and French colonized and competed for the resources of the Great Lakes and the Mississippi and Ohio River Valleys. Consequently, Chief Illiniwek is a highly constructed symbol that obscures as much as it presents, solidifying both the domination and difference of Native Americans.

MOMENTS OF PROTEST

In recent years, the existence of Chief Illiniwek as the symbol and mascot of the University of Illinois has been challenged by Native Americans and some white Americans, although these voices have remained a minority in the face of broad popular support for this icon of alterity. By following the course that this movement of protest has taken and by examining the forms of institutional resistance to such complaints, a clearer picture of how the neo-colonial power articulated in the early years by Zuppke, Leutwiler, Borchers, and the Illini Marching Band continues to create new spaces of practice. Ultimately, in response to the controversy surrounding the Chief, the University of Illinois began to resurrect and reconstruct the voice of the once-vanished Illini by encouraging the members of the Confederated Peoria to speak out on the issue. First, however, we trace the arguments of a small group of Native American students and faculty on campus who have dedicated themselves, in varying degrees, to having Chief Illiniwek permanently retired.

Historically, many universities and high schools have adopted Indian names and mascots, but sustained challenges to this trend emerged in the 1980s. Indeed, many institutions ultimately dropped their Indian symbols in response to these protests, although a majority continue to retain them. Stanford University actually was the first major institution to change, doing so several years before resistance to Native American mascots became a national issue. In 1972, it switched its moniker from the "Indians" to the "Cardinal," also retiring Prince Lightfoot—an Indian mascot who danced at games. More recently, Bradley University in Peoria, Illinois, known as the "Braves," changed their symbol from a hatchet-wielding Indian to a more circumspect letter "B" with a feather. However, they continue to maintain their nickname. In the 1980s a variety of Native American organizations, the most prominent of which was the American Indian Movement (AIM), began issuing resolutions condemning the practice of Indian mascots.

Owing largely to his conspicuous, highly produced, commodified performances and national stature, Chief Illiniwek has become the focus of many of these actions. In the middle and late 1980s, a few anti-Chief demonstrations took place on campus, and in addition to both Indian and non-Indian University students, these events drew the presence of such AIM notables as Clyde and Vernon Bellecourt and Michael Haney. However, the most effective and sustained voice of opposition regarding the Chief emerged amongst a group of Native American students, faculty, and staff at the university. After meeting among themselves, issuing complaints to the university administration individually and occasionally demonstrating publicly, they decided to form a body through which they might articulate their agenda. Called "Native American Students, Staff and Faculty for Progress" (NASSFP), this organization compiled a series of position statements and media packets outlining the arguments against the Chief.

The group consisted of Native Americans who, by and large, came to the campus either ignorant of or indifferent to the Chief, but as a result of exposure to the mascot and the environment that it helped to create, they eventually came to regard the Chief as being damaging to the interests of Indian people. In stark contrast to the experiences reported by Carlos Montezuma long before Chief Illiniwek came to be, these people often were ridiculed by the larger campus community and ignored by the administration, who simply found their arguments incomprehensible. Reactions ranged from the more grotesque, such as one Saturday, when a few students carrying anti-Chief signs at the football stadium were confronted by a large sign posted on a Winnebego RV that read "Save the Chief, Kill the Indians!," to the more mundane campaign of reentrenchment, in which the community redoubled their efforts to convince these protesters that the Chief was merely their way of honoring the Indians. Jean Edwards, a local woman representing the reactionary organization "Citizens for Chief Illiniwek," is quoted as saying, "What is it that they want anyway?" (Gone, 1995, p. 1).

The arguments articulated by NASSFP, as well as by other Native and Anglo-Americans against Chief Illiniwek, are complex and diverse. Here we attempt to outline the key points made in opposition to the Chief. First, as we argue above, it is suggested that Chief Illiniwek reinforces racist Indian stereotypes that turn on Hollywood images of warriors with painted bodies. Joe Gone (1994), a member of NASSFP, wrote, "Indian people were uniformly characterized as primitive barbarians, murderous savages, and godless heathens," suggesting that Chief Illiniwek is an extension of that type of discourse.

Second, Chief Illiniwek is maligned for misappropriating sacred ideas and objects, such as the war bonnet headdress, and relocating them in non-Indian, sacrilegious contexts. Basically, people insist that elements of Indian culture are misused and that their original symbolic meanings are misunderstood.

Third, it is argued that the very popular Chief Illiniwek becomes, for many non-Indian youth, the only image of Native Americans to which they are exposed. As such, it is a very narrow, limited representation that freezes the Native American, locking him or her into a mythical, unchanging past. To this extent, protesters argue, even if it is not an inherently negative stereotype (most believe that it is), it is still a stereotype, and a university has the responsibility to provide intellectually appropriate information about Native American societies that reflects their diversity and complexity.

Finally, many point out that insofar as Chief Illiniwek is an Illini Indian, he is a gross historical misrepresentation of the Illini tribe. Clearly, the mascot represents a Plains Indian—if not an Oglala Sioux Indian—and is not an accurate depiction of the Illini people. As noted previously, the Illini society did not include a warrior tradition similar to the Sioux, and the style of clothing and modes of subsistence of the two nations were distinct.

The following is a segment of the organization's position statement, dated January 1994:

> We find the routine public performance of the Chief to be a racist mockery of our remaining cultural institutions, insulting to our intelligence, and damaging to the psychological well-being of our many peoples. The very idea of university students parading around in traditional Native American clothing during athletics events for the purposes of inspiring sports fans is offensive and degrading to Native Americans, especially those Native Americans affiliated with the University of Illinois. (NASSFP, 1994)

The articulate members of this organization have dedicated an enormous amount of time and energy to make their voices heard. Several are graduate students with little time to commit to writing position papers and press releases, but they persisted anyway. However, dissatisfied with the lack of response they received, five members of the group jointly filed a federal complaint against the university in 1994. They argued that the University of Illinois symbol contributed to a racially hostile environment on campus. The case was litigated as a potential violation of civil rights at a federally and state-funded university through the Office for Civil Rights (OCR) in the U.S. Department of Education.

The plaintiffs eventually lost the case when, in late 1995, the OCR concluded that there was insufficient evidence to support the claims. In July 1995, several Republican U.S. Congressmen from Illinois met with members of the federal agency, urging them to discard the case and arguing that it was an issue to be dealt with by the state (Wojcieszak, 1995). Further, local Illinois Congressman Rick Winkel sponsored a bill in the state legislature, ultimately passed into law but vetoed by the governor, requiring the University of Illinois to retain Chief Illiniwek as its symbol, in perpetuity. The speed with which the state and federal legislative apparatuses mobilized to defend the presence of Chief Illiniwek reveals how colonial hegemony is reproduced through the novel tactics of postcolonial formations.

RESUSCITATING THE VANQUISHED VOICE OF AN INDIAN

The foregoing description of these protests, protesters, and supporters of Chief Illiniwek fails to fully reveal the neocolonial contours of the drama. The University of Illinois and the local community introduced a set of new tactics to defend the mascot when in the spring of 1995 they lobbied members of the Peoria nation in Oklahoma to make a public statement in support of Chief Illiniwek. Although the university had not, since the mascot's invention in 1926, attempted to formally acknowledge the Peoria as perhaps being the living descendants of the Illini people, it decided to do so in the face of mounting pressure by the small number of Native Americans on campus. Such efforts are ironic in the context of earlier scholarship, claiming that the Illini and, indeed, the Peoria, were virtually extinct. Some of this research was in fact supported by the State of Illinois and, in at least one instance, was carried out by a University of Illinois student (see Michelson, 1916). In his report to the Illinois Centennial Commission, which now rests in the university's archives, Michelson concluded that the true culture of the Peoria had by then been lost, and that, "There probably [are] no absolutely pure blooded Peoria Indians left" (1916, p. 8; see also Donaldson, 1886; King, 1998). Suddenly the University of Illinois began to resurrect the voices of these Indians, hoping that the public would perceive them as holders of the only historically *authentic* opinion regarding Chief Illiniwek. In fact, the idea to contact them originated with a member of the anthropology department who specialized in the archaeology of Native America. Initially, the elected leader of the Peoria, Don Giles, indicated through correspondence that the tribe had no official position regarding Chief Illiniwek and that it preferred to be left out of the controversy (Thomas Riley, personal communication). In March 1995, however, the university's administration redoubled its efforts to encourage Peoria support of the Chief.

The owner of a local television station, WICD-TV, a longtime friend of several University of Illinois administrators and already on record as being strongly pro-Chief, decided to send a correspondent and film crew to Miami, Oklahoma, to do a brief news series on Peoria opinion about the mascot issue. According to NASSFP members, as the network affiliate prepared to do this story in late March, the university again contacted the tribe—this time to extend to them an offer of scholarship money.[2] The first of three installments to the news story aired on the evening of May 1, 1995. Correspondent and news anchor Gwen Ellis interviewed Giles (tribal chief), Ron Froman (secretary-treasurer), and Ron Stand (program director) as they sat in chairs in a reservation civic center, all dressed in Western clothing. Froman told Ellis, "I think anybody who protests the Chief Illiniwek [mascot] would have to be a Peoria to begin with. I don't see where another tribe has any basis to make a protest." In the newsroom banter following this segment, Ellis remarked, "In fact, they say they're actually happy to have somebody come and talk to them about it, and let the public know how they really feel about this mascot." Her news colleague responded, "Wow, that's an important *voice* we haven't heard from before."

In the next evening's installment, Giles said, regarding the Chief, "I don't have a problem with it. I don't think it's demoralizing or demeaning, or in bad taste whatsoever." Then, actually confirming the claims by critics of Chief Illiniwek, Froman said, "It doesn't reflect anything from the Illinois Indians that was there, either today since they were driven out from Illinois or anytime since then." He added, however, that it is not a problem, "because I don't think they're trying to be historical . . . or accurate." Finally, Froman strongly condemned the protesters. "I think it would be the worst mistake in the world for the [university] trustees to ever bend to the people who see this somehow . . . as being a hostile learning environment. If it is, then they're in big, big trouble already, regardless of the Chief." Giles then echoed this sentiment, literally blaming the Native American students on campus for creating a hostile environment. The third segment focused on tribal efforts to teach its culture and history to younger Peoria.

These comments contain a contradiction that clearly undercuts the Peoria claim as the only Native Americans who can rightfully speak to the issue. On the one hand, Froman insists that the Peoria opinion is the only one that should matter (based upon the tribe's historical relationship to the Illinois), yet in nearly the same breath, he admits that Chief Illiniwek does not resemble anything authentic from either the Peoria or Illinois traditions. We have argued, and Froman seems to admit as much, that Chief Illiniwek is a highly idealized, naturalizing emblem of a generic Indian—if not a Plains Indian. Therefore, anyone with an interest in ensuring just representations of Native American people, which might include Native Americans and non-Indian people alike, has a significant voice regarding the matter.

Prior to this visit by an Illinois television news team, none of the Peoria leaders had ever seen Chief Illiniwek, on television or in person. The crew showed them reel clips of his performances as well as clips showing some of the protests. In fact, all the Peoria members would know about the protests was contextualized by the television crew. They were shown a protest that focused not on members of NASSFP but rather on the more flamboyant Vernon Bellecourt of AIM. After this series ran locally in the Champaign–Urbana area, the Native Americans on campus, who were members of NASSFP, were hurt and angered by the comments of the Peoria—comments that ostensibly represented a shift in the tribe's position. The Peoria comments in favor of the Chief and in opposition to local Native American voices quickly met the initial objectives of the university in setting out to relocate the once-vanquished descendants of the Illini. That is, local supporters of the Chief immediately began using this newly created "authentic" voice to bolster their own opinions.

These efforts underscore the perspective of the cultural critic that social voices must necessarily be considered in the first instance as social constructions. They are not merely collections of words or opinions; rather, they are dynamic, historically and socially positioned, politicized utterances that emerge at the intersections of multiple listeners and speakers. When Joseph Gone (1995, p. 2) wrote his position paper in February 1995, he seemed to anticipate these events even before they occurred, when stating, "By his very symbolic nature, the Chief means different things to different people as well as different things to different *groups* of people. Inattention to these details has resulted in a widespread misunderstanding and a genuine lack of communication."

The Native Americans on campus responded swiftly and creatively to these statements by the Peoria. A group of five met at Durango Mendoza's house to produce a videotaped series of "Open Remarks to the Peoria Tribe" from the NASSFP. An analysis of this video project reveals—midstream—the continual process of constructing and reconstructing identities and agendas central to all human interaction. The purpose of the video was to start a dialogue, to allow the Peoria to better get to know individual NASSFP members and their agenda. The manner in which these people represented themselves on tape indicates a strategic balance of emotion, sincerity, and agency. It was, indeed, a social performance designed to bridge a cultural and social distance between Native American people and ultimately to invite the Peoria to join them in their project of resistance.

In the video, the camera moves around the living room, where all five are seated, allowing each an opportunity to speak. Just as they do when listing their identities in the organizational literature, each utters his or her tribal affiliation before speaking. They seem to maintain a balance in articulating their identities as simultaneously marked by an Indian heritage *and* citizenship in the United States. Moreover, they distance themselves to a degree from the images of highly radical protesters. For example, Gone introduces himself as a Gros Ventre Indian who served in the U.S. Army, was stationed in Germany, and attended West Point, and is taking a doctorate in psychology in order to serve Native Americans. He states at one point, "I'm not interested in identifying with AIM folks." Karen Strong, an Alaskan Tlingit and a graduate student in language and literacy speaks about the personal pain that she has experienced as a Native American teacher and as a student on campus. At one moment, she challenges the Peoria. "Go to these games. See if they are honoring us." Wallace Strong, a Yakima-Nez Perce doctoral student in education, speaks about how he gradually was "sucked into" the issue of Chief Illiniwek. A Creek-Muskogee, Mendoza shares his experience—again in stark contrast to the experiences of Montezuma—of being spotted by several young children who then made highly caricatured "Indian" sounds in response. His experience is a striking reproduction of postcolonial writer Frantz Fanon's (1968/1952, p. 79) of being spotted by a young boy with his mother. "Look, a Negro! . . . Mama, see the Negro! I'm frightened!" Like Fanon, Mendoza was being confronted and constructed as the embodiment of a racial sign. Finally, we hear from Dennis Tibbetts (Ojibway), a one-time assistant dean of students at the university. He notes his tenure as a Vietnam veteran before angrily summarizing his objections to the Chief and his pain upon seeing the statements by the Peoria tribe.

Perhaps the most impassioned remarks are offered by Gone, who expresses personal pride in the fact that many Gros Ventre chiefs have hailed from his family and describes the traditions surrounding this role. He then shifts to Chief Illiniwek, with an emotional, sometimes admonishing tone:

> And when I see, on the sports field here at the university, a *white* boy dressed up to superficially resemble what my ancestors would have looked like in their appropriate time and place, of their leadership, it becomes difficult to express the damage that this has caused not just to me but to all of us here. And I think it is high time that we as Indian people around the country come to unite in causes which serve our collective interests and to no longer be *tricked* or invited to divide ourselves over issues such as this. It's my understanding that President Ikenberry has promised your people some scholarships, maybe some cash—I don't know all what was involved.
>
> I think it unfortunate that incentive has caused you to say harsh words—words which overstep your knowledge, clearly, of this issue and its effects on this community, and I hope through the making of this video that you can become more sensitive to our experiences and our positions here

and that perhaps you'll see fit to change your mind, to make
reparations, to make public statements demonstrating an alliance with us as opposed to—once again—allowing white
people to divide us and conquer us. (Videotaped remarks,
emphasis added, 1995)

The Peoria officials have not, to date, offered an *official* retraction
of the remarks made on television in support of the Chief.

A few days after the interview aired, Giles did apologize over
the phone to Tibbetts. Since receiving the videotaped response,
moreover, Giles has privately (although not "on record") restated
what had been the original position of the tribe—that it indeed has
no position and would rather be left alone. Giles and other leaders
of the Peoria have largely ignored the Native Americans on campus, and Giles has failed to respond to efforts by Joe Gone and the
author to communicate either through correspondence or over the
phone. At this point, seemingly unable to reconcile their conservative views with the agenda of these students and faculty in Champaign–Urbana, members of the Peoria Nation prefer to remove
themselves from the controversy and may be embarrassed over
how they were dragged into it in the first place.

CONTESTED SPECTACLES, UNEASY COMMUNITIES

Like many other athletic spectacles of Indianness, Chief Illiniwek's
existence is increasingly uncomfortable and problematic, especially
when contextualized by the efforts of the University of Illinois and
its supporters to incorporate the voices of Indian actors and communities. While the early meanings of Chief Illiniwek centered on
Euro-American students giving life to a 1920s' Indianness based on
romantic tropes and vanished natives, more recent investments in
this athletic icon turn on new experiences of a neo-liberal multiculturalism that thrives on flattened representations of cultural and
racial difference (see McCarthy, 1993). The predominant narratives of post–Vietnam multiculturalism envision a liberated,
post–integration America in which such simple tropes of difference
as the ubiquity of Thai restaurants, ethnic fairs, Habitat for Hu-

manity clubs, and suburban powwows signify a mode of *consuming* diversity, as merely a lifestyle practice. This powerful narrative of a white, consumer-class America is reproduced in myriad spaces. But as Stuart Hall (1991, p. 58) insists, "Hegemony is not the same thing as incorporating everybody, of making everybody the same . . . [It] is not the disappearance or destruction of difference. It is the construction of a collective will through difference."

Yet these discourses of difference do not sustain themselves magically. The University of Illinois—a site of institutional and state power—effectively promoted and framed consent, even relying upon a classic colonial tactic of divide-and-conquer the enemy. Importantly, these forms of power are never completely determining, and mascots such as Chief Illiniwek have become "uneasy because they have become contested" (King, forthcoming). King argues that the practices and identities once taken for granted by fans have "become debatable, questionable, and even negotiable." Efforts to challenge these spectacles of Indianness effectively allowed many to reclaim Indianness, to destabilize white supremacy, and to politicize the social. The politicization of the local, the everyday, and the social has, indeed, provoked vigorous responses that belie the prevailing sets of social relations between Native Americans and Euro-Americans.

A fundamental problem with the Chief Illiniwek mascot is one of *context*. It is difficult to understand how the heritage of an indigenous people can be appropriately celebrated in the context of big-time collegiate athletics. It is unlikely that the images of Indians on the sweaters of football cheerleaders and halftime Indian dances honor Native Americans when, almost without exception, these spaces offer little to the lives and interests of most Native Americans. That the Peoria leaders had never seen images of the mascot prior to 1995 underscores this point. If the very people who Chief Illiniwek ostensibly honors have never directly encountered him, then his existence fails, it seems, to fulfill university and community expectations that the performances "revere" Illinois Indians.

White people created and continue to reproduce the Indian. Performing Chief Illiniwek is a form of writing culture by inscribing relations of power onto the Native American body. The University of Illinois claims that its tradition honors the Illini people, as well as Native Americans more generally. Such a claim demands widespread criticism. Even if all of the specific concerns with the content of the Chief's performances were remedied—that is, for example, if the outfit was made more appropriate to an Illinois Indian the dances were redesigned to offer more accurate interpretations of early Native American rituals—his existence would remain fundamentally problematic at its core. Native Americans at the university have thus been unwilling to settle upon some sort of compromise that might include a more "authentic" performance or new curricula addressing Indian issues, although some administration officials have encouraged them to do just that.

In *Wassaja*, his monthly periodical pursuing justice, equality, and freedom for Native Americans, Montezuma (1921) blasted Euro-Americans who posed, acted, or otherwise played at being a Native American for profit and amusement. Assembling stereotypical items, objects, and attire associated with "Indianness," these "impostors," he insisted, duped their audiences, while severely damaging Native American cultures and histories: "[A] great majority of the people look on the feathers, the long false hair, and their Indian paraphernalia, and believe they are Indians" (ibid., p. 3). Montezuma, moreover, understood the power of enacting stereotypes, asking of the "Indian impostors . . . do they do any good to the Indian race?" Without hesitation, he (ibid., p. 4) responded, "They may do some good to other people, but they do more harm than good for Indian people . . . these impostors are working for selfish purposes, and not to benefit the Indian race. Anyone who poses as an Indian does not help the Indians."

Writing some seventy years later, Ojibway citizen Dennis Tibbetts (1993)—who in the 1990s found the University of Illinois, with Chief Illiniwek, much less palatable than Montezuma did long before the mascot was invented—penned the following verses, from a longer poem titled *Minstrel Show*, in which the narrator is speaking to an Anishinabe elder, "Grandfather Redsky":

> In the parking lot there were men
> with hairy chests, war whooping
> and jumping around without spilling
> the drinks they carried in their hands . . .

They have an authentic white Indian.
Impressive headdress, buckskins, and bare feet.
An imposing warrior, who danced quite a dance,
when the helmets scored a touchdown.

Tibbetts resigned from his dean of students faculty position in 1994 in order to remove himself from the discursive spaces of Chief Illiniwek.

Ultimately, when confronted with a symbol such as Chief Illiniwek, Native Americans and others must, in the final analysis, conclude that to the extent that he is an Indian, he is very clearly a white man's Indian (Berkhofer, 1979; see also Byrd, 1996). Indeed, images such as Chief Illiniwek are rooted in discourses of colonial hegemony that articulate categories and hierarchies of humanity. Inventing icons of alterity served the colonial project well in constructing Indians *naturally* as bellicose, and nomadic, and as warriors. The ways in which these images currently circulate, divide, are challenged, consumed, defended, and internalized are, however, characteristically emblematic of a postcolonial regime of power.

The practice of community emergent in the process of producing, consuming, and resisting Chief Illiniwek is profound and disturbing. A small group of Native Americans, having arrived variously at the University of Illinois to pursue professional and educational goals as participants in the nation-state that conquered their ancestors, is offended by the centrality of a dancing Indian. In their efforts to challenge it, they collide with university administrators, students, and alumni; scholars; Illinois and U.S. Congressional legislators; and reluctant members of the Peoria Nation, now in Oklahoma. Each of these groups attempts, in some way, to appropriate or dismiss the other.

> The postcolonial perspective forces us to rethink the profound limitations of a consensual and collusive "liberal" sense of cultural community. It insists that cultural and political identity are constructed through a process of alterity. . . . Culture becomes as much an uncomfortable, disturbing practice of survival and supplementarity—between art and politics, past and present, the public and the private—as its

resplendent being is a moment of pleasure, enlightenment or liberation. (Bhabba, 1994, 175)

The dances of Chief Illiniwek produce an exhibitionary space with many creases, folds, and interruptions. It is simultaneously a colonial and postcolonial space of subjectivity, and the dances are sacrificial spectacles whose discursive contours continue to expand.

4

Sammy Seminole, Jim Crow, and Osceola:
Playing Indian and Racial Hierarchy at Florida State University

To commemorate the appearance of the University of Tennessee in the National Championship Game at the 1999 Fiesta Bowl, *The Knoxville Sentinel* produced a special section. Emblazoned on the front was a (supposedly) humorous cartoon by R. Daniel Proctor. The image dramatized the pending competition between the University of Tennessee Volunteers and the Florida State University Seminoles. At the center of the cartoon, a train driven by one of the Volunteers in a coonskin cap plows into a buffoonish caricature of a generic Indian. As he flies through the air, the Seminole exclaims, "Paleface speak with forked tongue! This land is ours as long as grass grows and river flows . . . Oof!" The Volunteer retorts, "I got news, pal . . . this is a desert. And we're painting it orange!" Beneath this hateful drama, parodying the genocide, lies, and destruction associated with the conquest of North America, Smokey, a canine mascot associated with the University of Tennessee, and a busty Tennessee fan speed down Interstate 10, here dubbed, "The New and Improved Trail of Tears." They sing, "Oh give me land, lots o'land, full of starry skies above . . . don't defence me in."

Proctor depicts the impending game between the University of Tennessee and Florida State University as an interracial conflict, projecting the desired outcome through a popular, if misleading, pastiche of the past. As he imagines the glories of his team, the conquering Volunteers, he parodies, even mocks, Native Americans. The disrespectful and dehumanizing qualities of the image lay bare the practices and precepts animating Native American mascots. In fact, the image directs attention to those contexts in which individuals and institutions defend their uses of Indianness as expressions of honor, reverence, and tradition, more particularly, Florida State University, the institution denigrated in Proctor's cartoon.

While the cartoonist might be admonished for his insensitivity, it can be argued that Florida State University itself is guilty of propagating precisely the kind of environment in which Native Americans are likely to be "playfully" victimized by such forms of symbolic violence. The same year, 1947, that the public institution previously known as the Florida State College for Women became Florida State University, the student body voted to identify its athletic teams with the name Seminoles and "the student newspaper, *The Florida Flambeau,* carried a logo in its masthead illustrated with the profile of a Seminole man in a turban and kerchief" (Addonizio, 1998, p. 93). As we detail below, the Seminole "signs and symbols" created by Florida State University to inspire its athletes and supporters became increasingly elaborate and stereotypically flattened. Throughout the 1980s and 1990s, and continuing into the new millennium, the predominant spectacle at the start of Florida State University home football games was the entrance of a male student—wearing moccasins, a tasseled leather "Indian" outfit, face paint, and a large bandanna, hoisting a large feathered lance—who "charges down the field riding an Appaloosa horse named Renegade and hurls a flaming lance at midfield" ("Chief Osceola and Renegade," 1999). The student represents Chief Osceola, the famous Seminole who led an armed resistance against the United States in the 1830s.

This highly polished performance of Indianness turns on the traditional archetypes of masculinity, fierceness, and bellicosity, themes common to nearly all of the Native American mascots examined in this volume and understandably desired by aggressive athletic teams. Florida State University's Chief Osceola and Renegade inscribe a context which, indeed, openly invites violent-spirited salvos such as the Proctor cartoon. For example, Bobby Bowden, the celebrity coach of the perennial powerhouse Florida State football team, adds the slogan, "Scalp 'Em" to his autographs. By the late 1980s, a Florida State cheerleading group, The Marching Chiefs, and the student body, had perfected what the university itself called the "War Chant," and others have embraced (and criticized) nationally the tomahawk chop, a repetitive arm motion meant to symbolize the movement of a tomahawk.

Obviously, Florida State University's history of appropriating Seminole icons and inventing performances conveys a traditional set of stereotypes of Native Americans. These practices also underscore the production of whiteness. They foreground desires for impulses, experiences, and affects between and beyond the boundaries of the mundane, highlighting the dissociated identities and communities made possible in the liminal space of imagined Indianness. Importantly, the existence of Chief Osceola and the various ways in which he has been rendered by Florida State University is not just about redness and whiteness but also reveals the significance of blackness. Consequently, in this chapter we move beyond an analysis of familiar stereotypes to explore the ways in which Chief Osceola—from his lived, historical existence as a Seminole leader to his role as a contemporary college football cheerleader on horseback—has served as a canvas for the (re)creation of white identities and racial hierarchies.

Our argument unfolds through an interpretive history. We begin with a brief overview of the Seminole, noting their ethnogenesis, resistance, and removal. Against this background, we sketch the establishment of the Seminoles as the fight name of Florida State University in 1947, discussing early efforts to create a mascot. Next, we turn to the enshrinement of Osceola as the Seminoles' mascot after 1978 and more recent efforts to defend Florida State University's use of Indianness. This account offers a foundation on which to consider the racial hierarchy animated by Native American mascots, particularly in the American South.

THE EMERGENT SEMINOLE

Seminole is an English translation of a Creek (or Muskogee) transliteration of the Spanish word *cimmaron*, wild or untamed. Whereas the Spanish had originally used the term to describe the peoples they encountered and struggled with in the Southeast,

Native Americans in the mid-eighteenth century borrowed the term to communicate to the British that they were a distinct people (Wright, 1986, p. 4). As the naming of the Seminole underscores, a classic example of ethnogenesis, or the formation of a new people or an ethnic group. In short, the Seminole emerged, according to Sturtevant (1971, p. 93; see also Sattler, 1996), "in response to European pressure, for the tribe is an entirely post–European phenomenon." The Seminole, then, both as the imagined Indians staged by Florida State University and the embodied Indians who are enrolled members of either the Seminole Tribe of Florida or the much larger Seminole Nation of Oklahoma, were generated, fashioned, took shape, or (in popular scholarly parlance) invented under colonial conditions not of their own making. To appreciate the complex uses and understandings of Indianness animating the Florida State University Seminoles, one must apprehend the creation, attempted destruction, resistance, and persistence of the Seminole (McReynolds, 1957; Milanich, 1998; Wright, 1986).

Disease, raids by slavers, military conflicts between indigenous groups, and the imperial intrigues of European powers had largely depopulated northern Florida by the early eighteenth century. Lower Creeks, often at the behest of the Spanish, migrated into this area, providing a buffer zone between the Spanish and the English and their Native American allies. Initially, these communities lived their lives as they had before emigrating, for instance, building communities around central squaregrounds, playing stickball, ceremonially imbibing black drink, subsisting on horticulture supplemented by hunting, participating in intricate trade networks, and owning slaves. Each Lower Creek town maintained a unique identity and established loose regional alliances, while retaining its allegiance to the Creek Confederacy, perhaps as late as the American Revolutionary War. Over the course of the eighteenth century, others, fleeing armed conflict and slavery, moved south as well. During this period, the Lower Creek incorporated Apalachis, Yamasee, Hitchiti and others, following the Yamasees War of 1715, escaped slaves, and Upper Creeks, following the Red Stick War of 1813–1814. For much of the eighteenth century, the transplanted peoples in these Mestizo communities conceived of themselves as Creeks, but increasingly, in response to changing sociopolitical conditions as well as European and later Euro-American perceptions that the Indians of Florida were a unique, discrete group, one of the Five Civilized Tribes, they came to understand themselves a distinct people, the Seminole.

After the Revolutionary War, and particularly in the nine-teenth century, the Seminole presence proved problematic for the new republic. White Southerners in Georgia, Alabama, and the Carolinas were hungry for land and concerned about slaves es-caping to communities in Florida. The federal government, which acquired the territory from Spain, in turn sought to manage the escalating cultural, economic, and political tensions by removing the Seminole west of the Mississippi. During the first half of the nineteenth century, the United States waged three costly wars against the Seminole.

In 1817, misunderstandings, charges, and countercharges of theft, violation, and unjustified attacks, and nagging questions about runaway slaves, escalated into the First Seminole War. Led by Andrew Jackson, U.S. troops swept across Florida the follow-ing spring, destroying a number of African-American and Native American communities and capturing Spanish fortifications at Pensacola and St. Marks. While the Spanish ceded Florida to the United States during peace negotiations in 1819, the federal government did not make peace with the Seminole until nearly five years after the conflict. In 1823, a portion of the Seminole signed the Treaty of Moultrie Creek, requiring that they settle on a 4-million acre reservation in central Florida in exchange for an-nual food and cash payments.

A decade later, in 1832, a segment of the Seminoles agreed to the terms of the Treaty of Payne's Landing and endorsed their re-moval to Indian Territory. A number of Seminole balked at both the content of the agreement negotiated at Payne's Landing and the conditions under which it was negotiated. Rather than migrate, they actively resisted U.S. efforts to remove them, provoking the Second Seminole War (1835–1842). Under the leadership of the much-celebrated Osceola, Jumper, Alligator, Wildcat, and others, the overmatched Seminole waged a rather successful guerrilla war, receding deep into the Florida interior. After a seven-year cam-paign, costing in excess of $30 million, the federal government uni-laterally declared victory. At the close of the Second Seminole War, the United States had forcibly relocated more than 3,500 Seminole west of the Mississippi, leaving behind fewer than 500 renegades in Florida swamps.

In the 1850s, tensions between the Seminole remnants and Euro-American settlers and government agents resulted in the Third Seminole War (1855–1858). During the short-lived conflict, U.S. troops concentrated their efforts on locating small, scattered Seminole encampments in the Southern swamps. Although moderately successful in this venture, removing additional Seminole, several hundred lingered in Florida.

After the Civil War, which had devastated the relocated Seminole as a result of internal divisions over slavery and an external alliance with the Confederacy, governmental programs and policies increasingly sought to incorporate members of the native nation into American society. In contrast, in the half-century following the Third Seminole War, the undefeated remnants left behind survived on the margins of Floridian (and American) life, relying almost exclusively on "traditional" subsistence strategies and social institutions. Then, the establishment of reservations, combined with the pressures of development, particularly the draining of the swamps, compelled many Seminole to enter mainstream white society. Importantly, during this period, many Seminole integrated themselves into the tourist industry (Mechling, 1996; West, 1981), offering, if not embracing, Euro-American uses and understandings of Indianness. In 1957, the federal government officially recognized the Seminole Tribe of Florida. Today, the Seminole live on five reservations in Florida, one reservation in Oklahoma, and in urban and rural areas throughout the United States. They continue to participate in the tourist trade and in agriculture, and most recently they have established a vibrant gaming industry in Florida.

INVENTING THE SEMINOLES

After World War II, a number of veterans returning to Tallahassee wished to attend university. The needs of these soldiers served as the impetus for the Florida State College for Women to open its doors to men in 1947 (Hartung, 1998). Becoming a coeducational campus, the new Florida State University (FSU) entered into a process that would eventually transform it into a nationally recognized public university. Central to its national reputation has been its emergence as an acknowledged powerhouse in collegiate athletics, particularly football. In fact, Florida State University now regularly vies for the national championship in football and, to the delight of a national television audience, it annually revives its rivalry with the University of Florida.

It was in this not atypical collegiate context that Florida State University began to refashion itself as numerous other institutions had. In part, seeking to capitalize on the (imagined) identity of a regionally significant Native American society, the moniker "Seminoles" was formally adopted by students following a campus-wide competition. "Seminoles" was chosen over a range of alternatives, including the Crackers, Statesmen, Tarpons, and Fighting Warriors (Addonizio, 1998, p. 93). Apparently, "Seminoles" was the consensus favorite among the football players, who made certain of the outcome by stuffing the ballot box (McGrotha, 1987). From the outset, neither a formal nor a de facto relationship existed between the university and the Seminole Tribe, although at least by the 1970s, an ongoing, mutual conversation between tribal representatives and school administrators had emerged. But attempts were made to inscribe the very early FSU Seminole tradition as "authentic," illustrated, for example, by the patchwork skirts worn by FSU cheerleaders in the 1950s. These skirts were "made by members of the *real* Seminole tribe of Florida" (Addonizio, 1998, p. 93, emphasis added).

Choosing and retaining a mascot proved more difficult. A series of imagined Indians, actual and planned-but-rejected incarnations, took shape during the latter half of the twentieth century. Although cartoon caricatures of a Seminole figure, or even of Chief Osceola, appeared variously in campus literature and newspapers, the presence of an embodied mascot (or mascots) was unknown until the late 1950s. In 1958, Sammy Seminole became the first figure to perform as a football team mascot. He would lead the FSU team onto the field and follow with a series of back flips. During the game, he was an all-purpose cheerleader and acrobat. The carnivalesque role was played by a number of male students from the gymnastics and circus programs. The Sammy Seminole costume consisted of a breechcloth and a single feather. The practice ended in 1968, possibly due, in part, to budgetary constraints (see Ensley,

1997), but according to other news reports, the presence of a Sammy Seminole figure was swiftly reestablished at football games, although not—apparently—under the sponsorship of the gymnastics program (Stacey, 1970).

Even more carnivalesque than Sammy Seminole was FSU's Chief Fullabull, who emerged as the mascot at home basketball games. Little documentation exists which details the nature of these performances. According to FSU anthropologist Anthony Paredes (personal communication), the mascot ran around performing silly stunts and clownlike routines. Shari Addonizio (1998, p. 94) reports that his antics upset members of the campus organization, the American Indian Fellowship, which in concert with the support of other campus groups and "off-campus Seminole people" had Chief Fullabull eliminated and ultimately replaced by a figure in Seminole apparel known as the "spirit chief" or "Yahola." However, the first effort to "rehabilitate" Chief Fullabull failed. The individual portraying Chief Fullabull at the time, Jack Stacy, apparently enjoyed great control over the tradition, because unilaterally he changed "his" name to Chief Wampumstompum (Rutland, 1970). Of course, this change did nothing to appease those complaining that the name "Chief Fullabull" was derogatory, thus later the name "Yahola" was adopted.

In addition to the probable existence, by 1970, of two distinct Sammy Seminole figures at football games and a Chief Fullabull at basketball games, a lesser-known FSU logo had been "invented" in 1965 by FSU design and metalsmithing instructor Fred Metzke. The figure portrayed in the logo was a dancing, axe-wielding, feathered "Indian" named "Savage Sam." He was replaced by the present logo incarnation, a silhouette of a native figure, in the early 1970s (see Lindstrom, 1982).

As noted previously, the current and widely popular incarnation of FSU "Seminole Pride" consists of the home football game performances of a student portraying Chief Osceola, atop an Appaloosa named Renegade. The tradition was created in 1978 by Bill Durham, a Tallahassee businessman and an FSU alumnus, with the support of Ann Bowden, spouse of the football coach. Durham actually conceptualized the notion of a Seminole mascot on horseback in 1962, when he was elected to the FSU Homecoming Court (Coale, 1996). But in 1978, he was better positioned to enact his dream, and he provided the horse and the attire. The support of Bowden proved critical in securing various permits and approvals to have a live horse on the football field.

The first appearance took place at a Florida State University–Oklahoma State University game on September 16, 1978. Details of the performance have changed over the years, and the process has become more refined and more closely monitored by school officials. A self-proclaimed student of Seminole culture, Durham orchestrates all aspects of the contemporary Osceola–Renegade tradition. He trains a number of Appaloosas for the performances and selects the student riders himself. Only one Chief Osceola impersonator serves in the role at any given time, and to date, there have been ten such riders. In order to earn the honor, which is accompanied by a $1,200 annual scholarship, students must have a 3.0 grade-point average, must display a high moral character, and must serve a two-year apprenticeship. The Chief Osceola performer must ride bareback while carrying a 28-pound flaming spear. Near the end of the horse's gallop, the rider must urge the animal to rear up on its hind legs to strike a dramatic, defiant posture. Chief Osceola is required to remain "in character," affecting a solemn, bellicose persona, and is forbidden from smiling or responding directly to the audience (see Coale, 1996).

The appropriation and elaboration of the Florida State Seminoles, as well as the performances, costumes, and figures invented to represent them, turn on a complex dialectic of desire and dissociation in which Euro-Americans (and to a lesser extent, Native Americans) embrace difference, while refusing its significance, and claim Indianness, while erasing embodied Indians. To be sure, the tensions and articulations at Florida State University fit within a rich tradition that already was well established in American culture by 1947; however, the preoccupation of students, alumni, and fans with Osceola made the stagings and effects of the FSU Seminoles unique.

Osceola has long fascinated Euro-Americans (Perdue, 1992; Wickman, 1991). Beginning in the Second Seminole War, largely as a result of his position on removal and his exploits in battle, Osceola enjoyed great popularity, gaining prominence and influence that eclipsed most traditional leaders. He became a darling of the

American news media for his committed resistance to American encroachment, his uncompromising action, and his bravery in battle. A number of (largely fictional) biographies portrayed his life, and George Catlin rushed to South Carolina to paint the war leader after his surrender in 1837. Upon his death in 1838, his personal belongings were stolen and his head was taken as a trophy, later displayed in a museum in New York. Euro-Americans literally appropriated Osceola, making him their own. Then, as now, the repossession of Osceola has turned on erasure and control: romantic renderings of the Seminole war leader do not stress hybridity—he was of mixed blood, born to an English father and a Creek mother—but purity; they do not foreground his polygyny, religious practices, or other features of his everyday life but his more fantastic during a time of crisis; they do not reflect his complex engagements with American culture but offer a singular, flat vision of his ferocious rebellion. Importantly, for all of the revisioning, Osceola remains "a multifaceted symbol . . . the war hero, the worthy opponent, the 'savage,' the past" (Perdue, 1992, p. 488). He simultaneously encoded narratives of the hostility and backwardness of Indians, the romance of their (failed) opposition, the honor of conquest, the propriety of removal, and the Manifest Destiny of American civilization in the face of savagery. At FSU, Euro-American enactments of Osceola, their interpretations of who he is and what he means, remain polysemous and ambivalent. Put simply, they fashion Indians and Indianness in fairly formulaic terms, while locating whites and whiteness, what it means to be a white American.

When Osceola leads the FSU football players onto the field, he signifies armed resistance, bravery, and savagery, and his appearance builds on the prevailing understanding of Indianness that constructs Native Americans as aggressive, hostile and even violent. Although numerous other attributes would evoke qualities esteemed on the playing field, violence, competition, and force are invested in the FSU athletic symbol. When read against past and present representations of Native Americans within American popular culture, this association becomes clear: it draws upon the Euro-American knowledge of Native American cultures, misconceptions that paint them as savage warriors removed from the mores of civilization and constantly eager for combat. As we noted in the previous chapter, to characterize the indigenous Seminole people or any other native nation of North America as warlike dehumanizes and demonizes them. More importantly, it disregards both their cultures and histories and reduces them to a single aspect of life, namely war, ignoring the numerous other experiences and activities more valued than war.

Osceola, as portrayed at FSU, thus offers a stereotypical representation of Native American cultures and histories informed by racist notions and romantic sentiments. In fact, we would argue, the FSU icon represents a generic Indianness as much as it signifies the Seminole people as such. This sentiment undoubtedly derives from the cinematic and literary images of Native Americans most familiar to Euro-Americans. The Chief Osceola icon, then, not unlike its cinematic and literary kin, depends upon the dominant tendency to reduce all Native Americans to dehumanizing representations.

Within the limited space of the Indian warrior, Chief Osceola astride Renegade inscribes a complex, even ambivalent, narrative revolving around desire and dissociation. It conjures up an archetype, seeking the wildness and savagery at the core of the naming of the Seminole and white perceptions of them over the past three centuries. At FSU, the administration, fans, and athletes long for the attributes of the untamed other, particularly autonomy, individuality, defiance, and aggression, crafting rituals that enable them to imitate, materialize, and assume these qualities. That this archetypal, untamed other has been authenticated, really invented, by Euro-Americans, for Euro-Americans, only enhances the allure of the FSU Seminoles. The distance of time and the removal of imagination have domesticated Osceola, facilitating Euro-American identification and affiliation. Even more significant, the defeat and removal of the Seminole make them safe and desirable. "In the defeat of Osceola," as Perdue (1992, p. 484) asserts, "the quintessential 'savage,' Anglo-Americans confirmed that they were right: Failure to become 'civilized' resulted in death, albeit a heroic and romantic death." The performances of Chief Osceola do not so much celebrate his demise as lament it; they imprint a nostalgic drama through which they mourn the passing of a once-great and proud people who honorably and unsuccessfully defended their way of life against all odds. The honor and longing attached to these rites of incorporation enable supporters of FSU to fix the Seminole as noble savages, to enjoy the spoils of subjugation, and to embrace Indianness without encountering Indians. Through its stagings, FSU claims Indianness as a right of conquest, grounding white institutions and identities in the domesticated difference projected onto Osceola.

The identification and dissociation circulating as Osceola explodes onto the field merge in the stands, where thousands of people invoke signs and gestures associated with Indianness to cheer their Seminoles to victory. As players and fans gaze at the spectacle of a young Euro-American student wielding a flaming spear, galloping bareback to the center of the football field in the shape of an imagined Seminole warrior, they cross into a liminal space where they too "play Indian." This is illustrated, for example, by the FSU War Chant, which originated in 1984 during a game against Auburn University: the Marching Chiefs (the FSU marching band) began to perform this cheer. Several students behind the band joined in, and in subsequent games, more spectators participated and even added the now infamous chopping motion, symbolic of swinging a tomahawk. This was confirmed by an official student athletic booster organization, the Scalphunters, and by the more informal actions of individual fans, who dressed in paint and feathers and yelled war whoops. Such fantastic antics allowed the non-Indian audiences to momentarily transform themselves into a partial embodiment of Indianness. They fostered a form of *communitas*, in which the boundaries and distinctions of everyday life collapsed, giving way to a shared sentiment and identity (Turner, 1978). For the duration of the game, those who opted to join in the ritual became Seminoles.

ENTRENCHED INDIANNESS

As the FSU Seminole name, logo, and mascot have become increasingly controversial and contested in recent decades, a more sustained effort has emerged among campus administrators and supporters to engage members of the Seminole Tribe of Florida. Other than some early attempts to contextualize the FSU logo and mascot with minimal degrees of "authenticity," the evolution of the Seminole icon, in all of its incarnations, has been chaotic and, until recently, did not involve members of the Seminole nation. But by the 1980s and more publicly in the 1990s, once the university realized that some support for the embattled mascot did in fact exist among the Florida Seminole Tribe, it embraced this backing with enthusiasm. In fact, for FSU fans and administrators, these voices of the Florida Seminole Tribe seemingly came to symbolize *the* "authentic authority" on the mascot issue. The consent of the Florida Seminole Tribe, in fact, has been touted by the university as shield against criticisms from other Native American organizations and tribes.

A strategic relationship has emerged in which the Florida Seminole Tribe serves to lend a legitimacy to the FSU name and mascot. This Seminole–FSU relationship is of paramount significance, for it reveals a new turn in a long history of "invented" constructions (by both Seminoles and non-Indian people) of the Seminole figure in popular discourse, especially in terms of the idea of "Florida." Jay Mechling (1996, p. 149) revealed how both Florida and the Seminoles—for centuries—have been "locked in a dialectic dance of interpreting each other." He argued that, "The Seminoles played a key symbolic role in the social construction of the meanings of Florida though tourism, and the touristic visit is the quintessential act in the modern search for 'authenticity' and 'identity'," and further, he insisted, that while real Seminole people do exist, "it is also true that there are real historical circumstances and real institutions that work to determine how a person constructs his or her life as a Seminole." The circumstances under which FSU has engaged, staged, and coaxed contemporary members of the Florida Seminole Tribe conform to this older pattern of cultural appropriation.

Supporters of the FSU Seminoles and the Chief Osceola mascot now include official representatives of the Florida Seminole Tribe. Indeed, James E. Billie, chairman of the Seminole Tribe of Florida, has repeatedly stated that neither he nor the tribe has any objection to the use of the FSU name, logo, or mascot. As criticisms of the FSU Seminole mascot mounted in the 1980s, administrators purportedly sought the advice of Florida tribal members, and since that time, the regional Seminole voice repeatedly has been invoked as representing the authentic, thus legitimate, opinion regarding the mascot issue.

The current university Web site ("Chief Osceola and Renegade," 1999), for example, claims that, "The clothing and rigging
that Chief Osceola and Renegade wear were designed and approved by the Seminole Indian Tribe of Florida." On the same Web
site there appears a statement written by former FSU President
Dale W. Lick (1993), in which he defends the use of the Seminole
iconography. "Recent critics have complained that the use of Indian symbolism is derogatory. Any symbol can be misused and become derogatory. This, however, has never been the intention at
Florida State. Over the years we have worked closely with the
Seminole Tribe of Florida to ensure the dignity and propriety of
the various symbols we use." He does not, however, indicate the
length or nature of this relationship.

He then proceeds to essentially deflect blame for certain elements of the FSU mascot culture. "Some traditions we cannot control. For instance, in the early 1980s, when our band, the Marching
Chiefs, began the now famous arm motion while singing the 'war
chant,' who knew that a few years later the gesture would be picked
up by other team's fans and named the 'tomahawk chop'? It's a
term we did not choose and officially do not use." Who *knew*, indeed? At the very end of the statement, Lick writes, "Our good
relationship with the Seminole Tribe of Florida is one we have cul-
tivated carefully and one we hope to maintain, to the benefit of
both the Seminoles of our state and university." He closes by quot-
ing Chief Billie, who says that his people are proud to be Seminoles
and are proud of the FSU Seminoles.

The statement on the Web site appeared originally in *USA
Today* (May 18, 1993). In 1995, in response to a George Vescey
(1995) column in the *New York Times*, critical of the FSU mascot
tradition and the Indian mascot more generally, the new university
president, Talbot D'Alemberte, felt obliged to author a public defense. In his response (D'Alemberte, 1995), he describes how FSU
has consistently invited Seminole leaders to campus events. "Your
column acknowledges that we have always invited Seminoles, including the Chiefs, to our games, but the way you phrase it (that
FSU 'always trots out some real Seminoles') is insulting. . . . We do
not trot out anyone. We invite Seminoles and they often accept."
D'Alemberte (1995) also cites Chief James E. Billie.

Some critics are skeptical of the Florida Seminole support,
which apparently does not involve direct financial reward for the

tribe. However, the existence of the Osceola mascot and the Seminole trademark, owned by FSU, apparently earns the university as much as $1.8 million annually. Yet Billie has worked hard to involve his tribe in a number of economic ventures within the state, including the establishment of Seminole gambling casinos in Tampa, Hollywood, Brighton, and Immokalee. In essence, Billie is a politician, and he has many friends among state legislators in Florida. *St. Petersburg Times* journalist Jeff Testerman (1998) even suggested that tribal support for the FSU mascot served Billie well in terms of political advantage. Certainly a number of faithful FSU alumni serve in the legislature. At any rate, a carefully constructed system of mutual self-promotion has emerged in the context of the FSU–Florida Seminoles friendship.

Tellingly, concern for Seminole involvement and native responses to Chief Osceola apparently were never of interest to FSU supporters until the mascot became contested. Of further importance is the fact that none of the four Seminole tribes of Oklahoma nor any other well-known Seminole members have endorsed the FSU situation. In fact, Seminole Michael Haney is prominent among a national group of Native Americans who have protested the Indian mascots for many schools and franchises, including FSU. To further complicate matters, the Seminole Tribe of Florida apparently signed a statement condemning Indian mascots authored by the National Congress of American Indians. The precise nature of the FSU relationship to the tribe presents another complication, since it has never been spelled out in any detail by either party. For example, no one associated with FSU, whom the authors contacted, can state exactly when a formal consultation with the Florida Seminoles was begun. And while FSU's Web site claims that the Seminole leaders have worked closely with the university, this is never spelled out. Local journalists informed the authors that, indeed, little interaction occurs, and that Chief Osceola's creator, Durham, is in control of all aspects of the mascot performance and only seeks token approval from Chief Billie.

Under pressure, Chief Billie recently agreed to conduct a tribal referendum on the FSU mascot controversy, although no details regarding such a vote have yet been forthcoming. A vote could prove to be significant, however, and it might rectify the perception held by some, including the authors, that the nature of the FSU–Florida Seminole relationship bears resemblance to the common pattern of the way the United States negotiated Native American treaties. In the past, the practice of negotiating treaties with one or even a few native representatives, often under awkward circumstances, appears on the surface, at least, to have been replaced with the practice of negotiating mascot approval with a few tribal representatives, with perhaps questionable motivations.

As troubling as it may be that a portion of the Seminole community in Florida should find the image of the defiant Osceola appealing, even politically advantageous, conforms to a narrative pattern identified by Mechling (1996), who suggests that a series of stages characterizes the representation of the Seminole. The first stage located the Seminole as "noble savages at one with nature," and a number of tourist Seminole villages existed where one could witness a native wrestle an alligator. While the nineteenth-century Seminoles did utilize alligator meat and skins, they did not, in fact, traditionally wrestle alligators. A later stage characterized the Seminoles as "noble children of the swamp, but also as people who could pick and choose from modern conveniences without jeopardizing the virtues of their traditional ways." The current stage of Seminole imaging, according to Mechling (1996, p. 153), is that the "Seminoles 'interpret back' by gaining control of their own representations, yet these self-representations seem trapped by the narrative conventions of the first two stages." Perhaps the Florida Seminole relationship with FSU's Chief Osceola and his Renegade is indicative of having become ensnared in older, stereotypical narratives of Seminoleness. Or, perhaps Chief Billie, who himself once wrestled alligators for tourists, is merely being pragmatic, seeking to utilize whichever spaces of representation are opened up by the dominant public culture for the Seminole peoples.

To many supporters of mascots, the security of ideological hegemony and deep narrative structures is not enough; they desire the legal certainty and control. In March 1999, Florida State University alumnus Jim King was able to enact his love for his alma mater in a unique fashion. Rather than paint his face or wear a T-shirt, King—who also happens to be a Republican state senator—proposed an amendment to a minor bill to name various state buildings in the Florida legislature that, if it had passed, would have made it law that the FSU sports team would continue to be known as the Seminoles. It also would have mandated that the mascot be "Chief Osceola atop an Appaloosa horse." "For those of us" explained King ("Legislature . . . ," 1999), "who are of the garnet and gold persuasion [school colors] it is time, in fact it is long past time, for us to defend the heritage that is Florida State University." House Speaker, Republican John Thrasher, also an FSU booster, readily accepted King's amendment to the bill (SB 2244). The Florida Senate passed the bill by a vote of 30–0, but it failed to become law when the Florida House session ended without having taken any action. The reason for its ultimate failure may have been the actions of two state representatives, alumni of rival Florida universities, who attached additional amendments to the bill. King and Thrasher, at that point, decided to let the session end without a final vote. The bill is likely to be reintroduced again. In our opinion, this kind of legislation, which was similar to an attempt to make Chief Illiniwek's existence mandated by Illinois law, represents the very worst sort of effort to silence dissent. It embodies a fear of the potential outcomes of a democratic process. Indeed, it is a blatant misuse of legislative power. And yet representatives of the Seminole Tribe of Florida publicly did not object to the bill.

RACIAL HIERARCHY IN THE (NEW) SOUTH

The Florida State University Seminoles not only vividly illustrate the uses of Indianness and the fashioning of whiteness commonly associated with Native American mascots, they also reveal the centrality of blackness to the racial spectacles animated when whites "play Indian" at halftime as well. The image discussed at the outset of this chapter begins to reveal the entanglements of red, white, and black. Although central to the 1999 Fiesta Bowl, oddly absent from this depiction is the African-American athlete, student, or fan. We do not direct attention to this absence because we believe the inclusion of African Americans would improve it. Rather, we highlight this erasure because it mirrors current understandings of Native American mascots and points to the embedded racial hierarchy legitimating such athletic icons.

Interpretations of Native American mascots, whether condemning or celebrating them, almost invariably turn on rather narrow interpretations of race, history, and culture. Frequently, discussions hinge on understandings of Indianness; they debate images and intentions, noting perhaps the emergence of novel Indian agency and identities. Less common, particularly among defenders of mascots, is a concern for whiteness. African Americans (and other peoples of color) have no place in the current discussion of Native American mascots. This is an odd absence, given the presence of blacks and blackness. African Americans are fans of teams with such mascots; they are students, alumni, faculty, and staff members of institutions employing such symbols; and, on occasion, they have created and challenged Native American mascots as well. More importantly, they are athletes, central to the success, marketing, and revenues of big-time college sports. The erased presence of blacks and blackness complicates the racial hierarchies structured by and structuring Native American mascots.

Historically, redness, whiteness, and blackness have played off one another to give material expression to racial ideologies and hierarchies. Nowhere has this been truer than in the American South, marked as it was by the traumas of slavery, warfare, and removal, as well as more mundane "problems" such as miscegenation and acculturation. During the nineteenth century, precisely as they forcibly removed Native Americans, Euro-Americans painted their adversaries in rather romantic terms, stressing their bravery in battle, fidelity to place and people, and commitment to freedom. These renderings were not simply expressions of what Renato Rosaldo (1989) has described as "imperialist nostalgia" or a longing for what one has destroyed; they also were self-portraits that were made all the more heroic, honorable, and powerful by their association with noble savages. According to Joel Martin (1996, p. 139), "Romantic Indians were used to support the southern hegemonic class and its ideology. White patrician slave holders were men of honor: They should be in charge." These idealized images had implications, in turn, for popular understandings of African Americans. The romanticized Indian "provided a damning contrast to the African captive, who, according to white authors, loved bondage. . . . Antebellum literature typically portrayed Africans as happy in their captivity, obedient as dogs, eager to play their roles in the greater southern play. Romantic and rebellious Indians served to dramatize by contrast the docility of Blacks" (ibid.). Redness, whiteness, and blackness, then, worked in concert to establish an intricate racial hierarchy.

The largely uncontested FSU spectacles of redness in the 1960s were not the only racial performances taking place at athletic events. In addition to the presence of invented Indians, both on the field and in the stands, FSU teams were ostensibly inspired by large numbers of spectators brandishing the Confederate flag, often while the band chimed "Dixie." Actually, rebel banners had become ubiquitous at sporting contests and other public events in the Deep South since the 1940s—with the start of the eventual collapse of a segregated Jim Crow society of Southern states. These expressions of nostalgia for a bygone era of de jure white supremacy served to further complicate the racial spectacle at FSU athletic events, as members of a mostly white audience played at being Indian—with face paint and feathers—while also asserting a version of whiteness marked by rebel paraphernalia. Meanwhile, the presence of African Americans was confined to the playing field, even if frequently it was a presence more likely noted on the opposing team (given FSU's tardiness to integrate its sports teams).

In October 1968, in the wake of the recent formation of the Afro-American Student Union (later, the Black Student Union), an alleged racial incident occurred at a football game that sparked a number of protests by African-American students (see Palcic, 1979, p. 84). Using his lit cigarette, a white student burned holes in the shirt of a black student. This white student was a member of a fraternity that used the Confederate flag as a symbol, and members of this fraternity were responsible for a number of incidents in which Confederate flags were waved in the faces of black students. The black victim confronted his attacker, but security officers removed both students from the stadium before a fight could occur. However, the officers did not take the names of the students, and the black student was discouraged by an officer from filing a complaint. A white student, in support of the black student, attempted to identify the officer's badge number and was promptly arrested.

In response, the Afro-American Student Union issued a number of demands, including among them, first, that the incident be investigated by the administration, and also that black security officers and more black faculty be hired. The demand that stirred the most controversy, however, was a request that the school band stop playing "Dixie" and that students stop displaying the Confederate flag. The administration did make some effort to appear to respond to the students' demands, first by investigating the incident at the football game and dropping charges against the arrested student and then by actually meeting with and talking to representatives of the Afro-American Student Union. Regarding the matter of the Confederate symbols, FSU President Champion was reluctant to order students to desist from carrying the flag because it might infringe upon their rights of expression. As for "Dixie," his suggestion that the "Battle Hymn of the Republic" be played immediately following was unacceptable to the group.

In the fall of 1969, by the time the Afro-American Student Union had been renamed as the Black Student Union (BSU), the enrollment of African Americans had increased to between 300 and 400 (Palcic, 1979, p. 103). The new BSU president was John Burt, a junior, and particularly noteworthy, was that he also was a scholarship member of the basketball team. Of the team's total of 12 players, 8 were African American, including 4 of the 5 starters. Certainly today, but even during the rebellious 1960s, it was uncommon for athletes of any color, especially from revenue sports programs, to become politically outspoken. Burt, however, was not merely a token leader chosen for his popularity as an athlete. On the contrary, during the tenure of his two-year leadership, the BSU greatly advanced its campus presence and political power. His identities student and person of color superseded his identity as an athlete. "If you have to give up your manhood to be a basketball player," Burt reasoned, "then basketball isn't worth anything. If you can't be a man, and if you can't have dignity, then you're nothing" (ibid., p. 104).

Burt encouraged his teammates to strive to maintain politically relevant voices, reminding them that "whatever happen[ed] to those students in the Black Student Union [was] also going to happen to [black athletes]" (quoted in Palcic, 1979, p. 105). One of the first concerns tackled by the BSU under Burt's leadership was the nonintegrated cheerleading squad. Although many black women had auditioned to become cheerleaders, none had ever been selected. At the urging of black players, the FSU Athletic Department finally added a black woman, Gail Andrews, to the squad. However, a number of games had passed and Andrews still had not been allowed to cheer on the court ("Black Joins Squad," 1960; Palcic, 1979, p. 105). On January 27, 1970, the popular rivalry between FSU and Jacksonville University would resume in a statewide televised match. As the game approached, Burt consulted with the black basketball players, and all eight agreed to confront the coach. They made it clear that they would refuse to play unless a black woman appeared as an FSU cheerleader during the game. Andrews indeed made her first of many appearances during the Jacksonville game, and the cheerleading squad soon became more fully integrated. This incident reveals the power that student athletes wield, often unwittingly, as a result of their importance to a lucrative system of spectacle and sport. This platform would seem to be especially important to African-American students, since their presence, on the field and on the court, has so often provided the key aspect of "blackness" to these performances.

At the end of the twentieth century, in the context of post–segregation sports, racial stratification persisted in more ambivalent forms. Too often, redness, whiteness, and blackness, in spite of significant modifications, perpetuated racial ideologies and asymmetries, particularly at schools with Native American mascots. At Florida State University, the contours of this racial hierarchy have been plain. At the risk of simplifying, whites should be in charge; the conquered and removed Indians should be revered for the ferocity of their historical resistance; and blacks, applauded, if not celebrated, for their exploits on the playing field, should be appreciative of the progress and opportunities of post–civil rights America. The structures and sentiments resonating within this context have been more complex, more conflicted. Euro-Americans now occupy positions of prestige and privilege as coaches, administrators, entrepreneurs, politicians, and cultural workers. They "play Indian," and they play football. They cheer, idealize, and even idolize African-American athletes, while performing the tomahawk chop and dressing in feathers and paint. In stark contrast, Native Americans are largely absent, save for a handful of fans and students. They materialize at Florida State University home games most conspicuously in the form of a celebrated mascot enacted by a Euro-American student. The bellicosity, violence, and wildness of their invented Indian entertains, nay excites, the undulating crowd of primarily white spectators, channeling power to those who appropriate and mimic Osceola as a trophy, a totem. Importantly, the free, unconquered, and heroic warrior is ultimately safe, first because he was subdued by whites, second because this is a romantic rendering of the white man's Indian (Perdue, 1992), and third because the Seminole Tribe of Florida endorses it. African Americans likewise center the desires and aspirations of white public culture. They are not totems, but athletes, playing a key role in the success of Florida State University over the past two decades. Not surprisingly, an African-American student has never been selected to represent Chief Osceola, for this is an exclusive space where redness is engaged by whiteness. At the same, even though they have an important presence as fans, students, and alumni, African Americans hold few positions of authority in coaching or administration. Many would argue that the prominence of African-American athletes corresponds to their physical superiority. This popular interpretation does much to silently reinstate racial stratification: the physicality of blacks explains their athletic abilities and inability to succeed in other pursuits, because, as the story goes, they lack industry, intelligence, or character; consequently, it also justifies the continued control that whites exercise over public culture and black bodies. Romantic readings of redness further denigrate blackness. Whereas the Seminole fought passionately only to be subdued, resisting incorporation regardless of the costs, African Americans, evidenced by their presence on the football field, eagerly have embraced assimilation, acquiescing before white power for personal gain. In the end, blackness and Indianness, taken together, endow white individuals and institutions with identities, power, and meaning.

CONCLUSIONS

In 1993, Shayne Osceola graduated from Florida State University. His accomplishment was remarkable not only because he was the first Seminole to earn a bachelor's degree at the institution, but also because he is the great-great-great-great-grandson of Osceola. In agreement with the official position of the Seminole Tribe of Florida, he endorsed the FSU Seminoles as a tribute, honoring his people and their defiance. In fact, he excused, if not embraced, fans' antics associated with his esteemed ancestor: "I never took the Tomahawk Chop so seriously I could be offended by it. I never thought about it as anything but a bunch of kids out there having a good time—and I was one of them" (Wheat, 1993). In this chapter, we have taken the tomahawk chop, the war chant, and the tradition of "playing Indian" at FSU very seriously, finding that they are much more than kids having fun. We have analyzed the invention and defense of the Seminoles, probing the uses and understandings of Indians and Indianness, the formulation of whiteness, and the racial hierarchies structuring and structured by the mascot.

Indeed, in contrast to the sentiments of Shayne Osceola and other supporters of the Seminoles, both on the field and in the stands, "playing Indian" at FSU may be a good time for some, but it does not promote empathy, understanding, or respect. Instead, as fans applaud and enact Indianness, they perpetuate stereotypes, foster spaces of terror, warp social relations, and ultimately injure embodied people, especially Native Americans. To offer just one poignant example, Kiowa tribe member Joe Quetone, executive director of the Florida Governor's Council on Indian Affairs Inc., graduated from FSU. He described an experience he had in the mid-1990s, when he and his son attended a Seminole football game. As some students ran through the stands sporting "war" paint, loincloths, and feathers, and carrying tomahawks, Quetone and his son observed a man sitting nearby who turned to a little boy next to him and said, referring to the students, "Those are real Indians down there. You'd better be good, or they'll come up and scalp you" (Whitley, 1999). This episode shocks and saddens, clarifying the asymmetry, privilege, and terror that saturate Native American mascots at FSU and beyond. It vividly illustrates popular prejudices about Indian emergent around mascots and the role that such icons play in perpetuating them. At the same time, it underscores the ease with which Euro-American individuals and institutions appropriate and remake Indians in their own image, literally becoming the real thing as they displace the cultures and histories of Native America. It summarizes in a very poignant fashion a key point of this chapter: the Florida State Seminoles do not pay tribute to the Seminole nor honor their independent spirit, but they display both contemporary and historical leaders, especially Osceola, as trophies and talismans, precisely because they enact racial difference and structure a troubling racial hierarchy.

We close our discussion by returning to Osceola. We end by turning the dominant imagination against itself, asking a series of undecidable questions: How would Osceola interpret the Florida State University Seminoles? Would he recognize himself in the performances of Chief Osceola? What would he make of the Euro-Americans "playing Indian" at midfield and throughout the stadium? Would he be surprised, flattered, amused, insulted? How would he respond to the fact that descendants of the Seminole who successfully resisted relocation west now support such spectacles? Would he charge them with complicity? And what sort of conversation might he and his great-great-great-great-grandson have about mascots, race, and power? Although we cannot answer any of these questions for him, we would like to think that he would challenge the Seminole Tribe of Florida and Florida State University to stop "playing Indian" and the difficult (post)colonial conditions that have made it possible.

5

Body and Soul:
Physicality, Disciplinarity, and the
Overdetermination of Blackness

In common with many Americans, David Duke, a self-declared Nazi, a one-time grand dragon of the Ku Klux Klan (KKK), a former Louisiana state representative, and a presidential candidate, seems captivated by sports. And while he is not an average sports fan, his ideological platform, as extreme as it is, gives voice to many mainstream preoccupations with race and sports. In fact, his recently published memoirs, *My Awakening: A Path to Racial Understanding* (1999), with Glayde Whitney, which is less a personal narrative than a treatise on race in America, continually return to athletics, underscoring the supposed inferiority of African Americans while advancing the imperiled superiority of Euro-Americans. His attention to race and sport unfolds in the context of a broader effort to promote what he terms "white civil rights" (see Bridges, 1994; Hill, 1992; Moore, 1992). It punctuates, illustrates, and supplements his discussions of standard neoconservative and neo-Nazi concerns, intelligence, affirmative action, moral decline, integration, and welfare. Throughout, he reminds readers that African Americans are simultaneously dumber and largely at fault for America's financial and social ills, and that Euro-Americans who negligently support the equality of the races retard the achievement of a more perfect society. Others, occasionally even scholars, have expressed similar points of view (see Levin, 1997, pp. 114–115). Although we do not assert that Duke's views are representative of white America, his repeated engagements with sports and race in his nearly 800-page fascist text not only mirror many of the themes of great concern to a broader public, but his take on these "problems" frequently echoes more mainstream voices as well. His central preoccupation is with foregrounding, indeed explaining, the predominance of the African-American male athlete through a bizarre mix of folk genetics and intelligence theories.

The following are sample commentaries from Duke's analyses of sport, each of which was selected from the David Duke Web site because his cyber-commentary seems even less restrained than that found in the book (Duke, 2000):

> The truth is that many of the colleges sporting mostly black football and basketball teams have had some sort of scandal which included the assault or rape of white women by black players. Even the enemies of our heritage must shake their heads in amazement as seeing many whites who would angrily call for the maximum legal penalties against blacks who assaulted white women, cheering the same such scum on the football and basketball arenas of America.

> Some whites have wrongly suggested that blacks do not have the mental ability for certain sports and positions. Intelligence may be a factor at the quarterback position, but one must still understand that such play is still based on repetition and experience and fundamental skills. The quarterback does not have to design the plays or even call them, he simply has to have the physical skills necessary to execute them. Although there are some times when a quick-thinking quarterback will have an advantage over a slower-thinking one, and that probably is the reason for the preponderance of white quarterbacks in an 80% black sport.[1]

> During my race for the governorship of Louisiana, our sports crazy fans were told that our universities' sports programs would have trouble recruiting if I were elected. It pains me to acknowledge that I probably lost some votes because some members of our race were more worried about

their school's football team than the safety of our own kind from black crime or the racial discrimination practiced against thousands of whites with affirmative action.

The goal here is not to work through a careful critique of Duke's racist claims, nor do we attempt to (dis)prove in a scientific manner claims about the genetic bases of athletic superiority.[2] We do, however, suggest that Duke's inability to avoid the topic of sport, in offering readers his philosophy of race, politics, and power in the United States, does indeed reflect a national preoccupation with racial difference—in particular, *blackness*—in the context of American sport (see Davis, 1993; Entine, 2000; Hoberman, 1997). As extreme as Duke's thinking on race and sport appears to be, it exposes the centrality of white supremacy to mainstream representations, helping us think critically about the imprint of racist ideologies on sports spectacles.

In what follows, we examine the predominance of African-American athletes on the fields and courts where so many Indian and other collegiate mascots prevail. We analyze the inflated political economy of racial signs associated with intercollegiate sports spectacles through which particular formulations of blackness become meaningful and powerful That is, whereas in previous chapters we have directed our attention to the means and meanings of "playing Indian at halftime," the use of stereotypical images of Native Americans as mascots, in this chapter we seek to understand how gazing at black bodies at play mobilizes important Euro-American *desires*. We read the norms and forms of blackness emergent in collegiate athletics while pondering the location of the black athlete within this system as well. Identifying the various ways in which the black athlete has been constructed as a *site* of pleasure, dominance, fantasy, and surveillance, we argue that in a post–civil rights America, African Americans have been essentially invented, policed, and literally (re)colonized through Euro-American idioms such as discipline, deviance, and desire. White America has created certain spaces and opportunities for African-American athletes, and these openings have emerged in the context of a legacy of denied access and forbidden spaces.

Images and accounts of African-American athletes challenge, reproduce, transcend, and even deploy contemporary domains of blackness. At the same time, they continually (re)create an ambivalent conceptual space for European Americans to know, enjoy, and fashion themselves. Throughout American history, blackness has been mobilized variously in terms of at least three predominant tropes, each of which informed the other. First, the bodies of African Americans have been seen as grotesque, in a manner that contrasted the black body with the Native American body. Second, the black body has been rendered, aesthetically, as a superior body, in terms of strength, speed, and resilience, and this discourse articulates with prior conceptualizations of the black body as animalistic and hypersexual. Third, blackness has long signified deviance—sexuality, style and presentation of self, and criminality—and presently it animates the contemporary space of the black athlete in complex, pervasive ways. Each of these tropes have served as colonizing technologies, or ways that allow Euro-Americans to engage the presence of the African American—a mixture of fear, longing, and ambivalence that has long characterized the sensibility of European-American whiteness in relation to the nonwhite, transgressive Other.

CONDITIONS OF (IM)POSSIBILITY

Euro-Americans do not only "play Indian," they mimic African Americans as well. Repeating a pattern common throughout the twentieth century, Euro-American youth and popular cultures borrow, modify, recycle, and reinvent the style and stylings of urban African-American subcultures. Increasingly, they poach the language, dress, music, and bodily praxis associated with rap and hip-hop to fashion meaningful identities and imagined communities (Midol, 1998). These selective, romantic readings of marginalized people and practices have not facilitated the use of African Americans as club emblems, team spirits, or school mascots as they did a century ago, when Euro-Americans began adopting Native American iconography in association with athletic spectacles. Such an action, no matter how well intentioned, surely is absurd, literally unthinkable. What would such a symbol look like? What would the team be named? What would it convey? Would the rhetoric of honor and respect, often advanced to defend Native

American mascots, suffice as a rationale? How would players, alumni, and students respond? As thought provoking as such questions may be, they are ridiculous. Undoubtedly, in the wake of the civil rights movement, prevailing social and political circumstances would render any effort to fashion an athletic team in the imagined likeness of African Americans impossible. Importantly, save for the instance discussed in the opening chapter, such a context never really existed in the United States. In Euro-American public culture, both before and after emancipation, racist ideologies devalued and denigrated African Americans. Formerly enslaved, they did not embody the spirited resistance, aggressive defiance, or noble wildness ascribed to Native Americans but rather were thought to be shiftless, undisciplined, primal, childish, and dependent.

Although it would be unthinkable to invent a sports mascot that embodied such African-American stereotypes as "Sambo," the ubiquitous black athlete is celebrated in ways both more subtle and more obvious than halftime show spectacles. African-American athletes have emerged at the center of a multibillion-dollar collegiate and professional sports industry, and the black athlete has been transformed into an aesthetic commodity, controlled by the gaze of a largely white but also an African-American consumer (D. Andrews, 1996; V. Andrews, 1996; Cole & Andrews, 1996; Davis & Harris, 1998; Kellner, 1996). As the increasing presence of African-American students on many campuses in post–segregation America was often defined largely by the presence of the black student athlete, a new political economy of sport was already maturing. This economy deeply linked NCAA Division I revenue sports, such as football and basketball, to the professional leagues. It is difficult, if not inappropriate, to critique big-time college sports without also taking full account of this relationship to professional sports. By the time universities were commonly recruiting black student athletes, certainly by the 1970s, a moment had emerged in which the premier athletes of any race were invited to campus primarily as performers and players. Schools whose student bodies remained largely white often had athletic teams that were increasingly black. Significantly, these racialized social fields literally structured social relations and informed the production of social knowledge. It is essential to appreciate, for example, that white students are indeed relating to black students in particular ways when they cheer African-American celebrity athletes who also are fellow students. Likewise, the experiences of black student athletes recruited to play sports at a largely white university confront daily the consequences and stereotypes embodied in these social relations.

While imperialist nostalgia for Native Americans centered on courage, a sexualized wildness, bellicosity, and warring aggression, a particular nostalgia also emerged surrounding African Americans. Although these white discourses of racialized longing overlapped in some ways, as both the black and Indian body were hypersexualized, for example, in the white imagination, blackness arguably was evermore "grotesque," polluting, and transgressive than Indianness. Historically, a contradictory set of meanings has been ascribed to blackness. At once a lack (undisciplined, lazy, dumb) and an excess (strength, endurance, libido) (see Chideya, 1995; Cole, 1996; Cole & Andrews, 1996; Cole & Denny, 1995; Davis & Harris, 1998; Lipsitz, 1998; Lott, 1999; Pieterse, 1992; Wonseck, 1992), it has symbolized "the multiple, bulging, over- or under-sized, dirty, protuberant and incomplete" (Mellinger & Beaulieu, 1997). Popular, political, legal, academic, and religious discourses fashioned African Americans as infantile, animalistic, primal, base, servile, subhuman, unintelligent, and carnal.

Nineteenth-century postcards and advertisements exemplified this pattern. These media depicted African Americans with a series of exaggerated features, such as thick lips, bulging eyes, huge ears, and gaping mouths. In still other cases, black people were featured with opposable toes. A predominant theme that organized these imaginary images of black people was hygienic practice and toilet use: black figures are seen sitting on toilets, sweating and straining, and on others are seen farting and blowing their noses. Such excessive images of black bodies and lifestyles as dirty and "undisciplined" served to define a white bourgeois society in terms of a projected opposite. Black people were imagined ultimately to be what white people were not.

At the same moment Euro-Americans were using blackness to cement a playfully refined, civil version of whiteness, they began mimicking, actually mocking, African Americans within the increasingly popular tradition of black-face minstrel performances. To the amusement of paying audiences, particularly in urban centers, white men staged theatrical, caricatured portrayals of blacks. The minstrel show obscured the explicit and implicit terror that characterized the social institution of slavery by animating the slave as a silly, generally happy, buffoon (Lott, 1993). Further, these exhibitions embodied various black expressive traditions, such as song and dance, into passive, complacent, childlike figures who would then signify a sentimentality for the "good ole days" of plantation life (Hale, 1998). Indeed, icons emerging from this tradition linger into the present, from such subservient grocery emblems as Uncle Ben and Aunt Jemima to the folk narrations of Uncle Remus and Little Black Sambo (Manring, 1998).

The Harlem Globetrotters of recent decades appear in many ways to embody this discursive tradition. This all-black basketball team travels from arena to arena staging exhibition games against, most recently, the Washington Generals (their eternal opponent, whom they always beat). The performances turn on the humorous, comedic antics of the Globetrotters, who frequently interrupt the game to tease opponents, referees, and audience members. They display flashy basketball skills such as spinning the ball on their fingers, bouncing passes off of their knees and elbows, and rolling passes down their backs. These frolicking, happy Globetrotters have created such celebrity figures as Meadowlark Lemon, Goose, and Curly. Although conspicuously black, the Harlem Globetrotters have successfully effected a thorough erasure of race as a complicating factor of their existence. They play now before largely suburban white audiences, and they project accommodating and charming personas. They did not, however, as they do now, function almost exclusively as a traveling comedy troupe. This shtick emerged only after the NBA and collegiate basketball began to sign black players. Prior to that, the Globetrotters were a much more serious team, with black players who were among the most talented in the nation.

Abe Saperstein, a first-generation Jewish American of Polish descent who grew up in Chicago's North Side neighborhood, Ravenswood, founded the Harlem Globetrotters (see Vescey, 1970). They were actually situated in Chicago during their early years, but Saperstein wanted to include Harlem as part of the team's name to advertise that the players were black. Although the Globetrotters first official game was in 1927, they actually got their start a few years earlier. Saperstein organized the "Savoy Big Five," which played its games at the Savoy Ballroom on Chicago's South Side. Since the ballroom was an African-American establishment, the players, too, were all black. Soon, after it became clear that dancing and basketball would not mix, the team was without a job. They decided to stay together, however, and became the Globetotters, a team of traveling basketball performers. Saperstein was a savvy promoter, and the team soon became well known. It seemed to enjoy access to the best black players in the country since, until the 1950s, the NBA and most large universities refused to accept an African-American presence.

The Harlem Globetrotters scheduled a special tour for the spring of 1950. An all-white team of college all-stars agreed to play the Globetrotters in a twenty-game series, to take place on twenty consecutive nights in twenty different cities. Using an impressive combination of skill, pizzazz, and showmanship, led by Marques Haynes, the Globetrotters won thirteen of the eighteen contests (Vescey, 1970, pp. 42–43). Finally, that same year, professional basketball began to integrate, as the Boston Celtics drafted Chuck Cooper of Duquesne University, and the New York Knickerbockers paid Saperstein $25,000 for the contract of Globetrotter Nathaniel (Sweetwater) Clifton, the latter of whom became the NBA's first black player. Saperstein's response to the Celtic's drafting of Cooper belied the perception that he was committed to African-American progress. He was angered, thinking that he had earned the exclusive domain of black players, and he indeed boycotted the Boston Garden for years after the Cooper selection (Fitzpatrick, 1999, p. 61).

From nineteenth-century minstrel shows to twentieth-century sports spectacles, the tropes of the grinning, banjo-strumming, tap-dancing comic or of a happy, maternal (or avuncular) servant have characterized white longings for blackness (Early, 1994, pp. 155–162; Hale, 1998; Lott, 1993; Mellinger & Beaulieu, 1997; Turner, 1993). Read against this backdrop, contemporary sport becomes a troubling racial drama. Increasingly in the wake of integration, mass-mediated spectacles return the white gaze to the black body.

As with imagined Indians, performance paces the significance of blackness—physicality, play, and control of the body.

It is nearly impossible for many white people to think about sports without also pondering the predominance and success of African-American athletes. African-American Bill Russell, a Hall of Fame basketball player, wryly underscored this preoccupation when he claimed that, "A smart college basketball coach plays three blacks at home, four on the road, and five when he is behind" (Funk, 1991, p. 101). Russell's musing foregrounds also the ambivalence behind white *knowledge* of athletic blackness. This preoccupation of the African American as jock, with natural prowess, is one of several key white stereotypes of blackness, along with the African American as criminal, the African American as buffoon, and the African American as hypersexual.

If it is impossible for many white Americans to consider sport without thinking, at one level or another, about blackness, in 1966 it was impossible for Adolph Rupp to imagine his basketball team in terms of anything but whiteness. This is not to suggest, however, that Rupp did not have particular understandings of black America; by most accounts, he loathed and feared it. When on March 25 of that year, Rupp's all-white Kentucky Wildcats lost to the all-black Texas Western Miners in the national championship game, the nation was intrigued with the conspicuous racial mapping of the two teams. Rupp had long been a vocal opponent of integration, and he had steadfastly refused to recruit black players for his seemingly invincible Kentucky team (Fitzpatrick, 1999). Frank Deford, well-known *Sports Illustrated* writer, reported that Rupp referred to the Texas Western players as "coons" while speaking to his team before the game (ibid., p. 214). After the 1966 loss, he ridiculed Texas Western, accusing their coach of using players "out of the penitentiary and off the streets of New York" ("The Final Four," 1989; see also Funk, 1991, p. 102). Some Kentucky fans seemed oddly impressed by the "blackness" of Western Texas. Current Maryland coach Gary Williams, who observed the historic game in person, recalls, ". . . after the game, I remember hearing the Kentucky people saying , 'We gotta get us some of them' " (quoted in Feinstein, 1998, p. 128).

The game served, perhaps for the first time, as a national stage for what is often referred to as stylistically "black" basketball. The Miners' players, partly in response to the encouragement of their white coach, Don Haskins, had effected a style of play characterized by a certain flashiness, highlighted in particular by the "slam dunk." To perform a slam dunk, a player jumps up to the basket, usually with great force, and directly forces the ball through the hoop with both hands. Although he forbid his players from behind-the-back dribbling and passing, Haskins encouraged dunking because he recognized its potential to intimidate opponents. Frank Fitzpatrick (1999, p. 162) speculated, "That image of mean, muscular manliness was essential in Haskins' physical system. When he wanted to wound his players, he would challenge their manhood, calling them 'girls' or 'sissies.' They in turn took it out on their opponents in the same fashion."

Before the championship game, some supporters of Texas Western apparently heard Rupp claim on a radio broadcast that five black players could never beat his Wildcat team (Fitzpatrick, 1999, p. 205). Hoping to inspire his team, Haskins included this comment in a pre-game motivational speech. As the players were heading out of the locker room, Haskins grasped the arm of David Lattin, his large, flamboyant center, and demanded, "First chance you get, flush it. Flush it as hard as you can" [Haskins usually referred to the dunk as a "flush"] (quoted in Fitzpatrick, 1999, p. 205). During Texas Western's second possession, Lattin took a quick pass from the guard and "jammed the ball through [Pat] Riley's outstretched arms and down into the basket" (ibid., p. 210). Lattin then turned to Riley and shouted, "Take that, you white honky." Many, including Wildcat player Tommy Kron, sensed that Kentucky was intimidated. Kron commented on Lattin's dunk: "We were all just kind of standing there and he soared up and it seemed to be a real exclamation point. It really picked their team up, and I think we were intimidated by their quickness and power" (ibid., p. 211). Texas Western won, 72–65.

When Rupp relented in 1969 by finally recruiting and signing Tom Payne, Kentucky's first black player, he may have purposely set up the "integration experiment" for failure by selecting someone with both less scholastic and social preparation than many other available black recruits (see Fitzpatrick, 1999). Payne was a 7-foot center who sat out his freshman year with academic problems. After his sophomore year, he declared hardship status and entered the NBA. His brief career was unremarkable, and he ended up serving time in prison on a rape conviction.

By 1991, black players had become prevalent within the landscape of big-time collegiate basketball, as 19 out of the 20 players who comprised the starters of the Final Four teams were African American. The Nike shoe corporation had by then become inextricably woven into the political economy, uniting collegiate and professional sport. While their professional clients, such as Michael Jordan, were critical of the global rise of its trademark Swoosh, Nike was never technically able to highlight specific collegiate stars in its ads due to NCAA restrictions. Nevertheless, the company has regularly sponsored collegiate events, has held high school player recruitment camps, has pursued college coaches and universities to sign them to contracts obligating their athletes to sport Nike footwear, and has utilized nondescript college players in its advertisements. Acclaimed black filmmaker Spike Lee has been central to the success of Nike, ever since he teamed with Michael Jordan in a series of commercials that portrayed Jordan interacting with a youthful, urban black teenager known as "Mars Blackmon" (played by Lee). Viewers watch several scenes of Jordan's famous, elegant flight to the basket and then hear Blackmon, clumsily sporting large eyeglasses and a loose ball cap, exclaim, "It must be da shoes!" as if to explain the greatness of Jordan. David Andrews (1996, p. 140) has argued that, "Nike's promotional strategy systematically downplayed Jordan's blackness by contrasting him with Spike Lee's somewhat troubling caricature . . . Jordan was Jordan, he wasn't really black. Mars was a 'nigger'." Spike Lee, perhaps more than any other non-sports celebrity, is associated with a fanaticism of professional and collegiate sport. A fixture at New York Knicks games, he is commonly the focus of television cameras capturing his playful bantering of Knick opponents Jordan and Indiana Pacer star Reggie Miller.

One of the more significant spaces where the political economy uniting professional and collegiate sport is mobilized unfolds at the annual Nike summer basketball camps. One such Nike camp was featured in *Hoop Dreams*, as one of the documentary's stars, William Gates, was invited to attend as one of the best 100 high school players in the nation. Nike flies these students in, houses and feeds them for four days, and provides coaching and medical care, so that they can perform on the court before the eyes of college basketball's top coaches. Indeed, Bobby Knight, P.J. Carlisimo, and Rick Pitino are among those coaches seen in *Hoop Dreams*. In addition to playing basketball, students are required to attend a series of lectures, covering everything from study skills to financial advice. In one of the film's more significant scenes, Spike Lee appears before a large group of these high school basketball players, nearly all of them black.

The bespectacled Lee's advice to the players is cautionary as he urges them not to mistake the motivations of the system into which they are being recruited:

> You have to realize, that nobody cares about you. You're black! You're a young male! All you're supposed to do is deal drugs and mug young women. The only reason why you're here [is] you can make their team win. If their team wins, these schools get a whole lot of money. This whole thing is revolving around money.

Although Lee's comments do not run counter to the claims that we are making in this book, the context of his cautionary tale seems rife with contradictions. That a black celebrity of Lee's stature would be brought in by Nike to speak to high school students to warn them about their fateful purpose within an exploitative system is surprising since, in our view, for years Nike has been at the very center, valorizing the very spaces and narratives of this exploitation. Further, Lee's participation as an outspoken, youthful, liberal director and producer of films, which so often have eloquently critiqued America's relationship to African-American citizens, seems doomed from the outset. He does not appear to recognize that his very platform, the recruitment camps provided by Nike, is a significant commercial pillar of the system. Further, he has earned a great deal of money in partnership with Nike, himself valorizing the popular marriage of sport and blackness.

BODY POLITICS

In intercollegiate athletics, the body fosters the racialization of African Americans. It is an excessive, if ambivalent, semiotic nexus, (de)composed of historic sediments and emergent sentiments. Ultimately a social artifact, it naturalizes distinction, physically inscribing racial difference and materially legitimating social asymmetries. The body of the African-American athlete, as a site and source of (exceptional) ability, (criminal) deviance, and (spectatorial, if not sexual) pleasure, simultaneously facilitates imagination and exploitation. And as it entertains, inspires, troubles, and revolts, it legitimates, if not encourages, discipline, regulation, and control. In this section, we deconstruct the fabricated body of African-American athletes and the body politics inscribed upon it.

To return to the Nike camp and *Hoop Dreams*, shortly after William Gates and his fellow Nike campers are cautioned by Lee that their value within the system was predicated on their bodily talents as players, viewers witness a conversation among three college coaches, all coaches of color. As several campers stroll by, Bo Ellis, then assistant coach at Marquette, remarks, "Look at some of these young boys' bodies! They got NBA bodies already." In the next camp scene, Bob Gibbon, a white independent scout, innocently informs viewers that, "It's already become a meat market, but I try to do my job, you know, and serve up professional meat." While sport has commodified the bodies of all young student athletes, American sporting culture increasingly has turned on and has become decidedly "turned on" by the bodies of African Americans. Just as those Kentucky fans, amazed at upstart Western Texas's victory in 1966, began to embrace the idea of going out to "get some" black bodies, after Southern California soundly defeated powerhouse Alabama in football in 1970, due largely to the three-touchdown effort of a black running back named Sam Cunningham, legendary Alabama coach Bear Bryant muttered as he left the field, "He did more for integration in the South in sixty minutes than Martin Luther King did in twenty years." That very night, reportedly, he began to arrange to recruit his very first black players (see Lapchick, 1991, p. 227).

The longing for and appropriation of black bodies in intercollegiate sporting spectacles reveal an encrusted racial ideology that
explains the presence and success of African-American athletes
through accounts of their (supposed) natural physicality. Indeed,
this (Euro-)American fascination, even obsession, pivots on the
perceived excessive athletic agility, speed, and strength of the
black body (Davis, 1990; Hawkins, 1995/1996; Hoberman,
1997; Sandell, 1995). The intense interests and investments in the
athletic "essence" of the African American animate sports and
popular culture more generally, particularly films such as *White
Men Can't Jump*, *Blue Chips*, *He Got Game*, and *Hoop Dreams*.
Even as the rhetoric of integration and racial harmony prevails in
intercollegiate sporting contexts, the national media, administrators, coaches, analysts, fans, and players continually reinscribe
this ideology. Two infamous comments exemplify the logic of this
ideology. Jimmy "the Greek" Snyder explained the superiority of
black athletes as a result of breeding during slavery. Later, Al
Campanis, then vice president of the Los Angeles Dodgers, told
ABCs Ted Koppel that blacks "are gifted with great muscula-
ture and various other things. They're fleet of foot. And this is
why there are a lot of black major league ballplayers" (quoted in
Davis, 1990).

Sentiments about African-American athletic superiority are
both advanced and contested within the black community. For example, a few years ago, ESPN televised a program focusing on race
and sport. The opening segment featured African-American NBA
player Charles Barkley's visit to a sixth-grade school class to discuss the topic. Soon after Barkley introduced himself, the following dialogue unfolded in response to a question from a black child,
who asked "Do you think the movie *White Men Can't Jump* is
very racist?" Barkely answered politely:

No, I don't, and I answered that question when that movie
came out. Every time somebody speaks, they're not trying
to be racist. If you want to say the movie *White Men Can't
Jump* is racist, yeah, you can say that, but it's not true. But
if you want to be a real jerk or you want to start some
racial b.s. as I call it, you know, you can say, well that
movie's racist. You know but that's not true. It was just a

movie, they came up with a name. Now like when I said, like I'll give an example: Black guys can jump higher than white guys—most of them—you think that's racist?

A different student, an African-American boy, (bravely) responded, "Yes." Surprised, Barkley asked, "Do you think so? Why do you think that's racist?"

The boy who first asked about the movie then admitted, "Well actually I do too."

Barkley said, "I'm asking, well, I'm just asking why."

"Well, first of all, you didn't go out like, for a survey to see which, like you didn't have like ten people—five white guys and five black guys—and see who could jump higher. So if you didn't do that, then you are racist," reasoned the boy.

Barkley explained:

Well, I feel like, considering what I've done for the last 20 years, 25 years, I've had plenty of surveys. And my recommendation if I was asked a question, I said, can black guys jump higher than white guys, I would say yeah, I think they can, and I don't consider that statement racist at all. I mean if you want to make it racist you could, you could. But I don't see it as racist cause my, I guess my proper definition of racism would be with intent, if you wanted to debate whether what, what somebody says is racist or what they say is not racist, is the intent to harm or to belittle another group. I don't belittle white guys if I say I think black guys can jump higher. Like if I want to say um, I think um, basketball players, black basketball players are better than white basketball players, would you, would you consider that racist?

The boy said, "I have, like, a little problem with that because . . . there are like, there are . . . most white kids at this school could beat me at basketball, and they can jump higher than I can, and they're in the same grade. And like most of them are about, like at my old school, most of them were like the same height as me, and they could still jump higher than me and play basketball better than I could."

Barkley attempted to offer closure about the debate with the persistent youth. "Well, I guess I can't speak for you. I can only speak for my, my perception of the last twenty-five years. My opinion for the last twenty-five years, most of the black guys who I've been around can out-jump white guys. And they're better players at basketball."

These remarks revealed what scholars such as Kobena Mercer (1994) and David Andrews (1996) have argued is a historically significant racial epistemology based on a mind-body dualism in which brains and brawn are opposed in popular discourse. Indeed, Mercer (1994, p. 138) notes that, "Classical racism involved a logic of dehumanization, in which African peoples were defined as having bodies but not minds: in this way the superexploitation of the black body as a muscle-machine could be justified," and warns, "Vestiges of this are active today." Importantly, scholars have linked this preoccupation with natural strength and speed to the easy projection of criminality and intellectual inferiority onto the black body (D. Andrews, 1996, forthcoming; V. Andrews, 1991, 1996; Cole, 1996; Cole & Andrews, 1996; Cole & Denny, 1995; Davis, 1990; Hoberman, 1997).

While graduate students at the University of Illinois in 1994, the authors encountered clearly more than a mere vestige of this racial discourse. The Undergraduate Anthropology Student Association (UGASA) had posted a number of meeting notices in and around Davenport Hall, where the anthropology and geology departments are located. To attract attention, the students who designed the flyers advertised the meeting through an announcement for a new course, "Experimental Primatology 304 (same as Kinesiology 009)." The fictitious class promised to address subjects such as "Tree Climbing, Brachiating, and Termite Fishing," and "includes mandatory all expense paid field trips to Ecuador, Kenya, and Sumatra." Two images at the center of the flyer (over)determined its message. On the right, a photograph captures a gibbon hanging by its right hand from a tree branch; on the left is a photograph of the well-known bronze statue of Michael Jordan—in mid-flight, with right arm outstretched, preparing to dunk a basketball—which stands outside of the United Center in Chicago. The juxtaposition of the celebrated Jordan and the anonymous gibbon, the black athlete and the arboreal primate, dunking and brachiating—not to mention kinesiology and primatology—gives material expression to racial ideologies grounded in the black body, ideologies so commonsensical and invisible that students of anthropology perpetuate them without pause. In part, the flyer suggests that African Americans are base, natural, and animalistic; that they are better studied along with, if not as, lower-order primates; that their skills and talents, in turn, should be understood as natural, if not evolutionary, effects—that blacks dunk and gibbons brachiate.

European-American racial ideologies, as this example clarifies, have frequently terrorized their African and African-American objects by advancing hierarchies of humankind that directly question the humanity of nonwhite others. Specifically, for centuries the black body has been (mis)cast as a more primitive manifestation of humanness, often and without much subtlety, linked to apes and monkeys (Gould, 1996/1981; T. Lott, 1999; Pieterse, 1992; Smedley, 1993; Takaki, 1993). Tommy Lott (1999, p. 7) identifies this preoccupation as the mobilization of "Negro-ape metaphor," and claims, "The association of apes with black people in Western discourse was facilitated by the European discovery of apes and the continent of Africa at about the same time." Lott examines how the Negro-ape mythology informed ostensibly scientific discourse as well as the writings of colonial travelers and naturalists. Sir Thomas Herbert even contended that similarities between Hottentots (a black, southern African population) and apes implied that the black race might have been a by-product of sexual intercourse between humans and apes. Others believed that oversexed, libidinous apes would occasionally kidnap and "enslave" black women and children, and thus Lott (1999, p. 9) suggests that such beliefs allowed Europeans to rationalize the enslavement of Africans as a manifestation of the natural order of things.

Mediated by this discourse that locates the African American as animalistic, white America has imagined, exploited, regulated, desired, and feared the physicality of blackness throughout its history. Even today, such knowledge terrorizes humane sensibilities. For example, in the wake of the beating of Rodney King by members of the Los Angeles Police Department, the nation learned that one of the officers, Stacey Coon, harbored racist tendencies when, among other things, an audiotape was introduced during the King trial that featured Coon describing his intervention during a domestic abuse call in an African-American neighborhood as "Something out of *Gorillas in the Mist*" (Feldman, 1994). The history of attempts to position the black body, in particular, the black male body, as animalistic and bestial has fostered the cultivation of two overlapping, articulating discourses of blackness: the black body as naturally athletic and the black body as criminal.

In fact, these two discourses of blackness form a dialectic that illustrates well the ambivalence animating the white imaginary. This ambivalence turns on the tension between a fear of and a fascination with the black body (D. Andrews, 1996, p. 132). Consider, for example, the comments of Daryl Gates, who was the chief of the Los Angeles Police Department during the Rodney King beating and subsequent trial. Responding defensively to criticisms of his department for the high number of deaths of African-American men while in police custody, he reasoned, "We may be finding that in some blacks when [the carotid chokehold] is applied, the veins or arteries do not open as fast as they do on normal [*sic*] people" (quoted in Davis, 1992, p. 272). This (mis)application of folk biology underscores the deep investment of white America in racial difference. Fascination with the superior athletic black body too easily transmutes into the fear of the pathological black body.

This association has profound implications for African-American collegiate athletes. Indeed, increasingly in the wake of the Reagan revolution, Len Bias' death, the war on drugs, the Rodney King beating, and the subsequent trial and insurrection, the O.J. Simpson trial, and Latrell Sprewell, criminality indelibly marks the African-American athlete. Public perceptions and media representations transform minor infractions into moral dramas and major transgressions into scandals, often of national import. To be sure, popular attitudes toward and coverage of the illicit activities and wrongdoings of athletes, regardless of race, have attained unprecedented importance; however, the particular history of blackness and the peculiar return of race in sociopolitical discourse imprint all African Americans as deviant, not simply those who break the law. Comparing the reception of two University of Nebraska football players accused of criminal activity exemplifies this pattern. In 1994, Christian Peter, an outstanding (Euro-American) defensive end for Big Red was convicted of assaulting a former Miss Nebraska; a year later, Lawrence Phillips, the Cornhuskers' star (African-American) running back, was charged with beating his white ex-girlfriend. Although both athletes have extensive records and had committed offenses certain to evoke public contempt—violence against women—the scrutiny they were subjected to differed immensely. Whereas Peter's actions received little attention beyond Lincoln, Nebraska, Phillips' action ignited a firestorm of controversy, heightened when Nebraska coach Tom Osborne opted to let Phillips continue playing after a brief suspension. Phillips' story circulated far beyond campus, receiving intense national recognition, including a segment on *60 Minutes*. Given the similarity of their social standing and transgression, the (over)determining feature undoubtedly was race and the interracial relationship. For Phillips, and countless other African-American collegiate athletes, who more often than not do not break the law, the inscriptions of animalistic qualities, deviant capacities, and extraordinary abilities onto their bodies prefigure public understanding of their moral character, no less than their physical talents.

The excesses of the black body and the ambivalences of white public culture do not desist with either the athletic superiority or deviance inscribed upon it. Indeed, Euro-American fears and desires in post–desegregation sports support and rehabilitate another corporeal cliche, the myth of the hypersexual African American. Over the past several decades, precisely as they have desegregated, one of the greatest concerns of white universities and their communities—after integrating their sports teams—has been interracial dating. More specifically, there is evidence that once the black athlete arrives on the largely white campus, a fear—at times subtle, at times overstated—of the "primally driven" black sexual appetite emerges. At the University of Texas at El Paso, formerly Texas Western University, in the late 1960s, for instance, Coach Don Haskins commonly scrutinized the women his black players were dating, discouraging them from seeing white women. This policing was not limited to a single individual but was pervasive. Willie Cager outlined the shape of this context: "I used to talk to a white girl . . . but one day she said that she couldn't talk to me anymore, because some of the professors had been cornering her and telling her she would get a bad name" (quoted in Olson, 1968). Teammate Fred Carr highlighted the implications. "When you date a white girl, you get in trouble and she gets bad-mouthed all over campus" (ibid.).

Similarly, a report detailing the various forms of racial prejudice faced by black athletes at the University of Illinois in the 1960s suggests that "the most severely sanctioned social activity [of black athletes] was interracial dating" (Spivey & Jones, 1983, p. 946). A number of players were actually approached by a member of the Athletic Association in 1963, who warned them "to stop dating or being seen with white girls" (ibid.). In the early 1960s, at the University of Washington, football star Junior Coffey—the nation's third leading rusher at the time—was warned not to date white women. He refused to comply with the ultimatum and thus was never allowed to start another game (Lapchick, 1991, p. 245). This preoccupation with the imagined sexual appetite of the black male athlete is not merely an artifact of years-gone-by racism. Howie Evans, a one-time black assistant coach at Fordham University, once told sports-studies scholar Richard Lapchick that during his years of work at a black community center in New York in the 1990s, recruiters from white Southern schools would arrive seeking to sign black women to attend their schools. The reasoning, according to Evans, was that these women would be able to provide the black athletes at these Southern schools with *appropriate* female companionship (see Lapchick, 1991, pp. 244–248, 1996, p. 13). Lapchick, who suggests that a white paranoia prevails that views black athletes as potential rapists, reports that from 1988 through 1990, a total of thirty news accounts of female sexual assault by athletes was produced. Of these thirty assaults, twenty-one were by white athletes. He insists further that when an African-American athlete is the focus of such a report, it is indeed his blackness that is foregrounded, through text and image. On the other hand, reports of white athletic sexual crimes remain racially unmarked, even though they represent the majority of cases (Lapchick, 1991, p. 248).

As the foregoing discussions of the black body indicate, the set of beliefs and apprehensions about the blackness that has been constructed within the European-American imagination derives its meaning from the competing emotions of fascination and fear. On the one hand, the African-American athlete is engaged by collegiate institutions, as well as by the professional sports industry, as a highly desired corporeal commodity. On the other hand, the male African-American athlete, as well as the African-American male, generally, is the object of white paranoia. Increasingly, the ambivalent (physically) overdetermined black body has become the site of discipline, regulation, and management.

THE RULES OF THE GAME

Euro-American understandings of African Americans being excessive and transgressive have always fostered, if not demanded, disciplinarity, the application of regimes of control, regulation, and management; the bondage, beatings, surveillance, and dehumanization of slavery; and later, the lynchings, terror, spatial constraints, and segregation of Jim Crow. Although much kinder and gentler, veiled as it is in the rhetoric of opportunity, equality, and education, intercollegiate athletic spectacles construe African Americans as deviants in need of refinement, correction, training, and supervision. Informed by the taken-for-granted and largely white norms of etiquette, bodily practice, the life cycle and the good life, a succession of public panics has erupted in which fans, administrators, coaches, and media commentators have voiced grave concerns, if not blatant condemnations, of the choices, behaviors, language, and self-presentation of African Americans in paternalistic tones. The place of race in two recent public panics clarifies the articulations of paternalism, disciplinarity, and cultural difference in the domain of college sports—the increasing frequency with which African-American athletes opt out of college and African-American expressiveness on the field of play.

In the spring of 1997, Peyton Manning, the Euro-American quarterback of the University of Tennessee, decided to stay in school rather than to turn professional. Against the backdrop of

talented athletes, most of whom were African American, skipping
college or leaving college to pursue lucrative professional careers,
his decision was widely celebrated for its (apparent) endorsement
of amateurism, higher education, and (embattled) traditional values. Manning was hailed as an exemplary student athlete, balancing scholastic and sports to become a more complete citizen. Often
latent, these comments were assessments of the characters and
choices of those who had turned pro prematurely—immature, ma-
terialistic, disinterested in education, lacking discipline, and taking
the easy way out—or they were rationalizations of their deci-
sions—the athlete feels responsible for his family in the projects, so
this is a way for him to give something back. Neither media commentators nor fans evaluated Manning so cynically. The authors
do not recall hearing, "He is doing it to win the Heisman," or "He
wants to win the national championship." Although we do not
know why Manning opted to remain in college for his senior season, what is important about this, especially public reception of it,
is that it points to a deeper racialized structure.

In the mid-1990s, two young superstar athletes, Drew Henson
and Kobe Bryant, faced an exciting decision: to go to college or to
go pro. Whereas Henson opted to attend the University of Michigan and play minor league baseball during the summer, Bryant decided to play professional basketball and hoped to take college
courses on-line. Through their compromises and strategies, Henson and Bryant plotted very similar trajectories. In the media, their
choices were starkly different, presented in black-and-white terms
as polar opposites: Henson was applauded for his decision, and
Bryant, in contrast, was challenged, if not condemned, for his. Beyond incidental elements—hometown, sport, and grade-point average—two key differences distinguished Henson from Bryant:
first, their priorities, particularly the emphasis placed on college,
and second, race—Henson is white, and Bryant is black. And
racial difference is the difference that makes a difference.

Although they ultimately elected divergent paths, Bryant and
Henson were strikingly similar. Both were phenomenal athletes.
Bryant, 6'6", excelled at basketball, averaging 31 points, 12 re-
bounds, 7 assists, 4 blocks, and 4 steals a game; Henson, 6'5", distinguished himself in football, throwing over 50 touchdown passes
during his senior season, and in baseball, a 0.70 earned run aver-

age and a .650 batting average augmented his 95 mph fast ball. Both were from middle-class families involved in sports. While Bryant's father was a former professional basketball player in the United States and Italy, Henson's father coached high school sports in Michigan. And before either had played a single college game, professional teams expressed interest in the young superstars. Whereas Bryant's announced intention to go pro secured him a top slot in the NBA's draft and a $10 million contract, the New York Yankees openly courted Henson, offering him a $2 million signing bonus to play minor league baseball during the off-season. Importantly, the media attached great expectations to the untested pair as well, labeling Bryant "the next Michael Jordan" (Bamberger, 1996) and Henson "the next Michael Jordan" of professional sports (Montville, 1998).

Despite the fact that their experiences and possibilities nearly mirrored one another, media coverage, colored by popular racist stereotypes, painted a very different image. This difference begins with the titles of articles in *Sports Illustrated* about Bryant and Henson. The former is profiled in a piece called "School's Out" (Bamberger, 1996); the latter is heralded in a story entitled "Golden Boy: Michigan-Bound Quarterback and Yankee Bonus Bay Drew Henson—Who Also Averaged 22 Points in Basketball and 4.0 in the Classroom Is Almost Too Good to Be True" (Montville, 1998). From this beginning, the differences multiply in disturbing ways. Immediately after Bryant announced his intention to enter the NBA draft and to forgo his college eligibility, a public outcry questioned his decision. His physical and emotional maturity was debated in the media—was he ready to go pro? Did he have the necessary experience or strength to make it? Could he handle the pressure? Could he play with the likes of Shaquille O'Neal, Charles Barkley, and Michael Jordan? College, it was argued, would refine Bryant, granting him the opportunity to earn a diploma and to improve his game. It not only would make him a better player but a better person as well. In contrast, Henson's choices were celebrated by commentators. Their support persisted, even as the Yankees actively sought to lure him into a professional career. In the words of General Manager Brian Cashman, "We're selling, man. Selling the major-league experience and our tradition. We'd love for him to play only baseball, but if that's unrealistic, we'll try to help him decide to do both." This action and Henson's decision to take $2 million to play minor baseball went unremarked in the national media. There were no arguments about maturity, no assumptions about mobility, and no mention of the value of a college degree. The underlying assumptions in these feature stories and commentaries appear to be first that Bryant is lacking and second that he is breaking the rules of the game. In turn, commentators suggest that the African-American athlete needs training, regulation, and discipline, but that his Euro-American counterpart does not. He needs the refinement and upward mobility secured by college, in spite of his background, that Henson does not. In college sports, the linkage of race and deviance imposes discipline—control and improvement—on the black body.

The racialized contours of this public concern over the amateur and scholastic fates of high school and college athletes become clearer when considering the absence of such discourse in other instances. For example, as Russel Curtis Jr. (1998, p. 886) notes, when "blackness" was much less an issue, no one seemed disturbed that Ted Williams or Mickey Mantle entered major league baseball at age eighteen, bypassing college altogether. Additionally, neither the predominance of tennis stars in their middle teens or the decision of Jimmy Connors to forgo his eligibility at the University of California at Los Angeles to "turn pro" disturbed an American public. Perhaps such public concerns and panics are best understood as a form of racial paternalism, in which white America struggles to come to terms with its (exploitative) enjoyment of the African athlete by advancing a linkage between the ostensibly moral and disciplinary space of the university and big-time sports.

Even when they stay in school and play the game, African-American athletes unsettle as they entertain. Indeed, in addition to the (often contradictory) meanings associated with the black body, the means of using and practicing it often transgress the norms of civility, the hegemonic forms of whiteness governing intercollegiate athletics. In response, unspoken etiquette, team codes, and the rules of the game combine to police African-American expressiveness and style.

The emergence of end zone celebrations in college and professional football in the 1980s and 1990s offers a stunning illus-
tration of the disciplinary impulse central to racialized sports
spectacles. One of the author's acquaintances exclaimed, "Look
at those jungle-bunnies jumping around, slapping each other
silly!" while watching a televised football game in the late 1980s.
The blatantly racist remark was a reaction to several of the players—all African Americans—performing what is known as an
end zone celebration. To celebrate a touchdown, several players
gather in the end zone to enact an obviously choreographed
"dance" of sorts. Such orchestrated and extended expressions
of victory and triumph became increasingly common by the
mid-1980s. Vernon Andrews concluded that, generally, African-
American players performed the longest, most elaborate end
zone dances, and further, that African-American players were
more likely to enact their athletic roles with conspicuous individuality, defiance, trash talk, and taunting (V. Andrews,
1991). Researchers have argued that black expressiveness—
characteristically more colorful, improvisational, expansive, de-
liberate, and self-conscious—is a prevailing African-American
cultural mode of communication and style (Fiske, 1993; Gay &
Baber, 1987; Jones, 1986; White & White, 1998).

The National Football League (NFL), partly in concert with
spectator opinion, attempted to control and indeed erase such
colorful expressions of triumph by asserting that these were unsportsmanlike displays. It amended its rules in 1984 and 1991 in
order to temper "any prolonged, excessive, or premeditated celebration by individual players or groups of players" (quoted in
Fiske, 1993, p. 60). College football followed with its own attempts to limit on-field celebrations (see V. Andrews, 1998).
John Fiske (1993, p. 62) claims that such struggles to control
these embodied displays of success are, in essence, a struggle
over racial power:

> The argument is not *what* constitutes sportsmanlike con-
> duct, but over *who* controls its constitution. . . . Because
> the issue is not one of behavior but one of control. In dif-
> ferent social conditions, the same expressive behavior can
> be viewed by the power-bloc quite differently. In its TV

commercials for the World Football League (which is the NFL's attempt to spread U.S. football to Europe), the NFL relies largely on images of black expressiveness that it attempts to repress back home. [For European audiences presumably] the expressive black body signals not a challenge to white control but an American exuberance, vitality, and stylishness which European sport lacks.

Once again, the Euro-American reaction to both the expressive and spontaneous bodies of the nonwhite Other is decidedly ambivalent, characterized by adulation on the one hand and discomfort on the other hand.

Although not all black players have highly individualistic expressive repertoires and a number of white players do, black players are more likely to be identified and indeed penalized in these terms. Clearly, the scoring movement known as the "slam dunk" epitomizes the stylistic impact of black players since their presence became common in college and professional basketball by the late 1960s. Frequently, after making the basket, a player hangs, and then swings from the rim after the ball has dropped through. Such behavior has been considered by officials at both the collegiate and professional levels an unsportsmanlike way of "showing up" the other team, and indeed, referees were given the right to whistle players for technical fouls for hanging on the rims, unless a player was doing so clearly in an effort to avoid landing on another player. Interestingly, a year after the 1966 championship between Kentucky and Texas Western, in which David Lattin's dunks highlighted his all-black team's victory, the NCAA Rules Committee banned the slam dunk shot. The all-white committee, over which Rupp continued to enjoy a significant influence, explained that the ban would prevent injuries and equipment damage. This ban would remain until the 1976–77 season.

Perhaps the most famous singular group of college athletes that embodied what has been perceived as a flashy, showboating, in-your-face style of play was the University of Michigan's "Fab Five." The Fab Five was a group of five black, highly touted high school basketball players who signed with Michigan in 1991. Recognized as the best basketball recruiting class in the country, the Fab Five led Michigan to the championship in their freshman year, and in 1993, during their sophomore year, they returned to the championship finals again. Led by Chris Webber, the team had forged a flashy style of play and presence, characterized by shaved heads, long trunks, and glossy black shoes. They often would utilize extra passes, even bouncing the ball off of the backboard to set teammates up for slam dunks.

In the waning seconds of that championship game in 1993, Chris Webber had the ball with his team down by two when he called for a time-out. Unfortunately, since his team had no additional time-outs, he was whistled for a technical foul. Vernon Andrews noted the remarks by ESPN announcer Keith Olberman during the post–game coverage, who said:

> Webber failed to remember his team had no time-outs remaining and was thus penalized with a technical foul, thus losing the ball and the game by four points. Michigan played all this year with that in-your-face style and they got caught on a little fundamental. *It's a kind of morality play*, if you believe in that sort of thing. [emphasis added] (see V. Andrews, 1996, p. 53)

Olberman, in effect, claimed that Michigan was punished for its flashy, loud, if not black, style of play.

For years, then, such styles have been confronted by disapproving league eyes, which viewed these actions as rude, undisciplined, and transgressive modes of expression. Such concern, we suggest, is a tool of social control, in which the power bloc(s) within a state society localizes its power through an attempt to control and advance a surveillance of particular bodies in particular spaces (Fiske, 1993). Disciplinary mechanisms such as these limits on celebration and nineteenth-century prohibitions of Native American dance[3] are informed by a fear that these racial others have natural impulses that demand a civilizing force in order to rein them in. Michel Foucault would understand these league sanctions against victorious expression as disciplinary power, which allows the hegemonic forces within a society to manipulate the bodies of its citizens and to exact from them greater degrees of social control, so that imperial *discipline* might supersede *punishment* (Foucault, 1979).

CONCLUSIONS

Clearly, the racial spectacles of (intercollegiate) athletics overdetermine blackness, as they incorporate and exploit and discipline and display African-American athletes. Encrusted ideologies and well-worn stereotypes imprint the means and meanings of participating in, performing, and consuming the stagings of racial difference, both on and beyond the playing field. Indeed, as we have argued here, entrenched, often invisible, popular notions of blackness center on the black body and its purported excesses—extraordinary ability, criminal deviance, and libidinal pleasure. The excessive and transgressive physicality of African-American athletes, as we have further demonstrated, does not merely shape public perceptions—panics no less than pleasures—but structure the regimes of control, management, and even care applied to the black body as well. To close this chapter, we return to white supremacy, not as formulated by people such as David Duke but as a sociocultural field animated by the articulations race, corporeality, and disciplinarity.

In March 1992, during what has arguably become the nation's most conspicuous collegiate sporting spectacle—the NCAA Division I basketball championship, know fondly as March Madness—Indiana University's head coach Bobby Knight became embroiled in yet another controversy. During a press conference in Albuquerque, New Mexico, a photograph was taken of Knight, a large, white figure, brandishing a bullwhip and towering over Calbert Cheaney, one of his black players (Hurd, 1992; Wieberg, 1992). Cheaney apparently was following Knight's "playful" lead in this most incredulous form of theater, as he kneeled down under the coach with his practice shorts pulled down and faced the camera with a wide-toothed grin as Knight, softly struck his backside. The stunt by Knight, whose nickname is, tellingly, the "General," was an attempt to inject humor into public speculation about his abuse of players.

Naturally, the national publication of this photograph set off a firestorm of protest. The leader of Indiana's General Assembly's Black Caucus, Representative Hurley Goodall, wrote to Indiana University President Ehrlich urging that the popular basketball coach be fired. Meanwhile, the Albuquerque chapter of the National Association for the Advancement of Colored People (NAACP) condemned the stunt. Among many, the sentiment was that this caricatured performance was an insult to African Americans, for whom the image of a white man taking a whip to a black man might be expected to invoke a painful social memory. Of course, neither Knight, his players, or local supporters were willing to view the incident in racial terms.

We are not prepared to accuse Bobby Knight of being a racist based on this moment; neither, however, are we prepared to assert that he is enlightened when it comes to racial injustice and inequality. Our concern is not really with Knight at all but rather with the social and political milieu that made it possible (in the minds of Knight and others) to mock this deadly image of white authority and black subservience in a context already highly charged by contours of African-American exploitation, acknowledged even by other NCAA Division I coaches such as Joe Paterno and Dean Smith.

Black players on the University of California at Los Angeles team, which lost to Indiana just prior to the photo incident, were not amused. "That just shows," claimed Tyus Edney, "even though it's a joke, what some people may think about black players." Gerald Madkins confessed, "Fear is what comes to my mind when I see a whip, not motivation" (quoted in Hurd, 1992). It is Knight's position at Indiana University, however, that raises the greatest concern. He is the highest paid, most visible employee of the state institution, and while technically not faculty, symbolically he shares responsibility with faculty members for guiding the educational and ethical development of students. We cannot imagine a context in which Knight, having dreamed up this performance, approached Cheaney to ask for his participation; more difficult, however, is to imagine how a player on his team could muster up the energy to refuse to play his games, without being punished—either in the short or long run.

This spectacular moment exaggerates the racial contours of contemporary intercollegiate athletics, inscribing a hyberbolic instance of blackness, especially in relation to whiteness. That is, as Knight, the white coach, with bullwhip in hand, stands over and playfully strikes Cheaney, his smiling and stooped black player, this evocative exchange (rendered through the icons of American slavery) not only reduces the African-American athlete to a set of corporeal fragments requiring discipline but also affirms white supremacy. Indeed, it highlights the central ironies of post–civil rights college sports. African-American athletes have become central to college sports, yet institutional structures and ideological practices continue to control, marginalize, and disempower them, albeit in novel and unanticipated forms. Euro-American coaches, commentators, and spectators in turn remain dominant, retaining authority to define and discipline, interpret and enjoy, and exploit and appropriate African-American athletes. Pamela Wonsek's (1992, p. 454) interpretation of television coverage of the NCAA tournament nicely summarizes the significance of this reconfiguration.

> Although the sporting event itself is dominated by black players, these images are undercut by the overwhelming predominance of white images. . . . Not only does this place the black players in a secondary and entertainment role, but it may also serve to reassure the white majority that its dominance is not really being threatened.

Whites reign supreme, even as African Americans eclipse them on the courts. We have outlined in this chapter the constellation of signifying practices producing, problematizing, and policing blacks, while securing, at least for the moment, white supremacy.

In Chapter 6, we shift our attention to sporting spectacles of whiteness by examining some of those spaces where reformulations of embattled Euro-American identities persist. While certain constructions of blackness are indeed white technologies of appropriation and engagement, the cases taken up in the next chapter highlight conspicuous stagings of whiteness that thrive on invocations of a racialized past. While examining this white subjectivity at the University of Mississippi and University of Notre Dame, the reader should be conscious of the ways in which spectacles of whiteness continually rely upon constructions of blackness.

6

Of Rebels and Leprechauns: Longing, Passing, and the Stagings of Whiteness

On occasion, discussions of the racial politics of mascots and of college sports, more generally, linger on whiteness. Rarely does a critical or reflexive perspective emerge in such moments; instead, whiteness enters as a defensive reflex, a sign of resentment and rejection. Most commonly, individuals deflect attention and defuse tension around the circulation of racial signs by invoking ethnic, honorary, or historical whiteness, as if white identity and the ideologies and institutions legitimating it were fixed and transcendent. They ask, "What about the Spartans of Michigan State University?" "What about the Dutch of Central College?" and most frequently, "What about the Fighting Irish of the University of Notre Dame?" Others go farther, encouraging schools with embattled Native American mascots to opt for a safer, white symbol. For instance, Daniel E. O'Connell (1971), president of the Shamrock Club of Wisconsin, in response to the proposed retirement of Willie Wompum at Marquette University, urged the Jesuit institution to revert to its former symbol, the Hilltoppers, and to adopt a leprechaun for its mascot (King, 2001). This rhetorical strategy directs attention to the (often competing) stagings of whiteness hidden in plain sight. Indeed, whereas in previous chapters we have highlighted many of the ways in which blackness and redness—even multiple and contradictory stagings of these racial domains—have been performed in collegiate athletics, in order to implicitly, *invisibly*, inscribe whiteness, in this chapter, we turn our attention to some of the spaces where performances of whiteness are not only more conspicuous but literally are inflated. Importantly, though, the actors whose white identities emerge within these spaces generally do not understand them in terms of race at all. Further, in these instances, we see that class and gender continue to be interwoven in complex ways with stagings of race, as football, in particular, has historically served as a moral canvas for the transformation of boys into white men of strong character. We suggest further that the subjectivities that inspire these stagings of whiteness are complicated by a series of ambivalent desires, or longings, about nonwhite neighbors, opponents, and teammates.

A reading of two distinct sites structures the arguments in this chapter. First, in contrast to the ways in which so many other university athletics teams have identified themselves in terms of In-dianness, we address how the University of Mississippi has at-tempted to fashion an identity in terms of signs and symbols of the nineteenth-century Southern Confederacy. After examining this in-stance of Southern genteel whiteness, we turn to the experiences of Catholic, working-class whiteness that have inspired the emer-gence of arguably the nation's most prestigious and glorious col-lege football team, the "Fighting Irish" of Notre Dame University. Throughout, we foreground the ironies and contradictions negoti-ated by the influx in recent decades of black athletes into these very sacred, historical spaces of invented whiteness.

DEEP IN THE HEART OF DIXIE

> There is a spirit that sent three hundred University Greys to heroic death upon Confederate battle fields; there is a spirit that has made University men Mississippi's greatest states-men and foremost leaders for four score years; there is a spirit that makes old Ole Miss athletes give their utmost to win fame and honor for their Alma Mater upon the ath-letic field; there is a spirit that binds the sons and daughters of Ole Miss into the greatest fraternity in all the world— the fraternity of Ole Miss. (Dedication page from 1927 University of Mississippi yearbook, Ole Miss, 1927)

Throughout the course of the twentieth century, sports came to assume monumental significance in the United States, and by the century's close, football emerged as perhaps the most popular game in the country. Football has inspired narratives that have linked the game to patriotism, religion, and honor, and the sport has been championed as a "technology" for transforming boys into men of strong character. Andrew Doyle (1996, p. 74) argued that football has served the Southern United States, in particular, as a canvas for recreating a regional esteem in an era of progress:

> Progressive Southerners adopted the fashionable sport of the Northeastern elite in the early 1890s as a cultural component of their program of modernization. The Machine Age sport of "scientific football" provided a perfect vehicle for bringing bourgeois values to a region striving for inclusion into the American cultural and economic mainstream. Yet postbellum Southerners steeped in the mythology of the Lost Cause also imbued this Yankee game with the romantic trappings of the Cavalier myth and exalted their football heroes as modern incarnations of Confederate warriors.

Essentially, Southern manliness was at stake then, when college football teams met in what were commonly constructed as mythic battles. Prior to the mid-1960s, certainly, the powerhouses of Southern football were exclusively white, and the schools vested in the outcomes of these contests often were bourgeois spaces where the sons and sometimes the daughters of Southern elites enrolled.

The University of Mississippi was characterized by such a class discourse of social refinement and moral honor, rooted in a longing for the spirit of the Old South and the romanticized whiteness at its core. Although the legacy of the Confederacy has long imprinted Ole Miss, it entered a new phase in 1936, when the athletic teams were dubbed the "Rebels." The official "mascot," Colonel Reb, adopted the following year, was represented as an older, white gentleman with a mustache and goatee, dressed in a black suit and planter hat, symbolizing a genteel Southern aristocrat, if not a plantation slave owner.[1] Later, in 1947, this emerging restaging of white masculinity solidified when "Dixie" became the song of choice at campus athletic events and the Confederate flag was appropriated as a sort of college pennant. Completing these racial spectacles, planters' hats and black string ties were sold for people to wear to Rebel football games, allowing them to appear as "Delta aristocracy" (Butler, 1997, p. 133). At Ole Miss, the crystallization of these nostalgic enactments of whiteness not surprisingly coincided with the rise of Jim Crow and the ascendance of big-time college athletics.

Importantly, as the careers of two famous but very different sports cheerleaders for the University of Mississippi make plain, these statements of white supremacy were never simple nor certain; rather, they have always been marked by ambivalence and struggle. The first, known as "Blind Jim," was a popular fixture on the Oxford, Mississippi, campus for nearly sixty years, beginning in 1896. The second, John Hawkins, was an African-American student cheerleader in the early 1980s who created controversy by refusing to hoist the Confederate flag while leading the football team onto the field, a traditional campus ritual. We begin, however, with Blind Jim, whose real name was James Ivy, an African American who had lost his sight while working on a Tallahatchie River bridge in 1892 (see Sansing, 1999, p. 275). His eyes were permanently damaged after being accidentally sprayed with creosote. In the following years, Ivy emerged as a presence on the Ole Miss campus, where he operated a vending business selling snacks and drinks to students and faculty in order to feed his family.

According to local history,

> in the spring of 1896, Blind Jim was selling candy and peanuts at a baseball game between the University of Mississippi and the University of Texas. When told that Mississippi was losing, he began cheering for the home team. The students heard his loud booming voice and invited him to sit with them in the stands. With Blind leading the cheers, the baseball team rallied to beat Texas, and from that point on, Blind Jim was a part of Ole Miss. (Sansing, 1999, p. 275).

His popularity as an embodied good luck charm continued to grow throughout the early decades of the twentieth century. In the student yearbook of 1944, a photograph reveals a scene in which the thin, mustachioed Ivy, dressed in a black suit with a necktie and gripping a wooden cane, stands between two female cheerleaders in wool skirts. Behind the three of them, who are looking up into the stands, is the Ole Miss football bench, where several players are seated. Hanging from Ivy's neck, by a small chain, appears to be a musical score, with the implication that his momentary function is to serve as a post so that it can be displayed to the audience.

As the Blind Jim tradition matured, a custom emerged in the 1920s requiring the freshman class to assemble on the Lyceum steps during the first week of the fall semester "to receive a special greeting and words of advice from their dean" (Sansing, 1999, p. 275). From that time on, Blind Jim also was known as the "dean of the freshman class." The students, all of whom of course were white, had a great fondness for Ivy, a kind and entertaining black man. During these reflective chats, Ivy would dress in a formal, often white, suit, with a top hat of some sort. Each year he would receive a new ensemble, suitable for a Southern gentleman, as a gift from the Ole Miss students (Sansing, personal communication).

Ivy was likely the only visible African-American presence on this racially segregated Southern campus during these years. The athletic teams of the university were known as the "Rebels," a name chosen by a contest conducted by the student newspaper, the *Mississippian*. And the logo still known today as "Colonel Reb" first appeared both on the cover and on pages throughout the 1937 yearbook. The figure was a white man sporting a white goatee and mustache and a black suit with a bolo tie, reminiscent perhaps of a genteel plantation owner turned Civil War colonel. In a twist of great irony, according to some people (see Sansing, 1999), Blind Jim served in part as an inspiration for Colonel Reb. The aura and discourses of the University of Mississippi were particularly invested in the legacy of the Southern Confederacy. The campus is lined by streets with names such as Confederate Drive, Jeff Davis Drive, and Lee Loop, while a cemetery for Confederate soldiers killed at Gettysburg lies near the basketball arena. In fact, the whole university class was enrolled in the Confederacy. According to some reports, two black sorority houses are known among students as the "slave quarters." The entire student body enlisted in the Confederate Army in 1861, as a group of young men elected a captain, nineteen-year-old William B. Lowry, and formed themselves into a battle unit called the University Greys (Sansing, 1999, p. 106).

Ivy died on October 20, 1955, and students and alumni raised over $1,000 to endow a scholarship in his name. These Blind Jim Scholarships were available to assist African Americans in Mississippi to attend black colleges. Ironically, Blind Jim scholarships could not be used to attend Ole Miss, which did not accept a black student until 1963, when James Meredith enrolled and, with the protection of federal marshals, began to attend classes in one of the most famous spectacles of the civil rights era of the 1960s.

Central to this moment of suspense, hatred, and protest surrounding the Meredith controversy was a symbol that remains— even today—a conspicuous if contested presence at the University of Mississippi: the battle flag of the Confederacy. The flag re-emerged throughout the Deep South as an important symbol of Southern nationalism, only in the context of a burgeoning civil rights movement in the 1940s and 1950s. In fact, the presence of the banner at the University of Mississippi was uncommon prior to the late 1940s (Sansing, 1999, p. 254). By the time Meredith attempted to become the first African American to challenge the University of Mississippi's system of racial apartheid, the flag served to signify the most intense expressions of Southern pride and resistance to the civil rights movement. Not only a common banner at KKK rallies but also at civil government buildings and general protests against federal desegregation orders, the Confederate flag was the choice symbol of those many citizens who gathered in Oxford during the weekend preceding October 1, 1962, to protest the admission of James Meredith. Indeed, while visiting the campus in 1982, Meredith said, "There is no difference between these symbols and the segregation signs of 20 years ago" when asked about the controversial flag issue (Stuart, 1982).[2] Many Ole Miss students supported those demonstrations, whether actively or in silence, while others were ashamed. On September 1, less than two weeks prior to the day Meredith officially broke the school's color barrier, a small group of students on campus attempted to take down the U.S. flag and to replace it with the Confederate one. Their efforts were quickly interrupted by a larger group of concerned students.

Race also made its presence conspicuously evident in events such as Ole Miss football games in the 1960s, well before the team became integrated in 1972. One black student, Eugene McLemore, attended football games on Saturday afternoons and, in addition to the racist remarks hurled in his direction, he recalls that when teams with black players came to Oxford, local fans would shout such violent sentiments as "Kill that nigger!" (cited in Cohodas, 1997, p. 168). Cahodas explains in detail the contours of one of the racist rituals that too frequently punctuated these games:

> One of the more obscure taunts was "Give 'at ball to LeRoy," a catch phrase from a racist football joke that had been making the rounds in the state and was particularly popular at Ole Miss. "Two colored schools were playing," the joke begins. Late in the game, the coach of one of the squads knows he needs a score and tells the quarterback, "Give 'at ball to LeRoy." Instead the quarterback gives the ball to Sam, and he is pummeled to the ground. "Give that ball to LeRoy," the exasperated coach hollers. The quarterback turns around and yells back, "LeRoy say he don't want 'at ball." (1997, p. 168)

Thus, when the mood for such insensitive humor swept through the crowd, people would stand and shout, "Give 'at ball to LeRoy!" directing the comment to the opposing teams and their black players.

Twenty years after James Meredith breached the color line at the University of Mississippi, the student body elected John Hawkins to serve as its first African American on the cheerleading squad. As a male cheerleader, he would be expected to carry on a tradition in which the football team was led onto the field by a few cheerleaders running while hoisting very large Confederate banners from poles, as if to lead soldiers into battle. Hawkins finally, and forcefully, opened a heated public debate that had been poised to surface for some time when, during an interview that September with Jay Harris of the Gannett News Service, he declared that he would not wave the Confederate flag as part of his cheerleading role. The loud response of many Ole Miss alumni and traditionalists was immediate. For example, in a letter sent directly to University Chancellor Porter Fortune, John C. McLaurin—a lawyer in

Brandon, Mississippi—wrote that "a negro boy is now running the university. By now he has probably moved you out of the Chancellor's home and is occupying it himself. If he doesn't like the times and places for the games to be played, he will change that, too." At the end of the note, below his signature, McLaurin added this query: "Does the new king know who his daddy is?"[3]

The controversy presented university administrators with a problem. Surely they could not force Hawkins to carry the Rebel flag, nor could they remove him as a cheerleader. Such moves would generate far too much national criticism. On the other hand, popular sentiment for Ole Miss and its beloved symbols discouraged them from adopting what was likely the simplest solution—to eliminate any association with the flag from university events such as football games. Football season was fast approaching, and school officials examined several options, from actually adding the initials of Ole Miss to the Rebel flag, therein making it no longer an "official" Confederate symbol, to using the Mississippi state flag instead. Finally, officials decided that rather than having all male cheerleaders carry the banner, only one would do so. Hawkins, of course, would not be asked to be that one.

As the first football game grew near, Hawkins held a press conference to clarify his stance. "I am an Ole Miss cheerleader [which] makes me a representative of the whole student body—blacks and whites—but I am a black man and the same way whites have been taught to wave the flag I have been taught to have nothing to do with it" (Sansing, 1999, p. 326). He elaborated, "While I'm an Ole Miss cheerleader, I'm still a black man. In my household I wasn't told to hate the flag, but I did have history classes and know what my ancestors went through and what the Rebel flag represents. It is my choice that I prefer not to wave one" (cited in Cohodas, 1997, p. 200). Hawkins' refusal to ignore spectacles of whiteness could not have been easy. The litany of hateful sentiments and threats—even threats against his life—colored his remaining years at the university. His response served to complicate both whiteness and blackness for people at Ole Miss and within the state of Mississippi more broadly. Hawkins' stance was followed by increasing community criticism of the presence of the Confederate flag and other symbols at Ole Miss.

The head football coach at the time, Steve Sloan, voiced his concern also. He explained that the presence of the Rebel banner was likely compromising the ability of his staff to recruit black players, and he suggested that in turn the overall quality of athletics at the university was weakened (ibid., p. 201).

Once again, the ironies and contradictions so prevalent in the context of collegiate sporting spectacles of race, as we have demonstrated throughout this book, also have characterized the events at Ole Miss. The first black student to play football at the University of Mississippi was lineman Robert J. "Ben" Williams, who was a freshman in 1972. A decade later, half of the team was African American, overwhelmingly the most visible presence of black Americans at Ole Miss. The audience at football games remained almost exclusively white, however, and many of these spectators waved Rebel flags as they cheered. Although ironic, it is not surprising that the first University of Mississippi official to publicly question the Confederate flag was the football coach. The next Ole Miss football coach, Tommy Tuberville, also expressed concern about his ability to recruit black athletes, and he was even clearer with his public statements against the flag. In 1997, just after the new university chancellor made efforts to keep students from carrying flags to games, Tuberville issued a plea, urging fans to stop displaying the Confederate battle flag at games. "It's time to support our teams physically, mentally, and morally with enthusiasm and not symbols. . . . As stated many times before, the Rebel flag is not associated with Ole Miss" (Boling & Gregoire, 1997).

That an institution such as the University of Mississippi publicly attempted to come to terms with its archaic investments in whiteness only in the context of an increasingly lucrative, racially marked system of collegiate athletics is telling. To be certain, professors and students, both white and black, had expressed discontent with the Rebel baggage, outside of its connection to sports. In fact, by the early 1980s, recruitment of black students generally was down (Sansing, 1999). But, big-time athletics was indeed the context in which the confusing desires, spectacles, and badges of race predominated. This space of public culture foregrounded contradictions more than any other. For example, as recently as 1996, during a game between Ole Miss and its interstate rival Mississippi

State, former state Senator Brad Lott—an Ole Miss alumnus— reportedly "berated a black Mississippi State player with a barrage of racial slurs" (Sack, 1997). Dotson remarked after the incident, "I'd never been called the n word [nigger] until we played there. . . . At the game I saw a woman in the stands making ape gestures and pig noises at the black players" ("The Sound, the Fury," 1996, p. 22). Coach Tuberville would confess later that the resulting publicity "was devastating for recruiting" (Sack, 1997).

Soon after Hawkins' public stance and Coach Sloan's comments had generated a full-blown public debate in 1982—a mere twenty years after James Meredith was escorted to class by military guards—the KKK weighed in on the issue by holding a rally in Oxford on Saturday, October 23. About twenty-five hooded Klansmen gathered to voice support for the Rebel flag. The following fall, when the 1983 Ole Miss Yearbook was released, a new storm of controversy erupted. Black students were angered by a series of photographs that appeared in an early retrospective on the previous year's significant events. The photographs in question featured scenes from the Klan protest during the previous fall, including some shots centering on particular Klansmen waving Rebel flags. The yearbook editor attempted to explain to members of the Black Student Union that he did not intend to glorify the Klansmen but rather wished to drive home the connection between the school's beloved flag and this hateful group. A rumor circulated that black students were planning a ritual book burning of the annual on the steps of the Lyceum, the very building upon whose steps Blind Jim once greeted incoming freshmen. According to David Sansing (1999, p. 328), university history professor,

> on August 18, 1983, the night the rumored book burning was to take place, about 1,500 flag waving white students gathered at the Lyceum. Student body officers and fraternity leaders told the angry students that the rumors were not true and pleaded with them to go back to their dormitories and fraternity houses. After the larger crowd disbursed, about 600 students marched to the Phi Beta Sigma house, John Hawkin's fraternity, lofted their Rebel Flags into the night sky, and shouted racial slurs and threats.

Other responses to calls for the elimination of the Rebel flag were less violent but just as defensive. In a letter to the Clarion-Ledger, R. David Sanders sarcastically suggested that the university rename its sports teams "The Guilt" and change the school colors to blush red. In 1983, Chancellor Fortune formally banned the official use of the Confederate flag in connection with the Ole Miss campus, although students and community members continue to display the symbol at games and on campus.

The flag issue, which initially emerged with Hawkins' 1982 protest, resurfaced in the mid-1990s. Robert C. Khayat, the new chancellor appointed in 1995, played football and baseball for the Ole Miss Rebels in the late 1950s. He remembered the Confederate flags and the tunes of "Old Dixie," whose purpose was to inspire his teammates and him to victory. Khayat began his tenure as chancellor with a vision of enhancing the University of Mississippi's national reputation and even of establishing a Phi Beta Kappa chapter. He made a bold move in 1997 by announcing that the university had hired a private public relations firm to review the school's image and symbols. He spoke out against the Colonel Reb mascot and asked students and community members to not carry Rebel flags to games. Under his guidance, the Ole Miss student senators approved a resolution asking students to refrain from waving the flag and later approved a resolution forbidding sticks (for flags) in the stadium, citing safety concerns.

As in the 1980s, administrative efforts to reform the semiotic landscape of the university were met in some quarters with disbelief, sadness, and even defiance. Many in the campus community expressed concern that their attachment to Confederate and Jim Crow symbols could be construed as racist. "They're part of our southern heritage. . . . We hate to see [these symbols] censored simply based on offending or not offending somebody's sensibilities," reasoned Christopher Bridgewater in 1997, a senior who founded the Rebel Student Union to recruit members dedicated to "saving" the Rebel flag institution (see Sack, 1997). Beyond campus, neoconservatives and white supremacists, such as the Confederate Underground, the Southern Initiative, and the Nationalist Movement, launched vociferous critiques of the administration and its decision. They introduced the glory and sacrifice of the

University Greys, the honor and character of Southern heritage, the siege of traditional values, and the victimization of Southern whites to secure their position.

> There was a time when Senate Majority Leader Trent Lott joyfully rushed onto the field as an Ole Miss Cheerleader. . . . It was a time when we knew who we were and were not ashamed of it. . . . But now the dead hand of political correctness has descended upon the campus and the vision of the elitists have crushed the spirit of the people. . . . It takes more than denying your past to build a football dynasty. It takes more than spitting on your grandfather's grave to achieve academic respectability. ("There Was a Time," on-line)

State Senator Michael Gunn, speaking at a Confederate Memorial Day gathering sponsored by the United Daughters of the Confederacy and the Council of Concerned Citizens, defended "Southern tradition," suggesting that recent modifications at Ole Miss represented "a national conspiracy to exterminate the vestiges of our heritage" ("Confederate Underground," on-line). Later, as part of a statewide speaking tour in support of a petition drive launched by the Council of Concerned Citizens, he reiterated, "Make no mistake . . . we are the victims of a nationwide conspiracy perpetuated by the Left to exterminate any vestiges of our precious Southern heritage. When Ole Miss uses my tax money to pay hate-mongers like Johnnie Cochran to speak on campus and call my Southern heritage racist, I'm offended" (ibid.). Gunn called for legislation to protect citizens' rights to display Confederate flags at college sporting events. The Southern Initiative outlined a more populist program, directed at what it interpreted as the "treasonous attitude toward Southern tradition," including a boycott of athletic events at the University of Mississippi until the flag ban was lifted, a recall of the president of the Alumni Association for supporting the ban, and a boycott of his accounting practice. Similarly, Richard Barrett of the Nationalist Movement, rallying against the integration of Ole Miss, minority rule, and the "assault of a cherished symbol of freedom, spirit, and heritage," circulated a Petition in Support of Confederate

Flag Waving, which encouraged students and fans to defy the ban, and staged protests to return "the faith" to the campus community ("Stick the Ban," on-line).

Whereas earlier chapters have documented the ways in which redness and blackness have been privileged as *fantastic* commodities, at the University of Mississippi, whiteness emerged as a commodity in the form of an array of Jim Crow symbols, discourses of Southern pride and resistance, and an investment in victory. Importantly, these spectacles of whiteness have been contested in Mississippi by both European Americans and African Americans. The public culture animating Oxford, Mississippi, and its historic university did not emerge in a vacuum, as many other universities and high schools in the South have used Confederate imagery to mark their teams, and many communities have been forced to confront their attachments to figures such as Blind Jim and to symbols such as Jim Crow (Vanderford, 1996). In recent decades, as we have seen at Ole Miss, many white Southerners frequently have attempted to locate symbols and discourses of the Confederacy exclusively within the context of "Southern pride" and traditional Southern identity, as opposed to contexts of racism and whiteness.

We suggest, however, that these claims that such discourses are cleansed of any racist connotations are disingenuous. At best, they are instances of imperialist nostalgia and at worst, whether or not intentionally, they function as forms of symbolic terror. Further, they characterize the sentiments of a modern and contemporary Southern racial identity, the contours of which Grace Elizabeth Hale (1998) has sketched brilliantly. Focusing on the years 1890 to 1940, Hale argues that, after emancipation, in the American South a remaking of white identity took place, and in actuality, from the Civil War on, that whiteness emerged as an increasingly important category that could mark a new Confederate collectivity transcending, ideally at least, class and gender boundaries (ibid., p. 5). Against a postbellum philosophical backdrop in which Southern whiteness had to remain invisible while blackness had to be ever more visible:

> . . . it was racial identity that became the paramount spatial mediation of modernity within the newly reunited nation. Not self-evidently more meaningful, not more real or

natural than other markings, race nevertheless became the crucial means of ordering the new enlarged meaning of America. This happened because former Confederates, a growing working class, embattled farmers, Western set-tlers, a defensive Northeastern elite, women's rights advo-cates, and [an] increasingly powerful scientific community, and others, simultaneously but for different reasons, found race useful in creating new identities to replace older, more individual, and local groundings of self. (Hale, 1998, p. 7)

Central to this identity has been a narrative attempt to recast the Civil War and the institution of slavery as unmarked by the ter-ror of racial oppression, an effort that continues even into the pres-ent. Hale demonstrates that soon after emancipation, through literature, minstrel shows, and popular history, Southerners sought to repair their white subjectivities by imagining the bygone era of slavery as a time of paternal love of masters and mistresses for their slaves. A number of short stories, personal memoirs, and novels—from *Uncle Remus* to *Gone With the Wind*—feature black characters with avuncular, complacent, and happy counte-nances who often remained on the plantation out of affection for their masters. "Dramatizing the meaninglessness of emancipa-tion," Hale (1998, p. 73) points out, "became as common a trope in white Southern writing as having the slaves help hide the silver."

The relationship of the Ole Miss community to Blind Jim epit-omized this sentiment. Ivy embodied the ex-slave as a gracious if imaginary reminder of easygoing social relations between white and black people. In the 1980s and 1990s, the reasons large seg-ments of the Ole Miss community were deeply offended by criti-cism of the Confederate flag and other beloved symbols were undoubtedly complex. Such resistance of course is linked to a de-fense of particular identities, and these identities are based on a dual erasure. The first is an erasure that has emptied (on the sur-face, at least) these symbols of their past, but only because they had to be, to ensure their continued presence in a post–civil rights era. The second is an erasure based on a denial of the contempo-rary manifestations of white supremacy and the existence of racial stratification and institutional racism. It seems ludicrous, certainly, that many defenders of the symbolism of the Confederate banner can insist that it is not racist when the recent history of the flag's currency is marked by its use as a direct response to the civil rights movements, desegregation, Meredith's entry into Ole Miss, and its semi-official status as the KKK banner. A sensibility continues to thrive in which white Southerners are essentially asserting racial power by refusing to acknowledge complaints from African Americans and many European Americans who voice concern about the racist legacies of such symbols.

HONORING/HONORARY WHITENESS

The tradition linking football and the mythical, moral transformation of boys into manly men, especially in the context of whiteness, has not been exclusive to the South. In the second part of this chapter, we explore the ways in which identities of whiteness have complicated the evolution of a collegiate football legacy far more prominent than the one at Ole Miss. The history of the Fighting Irish of Notre Dame University contrasts in important ways to the regional institution of Southern football, described above. In fact, some readers will pause at this point, asking how *whiteness*, as a discourse and an ideology, can be implicated within the cultural spaces of Notre Dame football when obviously the Catholic–Irish origins of the university belie any argument about its whiteness. Indeed, the very KKK members, whose presence in and around the University of Mississippi was the source of so much horror, would be decidedly opposed to the very existence of Notre Dame University given its Catholic affiliation. Yet whiteness is a complex discourse, comprised of many planes of experience united though tangled webs of contradiction, and Notre Dame University has been a site for the diverse production of white subjectivities and for the platform of the whitening of the Irish (Ignatiev, 1995). Notre Dame went from being a university still lacking honorary whiteness, condescended to by a largely Protestant nation, to being a national embodiment of, simultaneously, the American work ethic, racial paternalism, Horatio Alger success, and winning whiteness.

A relative of one of the authors admires the Fighting Irish of Notre Dame. "I like them because they sort of represent white folks," he once reasoned. "They are kind of like the Boston Celtics in that regard, who I've always liked alot, with Larry Bird and Kevin McHale and those guys. I don't have anything against black players or teams. It's just that, with so many great black athletes, it's nice to see historically white teams dominate sometime."

We believe that many people view Notre Dame football as white in ways that are difficult for them to put into words. Certainly, Catholicism is not associated with African Americans, and the priestly hierarchy of the Church in the United States has always been decidedly white (Lucas, 1970). Although Notre Dame's football team became integrated relatively early, in 1953, by the standards of southern universities, in 1966—well into the era of civil rights advances—only sixty African Americans were enrolled at Notre Dame, and the football team had only one black player, Alan Page (see Delsohn, 1998). Terrence Moore, a sports columnist for *The Atlanta Constitution*, revealed that, "I'll never forget the Notre Dame–Michigan State game. It was 1966. I was ten years old. My aunt's house was packed. But except for me, my mother, and two brothers, everybody was cheering for Michigan State." He admitted that, "It was the racial issue. Michigan State had a black quarterback. Most of its starting defense was made up of black guys. Notre Dame had Alan Page, and that was it. So essentially, to my family, it was the white boys at Notre Dame against the black Michigan State team" (ibid., p. 141).

On campus, race was more conflicted, less certain, and surely as saturated with power and significance. Institutional discourses sought to balance academics and athletics, progressivism and paternalism. Father Theodore Hesburgh was the president of Notre Dame University from 1952 through 1977, thus he oversaw several significant events in the development of the school's renowned athletic programs, including the recruitment of its first black players. Hesburgh is known for his philosophy of giving education priority over athletics and for championing civil rights. He was one of the original members of the U.S. Civil Rights Commission as well as an outspoken critic of the draft during the Vietnam War. Within the context of his biography, there is no doubt that he was a progressive thinker in prior decades. Like the American Catholic Church, he assumed a series of liberal positions on issues such as international politics, domestic welfare, civil rights, and academic freedom; but also like the church, some of his views seemed old-fashioned, if not also paternalistic. And while he came to his administrative duties at Notre Dame with no particular enthusiasm for sports, he quickly grew into his role as a de facto athletic director of the nation's most famous collegiate football team. During his tenure, he engineered Notre Dame's precarious balancing act of synthesizing, at once, its continually emerging Catholic, secular, American, athletic, academic, and Irish identities.

Interviewed in *Black Issues in Higher Education*, in 1992, Father Hesburgh acknowledged the existence of racism in the Catholic Church, but he noted that its prevalence mirrored the presence of racism in the United States generally. He also criticized what he termed *Afrocentric scholarship*, *ghetto schools*, and *black English*. On inner city schools, he said:

> Schools are so bad in the ghetto . . . I think we need to clean the place out and have a campus like we have here at Notre Dame or at most state universities. Organize the thing just for educating poor kids, but make the schools so good that white kids will want to attend. I'm talking about 500 acres of a park or something. You could create it in Harlem; you could create it in Chicago. In fact, the first thing I would do [after it is built] is put a fence around it. In fact, two fences, 20-feet high with wild dogs running between them. (Phillip, 1992, p. 11)

Hesburgh has always been known for a frank, outspoken style of expression, and these remarks are clearly motivated by a desire to improve lives and educations. Yet his solutions oversimplify matters and his unwillingness to understand the cultural and political complexities of inequality. On black English, he remarked, "Black English is not good English. It may be spoken by a certain class of people, but [they are not] the most successful or educated."

During the same interview, Hesburgh attempted to address the question of why so few African Americans attend Catholic universities such as Notre Dame:

> I often ask myself why we don't do better. I think one problem is most blacks are City people. They tend to be in large

cities where there is work. For someone from Harlem to come to Notre Dame it would be a culture shock. It's a different atmosphere. It's rural. We have everything we need here to live, have fun and learn. For city kids used to jive and Black kids around, that might be a bit strange. It's a very quality school. The average SAT's are about 1,250. Another problem would be social adjustment. (Phillip, 1992, p. 10)

The Notre Dame football coach during the 1960s, Ara Parseghian, reported in an interview that Hesburgh, at a post–game party at Parseghian's house in 1972, asked the coach, "How come we don't have more blacks on our football team?" Parseghian's response at the moment was that the university admissions office kept turning down recruits (Delsohn, 1998, p. 144).

It is emblematic of the overall significance of sports and football at Notre Dame that Hesburgh's autobiography, *God, Country, Notre Dame* (1990), contains one chapter exclusively dedicated to the subject. He offers various anecdotes about his relationships with famous coaches such as Frank Leahy, Ara Parseghian, and Lou Holtz. His narrative positions himself as a hard-liner who often had to temper the desires of coaches and athletic administrators. He articulates a philosophy, also the reputed philosophy of Notre Dame, wherein athletics must never come before academics. At one point, he candidly addresses the issue of recruiting athletes:

Do we take athletes who don't meet our normal admission requirements? Yes, but not very many. Every year we accept a small number of students who excel at something—music, art, whatever—but who do not meet our normal academic requirements. We once, for example, admitted the best high school tenor in the country. He did not have the grades or the test scores that we normally require, but we felt he deserved to come to Notre Dame because he had tremendous talent. (Hesburgh, 1990, p. 90)

A controversial book released in 1993, *Under the Tarnished Dome: How Notre Dame Betrayed Its Ideals for Football Glory* (Yaeger & Looney, 1993), charged the university with failing to live up to its own standards of academic excellence and the university's claim that its athletes were no different than its other students. The authors focus mainly on Lou Holtz, the Notre Dame football coach from 1986 to 1996, and they accuse his administration of allowing for steroid use, payoffs, recruiting violations, and violating other NCAA regulations. But of greater interest is the manner in which Notre Dame, under Hesburgh's eye, transformed itself from an institution with an at best modest financial foundation—viewed as the place where marginalized, poor Catholic boys went—to an elite academic institution as its football team simultaneously became the epitome of collegiate athletic achievement.

The relationship between amateur football coaches and the young men who they coached often has been understood in paternalistic terms. This tradition was already in place as Notre Dame University began to map itself onto the American institution of football, which brought with it its own brand of paternalism. Indeed, the very hierarchy of church authority is fashioned in terms of a priesthood known as fathers whose purpose is to look out for the moral state of the congregation and community. Perhaps more than any other American church, the Catholic Church established a history of providing for the needs of impoverished, often orphaned, children through "boys' homes" and other kinds of orphanages. Hard-nosed discipline was paramount within this tradition, as tales of priests and nuns victimizing students through corporal punishment are legendary among those who attended Catholic schools. And fighting, in the form of boxing, was a popular method used by priests to teach boys moral fortitude, fairness, and toughness.

As long as the children in these institutions were either Irish, or otherwise poor and white, the paternalism was understood in benign terms. But as Notre Dame, as well as the Catholic Church, more broadly became part of mainstream white America, its own history of custodial paternalism was overladen with symbolic baggage, as the overwhelmingly nonblack school and the Church began to address issues such as African-American poverty. Paternal authority quickly became racialized paternalism when black students were offered opportunities to learn and play at Catholic institutions. Indeed, as Notre Dame became progressively more integrated, it characterized its own efforts as generous and charitable, while appearing generally to have little interest in the social world of many African Americans.

The legacy of Notre Dame football really began to crystallize with its teams in the early part of the twentieth century and became literally mythologized during the 1920s and 1930s, the decades when Knute Rockne was the football coach. The university was already committed to the creation of a dominant athletic culture by the turn of the century, and its football teams regularly had winning seasons. But it was the legendary Rockne who transformed Notre Dame's football tradition into a national, mythical spectacle. Rockne was neither Catholic nor Irish, but he came to study at Notre Dame University because he was attracted to the school's reputation as a "poor boy's institution, a place where students with little money but a willingness to work could succeed" (Massa, 1999, p. 198). After Rockne graduated and became the head football coach in 1918, he took what was already a history of winning and, with much savvy and conscious design, invented the mythical juggernaut that is Notre Dame football. In addition to being perhaps the most innovative football tactician, he also attended to concerns such as the team's uniform design, its nickname, its press coverage, its financial success, and even its psychology (see Chowder, 1993; Massa, 1999; Sperber, 1993). By any account, Rockne loved Notre Dame and sensed that his contribution to its success had to be the elevation of its football program to legendary status. He clearly succeeded. By the early 1920s, the Notre Dame football program already had generated immense revenues, an annual average of about $200,000 (Massa, 1999, p. 198).

George Gipp was Rockne's star back in his first years of coaching, and he became Notre Dame's first first-string all-American player. A brazen, rebellious, undisciplined student, Gipp skipped many a class and even some final exams. He lived at an off-campus hotel so he could carouse at night. He was honored during his senior year, 1920, when the university designated the Northwestern game as "George Gipp Day." Due to a high fever, he sat on the bench until the fourth quarter. In response to the crowd chanting his name, he entered the game and threw two touchdown passes to help Notre Dame pull out yet another victory. His fever turned into pneumonia, and in the hospital, with Rockne at his bedside, he died on December 14. Posthumously, Rockne transformed even the death of George Gipp into a spectacle. First, he remade Gipp's image during interviews with journalists, recalling that he was a "great guy," a generally upstanding citizen. Eight years later, during halftime of his team's big game against Army, which they were losing, Rockne delivered a famous speech in which he told his players that upon his deathbed, Gipp had said, "Some time, Rock, when the team is up against it . . . tell them to go in there with all they've got and just win one for the Gipper. I don't know where I'll be then, Rock. But I'll know about it, and I'll be happy." The speech was effective as Notre Dame won, and Rockne's speech and purported recounting of Gipp's request were memorialized in the 1940 motion picture, *Knute Rockne—All American*, starring Ronald Reagan as Gipp (see Sperber, 1993, pp. 773–783).

Well after Rockne was killed in a plane crash in 1931 while en route to Los Angeles to make a football demonstration movie, Father Hesburgh's central preoccupation in the 1950s was in advancing the quality and reputation of academics at Notre Dame. But he knew that such an agenda required a great deal of money, and he quickly realized that the football program represented a financial treasure chest. Rather than situating athletics in opposition to the other, scholarly functions of the university, Hesburgh celebrated his coaches and football players. As Mark Massa (1999, p. 212) characterized the results of Hesburgh's agenda, "[He] . . . had crafted a Notre Dame whose reality was somewhat different from the perception of both fans and critics, a place where successful football teams were merely a metaphor for other, more serious pursuits." Although the annual financial windfalls from football were used to enhance the university's academics, we suggest that the relationship between scholarship and athletics and between race and opportunity at Notre Dame—just as with all top NCAA Division I schools—is rife with awkward alliances, uneven opportunities, and contradictory spaces.

For centuries in the Old World, the Irish were viewed as being racially inferior by the English, and Irish Americans also were victimized by virulent racism in the United States. The epitaphs and slurs used by non-Irish Americans to commonly refer to Irish Americans actually questioned their humanity. Popular eighteenth- and nineteenth-century terms for the Irish, such as savage, bestial, wild, and simian, are reminiscent of terms also used to describe black and Native American people, even today. Further, David Roediger (1991, p. 133) reported that in antebellum Philadelphia, to be called an Irishman was tantamount to being called a "nig- ger." In fact, the Old World Irish apparently sympathized with blacks in the United States, sensing clear parallels between them- selves and American slaves (see Takaki, 1993, p. 150). Many Irish also supported the abolition of slavery, but once they crossed the ocean, it seemed, such sympathies tended to vanish. Irish Ameri- cans had entered into a historical process by the 1850s that would transform their identity from one of an inferior race to one char- acterized by all of the privileges and assumptions that came with "whiteness." The way in which the Irish in the United States be- came white, and in which their Irishness became merely a marker of a particular Euro-American ethnicity, has been studied by Roediger (1991) and Ignatiev (1995). It is a story that involves the making of a working-class identity that ultimately would include the Irish.

The Irish emigrated to the United States in waves during the early part of the nineteenth century, and once in the New World, they continued to face racial prejudice. As a population, they began to occupy various unskilled labor positions, from domestic service to factory work to shipyards. They also quickly threw their political support behind the Democratic politicians, who at the time were anti-abolitionists. Competition for these as well as for somewhat more skilled industrial positions later was a concern for Irish Americans. In various Eastern cities, Irish workers occasion- ally clashed with black workers, whom they feared might take their jobs. But as Roediger (1991, p. 147) has argued, "Free Blacks were *not* effective competitors for jobs with the Irish." He at- tempts to understand why, then, Irish Americans stressed job com- petition with black workers instead of with other white groups, with whom they had much more protracted competition.

One reason, Roediger suggests, is that the Irish-American com- munities realized that blacks were a largely defenseless target, and denigrating them actually united them with other white populations. Irish Americans were heavily invested in merging themselves into the process of becoming white, thus joining other groups, such as Germans and Scots, to capture the privileges of a new working-class whiteness. This working-class identity defined itself against a largely imaginary concept of blackness, as African Americans as a group would serve as the very bottom racial rung on a stratified social ladder previously based on class. Southern and Eastern European immigrants, who arrived in large numbers near the end of the century, did not receive free access to this space of the white wage laborer. First identified variously as colored, and racially marked, they later were able to generate identities of whiteness that would always continue to be closed to non-European peoples.

This reorganization of working class and ethnic social relations was never a completed project but rather always an unfolding process structured by racial ideologies and economic circumstances. For example, Irish immigrants continued to emigrate to the United States, and upon their arrival, they faced hardships and competition for jobs characteristic of African Americans and the first-generation ancestors of Irish Americans. Of course, they were able to assimilate whiteness in ways, again, that were unavailable to black Americans. But during these difficult times, Irish Americans shared many experiences with African Americans, from hiring prejudices to poverty to denied opportunities for education. Further, both groups created similar opportunities for themselves, such as sports. In the United States, Irish Americans were in fact the predominant athletic superstars in prize fighting, baseball, and football, well into the twentieth century, before these "working-class" sports were even open to African-American participation.

Some suggest that the nickname "Fighting Irish," used to identify the athletic teams at Notre Dame University, began as a result of the association between boxing and Irish-American identity (see Sperber, 1993, p. 79). Various stories about the origins of the name continue to circulate, from the claim that Northwestern University students began yelling "Kill those Fighting Irish" during a game in 1899, to the report that Notre Dame halfback Pete Vaughn admonished his teammates by crying, "What's the matter with you guys. You're Irish and you're not fighting!" during a tough battle with Michigan in 1909. The term begins to appear in various regional and national news columns by the early 1900s, and the moniker was ultimately adopted by the Notre Dame community itself by the 1920s, although university administrators initially disapproved of it. Knute Rockne very much liked the name, and after he was hired to coach football, he encouraged its use among his many student press agents and journalistic contacts. As for a mascot, various Irish terriers roamed the sidelines with cheerleaders for years, beginning in 1923 and ending in 1966, ultimately replaced by the current figure, a redheaded, five-foot-tall character dressed in a green suit and an Irish country hat. He represents a leprechaun and, brandishing a shillelagh, he leads the spectators in cheers.

Since the "Fighting Irish" of Notre Dame nickname and the leprechaun mascot are highlighted so frequently as a way of responding defensively to critiques of Native American mascots, it is worth underscoring here the historical significance of this moniker. Notre Dame and its teams and students were labeled a number of disparaging things at the turn of the century, into the 1920s. The press typically referred to Notre Dame variously as the "Catholics," "the Papists," or "Horrible Hibernians." The more common labels foregrounding the team's Irish affiliation included "Dumb Micks," "Dirty Irish," and then ultimately, of course, "Fighting Irish" (Sperber, 1993, p. 80). By slowly but eventually embracing a version of what had been one in a litany of perjurious nicknames, some subtle and some obvious, the school's students and faculty actually embraced, if not co-opted, the symbols originally used by outsiders to refer to themselves.

The racial contours of Notre Dame's athletic signs and symbols were mobilized during the 1990s during two football contests against Stanford University. In hosting the Notre Dame football team at Stanford Stadium in 1991, a Stanford drum major mocked the opponent by wearing a nun's habit and beating his drum with a cross. In response, Notre Dame University officially banned the Stanford marching band from appearing at the South Bend campus. More recently, Stanford University itself forbid the Stanford band from performing during contests against Notre Dame after it staged a 1997 skit parodying the Irish potato famine. The skit, performed before the game and during halftime, included a mock debate between a Catholic cardinal and the devil. The clergy was portrayed as an anti-intellectual advocate of a flat earth and other scientific theories (Workman, 1997).

The legacy of whiteness, as a particular subjectivity, continues to color the atmosphere and the social relations that exist on the Notre Dame campus, even in the context of a post–civil rights era of multiculturalism. Although in important ways, Notre Dame University remains both Catholic and Irish, newer manifestations of its identity have emerged in which a post–civil rights United States can embrace Notre Dame for its quintessential "Americanness." Achieving this Americanness was an arduous process, and Notre Dame offers many Americans a shining example of how a circumscribed racial identity, Irish, was whitened as Irishness became not only an ethnic domain but literally everyone's "favorite" charming ethnicity. Indeed, this is underscored by the broad participation of the non-Irish public in St. Patrick's Day celebrations when, ostensibly, anyone can be Irish.[4] Perhaps the single most important means through which Notre Dame created these new identities was its football team, which went from being the poor Catholic boys' team to being, in reality, the national team of college football, simultaneously more loved and hated by fans than any other team. But passionate spectator hatred for Notre Dame today almost never results from anti-Irish or anti-Catholic bigotry. Many people dislike Notre Dame football for its dominance, some for its whiteness, and even a few for the contradictions underlying the combination of its commitment to winning and teaching.

CONCLUSION

Although whiteness centers the racial spectacles of intercollegiate athletics, its contours are rarely as apparent as the stagings and struggles at the University of Mississippi and the University of Notre Dame. At both of these institutions, whiteness materializes through the complex entanglements of identity, ideology, and institutional context (see Dyson, 1998). Clearly such materializations are not singular or teleological, but rather multiple, ambivalent, and conflicted. What it means to be white at Ole Miss has always been quite different from what it means to be white at Notre Dame. At the University of Mississippi, whiteness has served as a conceptual space for desperately clinging to social relations of an imagined past, while the racial process that has informed the evolution of Notre Dame's collegiate dynasty centers on efforts to invent a new membership in an emerging national whiteness of the twentieth century. At Ole Miss, racial paternalism was manifest as a patrician, Southern whiteness which, when mapped onto the newly racialized collegiate sporting world, turned on the assertion of difference, supremacy, and generosity. At Notre Dame University, which confronted America's preoccupation with its own Irish–Catholic difference, racial paternalism emerged in the form of a white, priestly administration. It only begrudgingly opened its campus and sports teams to African Americans, then it extolled the virtues of competitive, high-revenue, collegiate athletics while refusing to acknowledge that it contributed—perhaps more than any other school—to a Euro-American and an African-American culture obsessed with "hoop dreams" and visions of athletic achievement that often undermined education. Importantly, these formulations of whiteness increasingly have distinct resonance: the (honorary) whiteness of the Fighting Irish remains invisible, unmarked, and largely unquestioned, often eliciting praise, affection, and even celebration; the embattled (neo-Confederate) whiteness of the Ole Miss Rebels bears an indelible stain and frequently evokes discomfort, if not disdain, precisely because it represents a problematic or vile formulation of whiteness, relying as it does upon symbols and sentiments of white supremacy that are no longer deemed acceptable or appropriate.

7

Postcolonial Arenas:
The Dis-Ease
of Desire in America

In this book, we have begun to unravel the political economy of racial signs structuring and structured by intercollegiate athletics. We began this book with the understanding that the American university has become deeply vested in a relationship to athletics and that a deeply imbricated constellation of racial spectacles and commodities anchors this relationship. Throughout, we have taken race, power, and culture to be slippery, conflicted, uneasy, and, at times, paradoxical—both "obvious" and "invisible" (Omi, 1997, p. 493). Foregrounding, even disrupting, common-sense ideas about race in the context of college sports, we have deconstructed the institutions, economies, and social relations with which these ideas *articulate*. While to this point we have mapped the erasures, inflations, and elaborations of redness, whiteness, and blackness, in this closing chapter we aim to critically assess the current state of the university as a conspicuous site of public commodification and consumption of "culture." In particular, we clarify the importance of the fundamental concepts animating our analysis. Such a clarification will allow for additional considerations of blackness, redness, and especially whiteness, while highlighting the networks of power and the play of signification facilitating and contesting these dominant formulations of race in intercollegiate athletics.

ACADEME

The American university, in particular the public university, is a relevant, significant cultural site comprised of complicated, often contradictory sets of practices. As we have argued so far, fixing Native American images as athletic icons is best appreciated as a conspicuous institutional practice that both collides and colludes with other university practices, discourses, and values. Myriad flows of (post)colonial power continually parse the space of the university, informing its visions and values. University curricula are characterized by a variety of technologies of symbolic violence that locate particular cultural tastes, class occupations, political histories, and social statuses within the blind spots of elite education (Bourdieu & Passeron, 1977). For example, consider the awkward spaces of interaction that often inhere at the university, such as a Marxist scholar who teaches and theorizes class exploitation and who seldom if ever greets or engages the presence of the custodian who nightly cleans her office. Or consider dormitory students that pass by the janitors who clean up their daily messes, with whom they might be cordial, even friendly, but who clearly represent an occupational space that—by their very enrollment at university— these students likely intend to avoid. To be certain, within these scholastic spaces many enlightened critiques of and even successful challenges to imperial dominance have arisen; but we would argue that situated prominently at the front and center of university public culture is an odd intersection of several articulating systems of exploitation.

In March 1989, the authors recall the atmosphere in Davenport Hall, where the University of Illinois Department of Anthropology is housed. The NCAA Division I basketball tournament, a single-elimination televisual spectacle involving some sixty-four teams in four regional brackets, always produced a near-carnivalesque environment, but this year was particularly noteworthy, for the talented Illinois team, led by Kendall Gill, had won the East Regional to advance to the Final Four. At least one of the players had taken an anthropology course that year. And many of the anthropology faculty intently followed the course of the tournament; one professor even brought his own television into the office. Secretarial staff, as well as two professors, wore Chief Illiniwek clothing throughout the week preceding the Final Four. Various faculty, staff, and graduate students partook in a ritualized gambling pool in which participants attempted to predict the winners of all of the games, beginning with round one. Contests to predict the winners of the March Madness tournament brackets have likely emerged as the most common form of casual office betting in the country. We find this scene of mania for March Madness in Champaign–Urbana rife with contradiction. For example, some of the same professors and graduate students so heavily invested in the outcome of the Final Four frequently poked fun at the lack of academic preparation of student athletes, while in fact they were literally betting in the department pool. Further, the Fighting Illini were then, as now, characterized by an overdetermined nexus of locations and images, with a largely black basketball team and an ostensibly Native American mascot but no ample social space where African-American students could unite with or even engage Native American students.[1]

SPECTACLES

Spectacles, particularly racial spectacles, pace intercollegiate athletics. Guy Debord linked his concept of the spectacle to capitalism and necessarily then to the commodity. Within the spectacle emerges particular, empowered ways of seeing the world, which is mediated in late capitalist societies as a series of images, dramas, and visual narratives. Debord (1970/1967, p. 42) was convinced that, "The spectacle is the moment when the commodity has attained the total occupation of social life." Clearly, sport has become one of America's prevailing commodity forms that mediates our experiences of daily life, as well as more broadly, class, gender, nation, and race. Debord's intellectual project of the spectacle was largely Marxist and in our view failed to completely grasp the implications of the imaged and imagined society of late capitalism. He considered the spectacle to function as a sort of modernist, stupefying tool that engendered passivity and disrupted creative praxis. We suggest a more dynamic reading of spectacle that bypasses overly simplistic notions of class divisions and hierarchies of consumption. Certainly we aim to foreground the uneven fields of empowerment and disempowerment, but we view our task as one of complicating the relations between signs and social relations, and as one of advancing a notion of culture as mutually constructed along multiple lines of experience and power. In so doing, we believe that Stuart Hall's model of public culture perhaps anticipates, more insightfully than other orientations, the sites and images engaged throughout these chapters:

> I think there is a continuous and necessarily uneven and unequal struggle, by the dominant culture, constantly to disorganize and reorganize popular culture; to enclose and confine its definitions and forms within a more inclusive range of dominant forms. There are points of resistance; there are also moments of supersession. This is the dialectic of cultural struggle. In our times, it goes on continuously, in the complex lines of resistance and acceptance, refusal and capitulation, which makes the field of culture a sort of constant battlefield. (Hall, 1981, p. 233)

It is necessary, further, to conceptualize the relationship between spectacle and power in terms of its affective dimension. That is, all of these sites of athletic spectacle persist not merely because they incorporate particular ideologies of whiteness but because they mobilize cultural desire, pleasure, and emotion. They *work* because, clearly, they "matter" to people (Grossberg, 1992, p. 83). The desire for Native American mascots and other racial icons locates the non-Indian self within a space of impossibility, wherein spectators, students, and administrators fail to recognize the uneven, historical significance of the convergence and then slippage of professional sports, the American university, scholastic athletics, the embodiment of the Indian, the predominance of the bodies of African-American student athletes, and the absence of Native American students and faculty. Grossberg argues that cultural formations, such as the one comprised of the images and social relations of college sport, cannot be understood in dichotomous terms of groups, with or without access to power:

> Different social groups have differential access to specific clusters of practices, and these relations are themselves part

of the determination or articulation of the [cultural] formation. Moreover, at different sites, for different fractions,
the distribution and configuration of the formation itself
will determine different relations to and experiences of the
formation itself. (Grossberg, 1992, p. 71)

In these chapters, we have attempted to highlight the *multiple
vectors* of commodification and exploitation of the black student
athlete (as well as all student athletes more generally) and imagined Native American subjectivities. The cultural formation of
racialized collegiate spectacle turns on a particular sensibility, in
which Americans can and do feel that their society has arrived at
the moment in time when sport has transcended problems of race.
Such a sensibility, of course, obscures the fact that racial signs and
symbols matter immensely to the lives of people.

RACE

In the afterword to a recent collection of essays, *White Reign*, education critic Cameron McCarthy reminds readers, importantly,
that white people also practice and benefit from identity politics,
even if unwittingly (1998, p. 330). McCarthy (ibid., p. 331) realized, as our readings in previous chapters have demonstrated, that
"Racially dominant identities do depend on the constant ideological appropriation of the Other. Racial identity, racial affiliation,
and racial exclusion are the products of human work, human effort. . . . The field of race relations, in popular culture, but also in
education, is one of simulation." McCarthy (ibid., p. 333) insists
further that,

> Education is indeed a critical site in which struggles over
> the organization and concentration of emotional and polit-
> ical investment and moral affiliation are taking place.
> These battles over identity involve the powerful manipula-
> tion of group symbols and strategies of articulation and
> rearticulation of public slogans and popular discourses.
> These signs and symbols are used to make identity and de-
> fine social and political projects.

Whiteness is simultaneously a practice, a social space, a sub-jectivity, a spectacle, an erasure, an epistemology, a strategy, a his-torical formation, a technology, and a tactic. Of course, it is not monolithic, but in all of its manifestations, it is unified through privilege and the power to name, represent, and create opportunity and to deny access.

While we agree with McCarthy that whiteness, as well as red-ness, blackness, and other racialized domains, is evermore a prod-uct of simulation, we emphasize that these simulated spectacles have significant impacts on patterns of social relations, economic and cultural opportunity, the design of material space, and the flow of capital. That is, each of the instances of spectacle that we have examined relates in rather specific ways to how these ques-tions can be answered: who plays whom; who plays *for* whom; who plays *by* whom; who plays mascot for whom; who watches whom; who goes to college, who does not; who studies by whom; who teaches whom? In sum, who wins and who loses.

In recent decades, whiteness has become identified in terms of its diverse desires for difference. Indeed, capitalism has driven whiteness, and "Consumer utopias and global capital flows rearticulate whiteness by means of relational differences" (Mc-Laren, 1998, p. 67). Native American mascots, spectacles of white racial longing, and African-American athletes occupy conspicuous, crisscrossing locations within the landscape of American collegiate athletics. For the everyday consumer of college sport, they signify popular nodes of racial difference. Whiteness has centered these stagings of racial difference, although the experiences and re-sponses of nonwhite communities have repeatedly complicated these spectacles. Upon this racial terrain of sport, the desires, fears, preoccupations, and privileges of many Euro-Americans have as-sumed material expression. Individuals and institutions colonized the nonwhite Other, appropriating but redefining stylistic render-ings of cultural difference in order to secure versions of whiteness and frequently white masculinity that resonated with local, re-gional, and national audiences. By establishing exhibitions such as Sammy Seminole or Colonel Reb, or by authoring the terms and explanations by which collegiate athletics was opened to African-American students, signifying "regimes of naming" are enacted. Naming here is to be taken broadly, as in the power to label a group of people, the power to mimic, or even the power to have one's values be society's dominant values.

Ambivalence, more than any other social, historical affect, has structured the various formations of what we have termed *whiteness*. Ambivalence here is construed as a social and psychological discourse centered on a (dis)comfort with an imperial bloc's own mechanisms of identity, modes of power, and relations with the other. Postcolonial scholars such as Homi Bhabha (1994) have argued that at the very center of colonial discourse is a constitutive ambivalence. During such imperial moments, ambivalence often manifests itself within overlapping responses and contradictory projects: disgust paired with desire, fear joined to longing, emulation embedded in condemnation, nostalgia arising from acculturation. In postcolonial contexts, such as post–civil rights America, ambivalence colors power in terms of a love-hate response to hybrid cultural formations, such as the popular fascination with black athletic style (e.g., slam dunks, end zone celebrations) juxtaposed with institutional discomfort with such styles. But, more importantly, the postcolonial moment is framed by an emergent hybridity "in which the discourse of colonial authority loses its univocal grip on meaning and finds itself open to the trace of language of the other, enabling the critic to trace complex movements of disarming alterity in the colonial context" (Young, 1995, p. 22). By moving into, onto, and over the historical and cultural terrains of nonwhite Americans, white America secures a partial recovery of its erased selves, from imaginary expressions of libido, bellicosity, aggression, expressive spontaneity, and deviance.

But at the same time, we have argued, whiteness has remained unmarked, literally masked, even as these practices of spectacle have been effectively doing the cultural work of mobilizing forms of whiteness. David Andrews and Cheryl Cole (see Andrews, forthcoming; Cole, 1996; Cole & Andrews, 1996; Cole & Denny, 1995) have written extensively on how the management of the images of black athletes has mediated important narratives that define the boundaries of personal, social legitimacy. That is, once such constellations of capital as the NBA, the NCAA, television networks, and Nike and Reebok, among others, recognized that if America were to engage, indeed embrace, the growing presence of the black athlete, certain black sports stars who embodied the cluster of political ideologies regnant in the 1980s would have to be mobilized for the consumption of an increasingly conservative white public. For example, Michael Jordan has, more than any other player, been mediated as the culture hero who transcends race and racial divide; who embodies discipline, drive, and integrity; who took advantage of the opportunity provided by America; and who "flew" metaphorically over insignificant social stumbling blocks, signifying an "open class structure, racial tolerance, economic mobility, the sanctity of individualism, and the availability of the American dream for black Americans" (Gray, 1989, p. 376). Many black college stars have assumed this script, if less prominently than Jordan, from Grant Hill to Danny Manning.

Most importantly, however, is that these new African-American stars are nonthreatening, insofar as they generally avoid political activism, especially black politics, and they are presented as the cultural peers of white America. In a sense, they resemble Bill Cosby's popular 1980s character, Heathcliffe Huxtable: educated, wholesome, attractive, responsible, and "middle class." The narratives that construct the black athlete as transcendent of race—such as the common notion that Michael Jordan allowed Americans to rise above their obsession with race (D. Andrews, 1996, p. 138; LaFeber, 1999; Wideman, 1990, p. 140) and that he effectively displaced race in the spirit of Reagan discourse—work because they oppose alternative narratives about the transgressive black athlete. Indeed, we outlined in an earlier chapter how African-American athletes who fail to conform to prevailing standards of integrity, opportunity, and achievement are (re)located by the public as immature, incomplete, and even dangerous.

The racially transcendent black athlete opens a space for white America to modulate its own desires and racial ambivalence. David Roediger's (1995) essay, "*Guineas, Wiggers,* and the Dramas of Racialized Culture," clarifies well the postcolonial significance of white ambivalence in terms of appropriating the spaces and places of the nonwhite Other. "What *can* be 'made of'," he queries, "the impulses that at once and often in the same person lead to tremendous attraction toward "nonwhite" cultures and toward hideous reassertions of whiteness?" (ibid., p. 659). In particular, Roediger seeks to unearth the cultural genealogy of the fairly recent term *wigger*, which he first heard in 1989 when it was used as a slur at Cabrini High Schools in a Detroit suburb. White students from Detroit had begun to enroll in the school, bringing with them black friends, black styles, and modes of black communication. Some of the suburban white students referred to these newcomers as "wiggers" which, Roediger clarifies, was intended to mean "white niggers."

Certainly, a segment of white, middle-class American youth, especially males, has embraced certain elements of "blackness," from rap to hip-hop to clothing styles to speech patterns, or even a unique mélange of these effects. Hip-hop magazines will often market to a young Euro-American audience, which now buys as much as half of all rap and hip-hop music (see Ledbetter, 1992; Roediger, 1995). Greg Tate (1992, p. 15), a columnist writing in one such magazine, taunts these white consumers of black style, referring to them as "all the B-boy wannabes who like to say *ho*!" As Roediger (1995, p. 661) muses, this youthful investment, which often fades after adolescence, underscores Leslie Felder's claim that white American boys often spend their early youth, "playing Indian" and their teens as "imaginary blacks" before entering into white adulthood. The marketing and consumption of NBA and college basketball, more than any other game, has effectively targeted this segment of the population. The music of black rap and hip-hop artists serves as the backdrop for many highlight shows and even as halftime entertainment at games (Nelson, 1997). Nike commercials and the documentary *Hoop Dreams* also make frequent use of these performances.

In one sense, this hybridization or pastiche of cultural elements can be viewed in a positive light, as a parsing of intercultural/ interracial boundaries, especially when it involves new, multiracial friendships. But, in another sense, such appropriations may reveal a deeper ambivalence about the Euro-American relationship to blackness, and too often they rely on performance and mimicry while obscuring the social experiences of African Americans. Consider, for example, the white teenager who likes to play rap music, wear gold chains (imitating his favorite NBA star), and mimic black, "Cool Pose" gestures, but who is oblivious at the same time to his father's open hostility to the NAACP, affirmative action, and the legacy of Martin Luther King Jr. Or perhaps this young man relishes these newfound adornments of blackness but continues to fear interaction with African Americans.

AGENCY

We hardly intend to suggest that African-American communities have done only what a white America has allowed them to do. The situation is much more complicated indeed. Identities of whiteness and blackness are in the first instance, historical and multiple, and in the United States, each has had a profound influence on the other. We do insist, however, that insofar as the political economy of racial signs and social relations in college sport advances systems of exploitation, contradiction, or inaccurate representations, it does so largely informed by Euro-American agendas and preoccupations.

Throughout this analysis of racial signification in college sport, we have sought to bypass simplistic dichotomies, such as subordinate/dominate, resistance/submission, or subject/agent. That is, we have traced the political economies of these colliding sign systems without the illusion that they merely exist in social space as objects that generate their own energy and domination. Rather, these racial signs are at once simulated, performed, and materialized as well as being social, political, and personal. They are historically articulated social fields, always provisional and in production. And, at the dawn of a new millennium, perhaps the primary mode through which people create these fields is the practice of consumption, as a mode of late capitalism. Grossberg (1992, p. 290) reminds us, "Consumerism marks an affective investment in capital, an investment within which people are both the subject and the agent." This point is crucial, because it organizes diverse citizens, often with opposing interests, into particular relationships of exchange and interaction.

In highlighting these regimes of signification—redness, whiteness, and blackness—we have implied that they are powerful, that they have effects, and that they always have the potential to oppress, in both psychosocial and material ways. But social power is emergent in human practice, and it is never complete, monolithic, or deterministic. Power is neither a substance nor a conscious apparatus. Rather, "Cultural hegemony is refused, diffused, absorbed, reproduced, and reconfigured" (Palumbo-Liu, 1997, p. 4), but at the same time we do not wish to valorize resistance. As we ponder the social existence of the university community and its student athletes, especially African-American student athletes, we seek to understand the nature of this constraint, opportunity, and strategy. Thus we must attempt to understand the role of *agency* in this context of sporting spectacles and the global economy that drives them. While numerous studies in recent decades have attempted to locate the agency, or the power to act and resist (hierarchical) social structure (Fiske, 1993; also see Brown, 1996), here agency is viewed not as a matter of individuals, or even of groups. Best conceptualized, after Antonio Gramsci, as "tendential forces," we understand "such forces, which often seem to have a life of their own but exist only conjuncturally, represent a movement and a direction which appears to be independent of the desires or intentions of any and even possibly all social groups" (Grossberg, 1992, p. 123; see also Hall, 1985).

All people and all groups, then, are agents, living and acting with historical structures (which they had no part in creating in the first instance), colliding with other social agents in ways that are difficult to anticipate and seldom direct (Grossberg, 1992, pp. 123–127). As regimes of signification, then, redness, whiteness, and blackness are engaged, consumed, and inscribed by all individuals and groups in the United States, regardless of race. But these social agents are uniquely located along uneven planes of action and existence.

How, then, should we understand the location of the athletes in particular who labor within this political economy of racial signs? Perhaps it would be instructive to revisit here the circumstances of the African-American students who comprised the all-black 1966 Texas Western championship team, discussed in Chapter 5. While most accounts of the famous national championship contest against Kentucky positioned (usually with justification) Adolph Rupp and his Wildcats as the racist antagonists in the drama, the Texas Western players suffered racial indignities in their own university community. First they suffered forms of exploitation that were, and remain, generic to the Division I collegiate athletic experience. For example, Haskins had his players in the gym at 2 P.M., and they would often not return to their dorms until 7 P.M., after the cafeteria was closed. They practiced seven days a week, getting reprieves only on Christmas and Easter, and this includes the travails of cross-country travel, often during the middle of the class week. Texas Western, moreover, as an all-black team, was the victim of intense racial hatred at home. The Texas Western campus was located in El Paso, which lacked a recognizable African-American community, and the university enrolled few black students beyond the athletes.

Players complained of extreme social isolation and racism on campus and in the classroom, and some pointed to Texas Western athletic director George McCarty's use of the word "nigger" (Fitzpatrick, 1999, p. 31; Olsen, 1968). Haskins began to recruit black players, not out of some commitment to social justice but rather to win games. College President Joseph Ray insisted that his athletic director inform Haskins that he was playing too many blacks in 1966, but Haskins would not relent, and Ray finally backed off. After the victory, Haskins began to receive thousands of nasty letters.

> It started a week to ten days after, and all of a sudden we were just flooded with mail. . . . It was just all "nigger lover" stuff, all from Southern states. One in particular I got the biggest kick out of was from a professor at Alabama. He wrote this neat letter saying they'd never have a "black nigger" on their team. . . . I got letters from black leaders too calling me an "exploiter." . . . The next year was about the toughest of my life. There were death threats. One guy called and said he'd shoot me if the "niggers" stepped on the floor for a game in Dallas. (quoted in Fitzpatrick, 1999, p. 228)

One can easily imagine that if these were the experiences of the white coach, the black players themselves must have endured a horrific barrage of terror as they attempted to negotiate exams and practices.

Since power is multiple and indeed unfolds in terms of a number of vectors, it is necessary to underscore that the pursuit of avenues leading to collegiate and then possibly professional athletic careers exists as a viable strategy in numerous communities. Although the systems to which these avenues lead may be plagued by exploitation, the decision either wittingly or by default to commit to developing one's athletic potential may allow a young person to accrue significant amounts of prestige, first in the local community, then regionally, and even nationally. Success upon the athletic field, in a very localized, immediate, and visceral sense, opens up the athlete to a barrage of intense, largely positive emotions that emanate both from within and from spectators and teammates. At an affective level, one feels empowered upon scoring a touchdown or sinking a three-point shot. And if such feats should win games, even championships, the surrounding community shares in this empowerment. In school, at the cafeteria, next to the lockers, and in the parking lot, one's presence as a star athlete works to generate adulation among peers, for better or for worse, often inflating a sense of self-worth. In fact, we would suggest that in some circumstances, the social responses to remarkable athletic achievement in high school can literally engender a euphoric, godlike complex.[2] These emotional and social outcomes rarely, if ever, accompany other forms of scholastic achievement.

A typical practice in the recruitment of high school athletes, in our minds, embodies many of the ironies and inflations of postcolonial America: the ritual of signing a letter of intent. The most highly desired and sought-after high school athletes, when ready to accept a scholarship offer from a particular university, are often visited in their living rooms or high schools by university athletic representatives, if not the head coach, to sign an informal contract known as a letter of intent. This act often is framed as a photo opportunity, including the student's parents and the high school coach. A poignant scene in *Hoop Dreams* reveals this ritual, as cameras capture Arthur Agee sitting with his parents in his living room as Mineral Area Junior College basketball officials hand him a letter of intent. It is a moment of suspense, and his father offers encouragement. The school is a two-year junior college, a level of higher learning whose sports stars are recruited by NCAA Division I universities to start their junior years. After a period of silence in the Agee home, a Mineral Area official asks, "Ready to sign?" Agee does indeed sign then, with his parents looking on.

This ritualized affair, common in the recruitment of high school athletes, has no effective parallel outside of the sports arena. Teams of representatives do not visit the living rooms of prospective math or French students. However difficult, it is important to try to imagine the sense of anticipation, excitement, and enhanced esteem that a student experiences when college scouts are watching his games, calling his coach and parents, and arriving on his doorstep with contract in hand. We believe that such rituals must only confuse the relationship between the spheres of classwork, classmate, sport, and career. Such confusion assumes greater significance in impoverished, urban communities, where representatives from Penn State, the University of Michigan, or Notre Dame cannot visit without creating an ambiguous spectacle of their own.

Such charismatic power tends more often to accrue around spaces of masculinity (Bass, 1996; Katz, 1996). In fact, while women's sports, importantly, continue to gain in popularity, we suggest that certain (contested) bastions of masculine identity are linked to sport, if not militarism (see Messner & Sabo, 1990). In terms of race, we suggest that the confluence of the more aggressive scripts of masculine identity commonly associated with sport has a particular relevance for understanding the African-American experience in many communities where racism has shut off economic and educational opportunity (Majors, 1998). Richard Majors (1998, p. 15) believes that, "Contemporary black males often utilize sports as one means of masculine self-expression in an otherwise limited structure of opportunity." This participation in sport is mediated, in particular, by the stylistic practice of "cool pose," or the conspicuous forms of creativity characterized by demeanor, gesture, posture, clothing, hairstyle, and handshake (ibid., p. 17). Masculinity, in any community in the United States, often is a highly charged, even ambivalent identity (see Kimmel, 1996; Messner & Sabo, 1990, 1994; Springwood, 1996). Black Americans, and black American males, have been forced to negotiate severe forms of emotional and physical emasculation through slavery and racism, even into the present. The black male in particular has been the highly charged locus of racist preoccupation for over two centuries. As Euro-Americans enslaved Africans and black Americans, they whipped males and raped females. Upon Reconstruction, white supremacist attacks on African Americans frequently centered on a fear of the black man's sexuality, and violent castrations were a popular mode of "discipline" (see Turner, 1993). In more recent decades, as African-American males have become the most likely U.S. citizens to be killed, imprisoned, and sentenced to death, popular and intellectual sources lament the "absent," "weak," and "ineffective" black male.

Against this backdrop rests the powerful institution of sport, the social field that has always been the quickest path to economic and social achievement for nonwhite, immigrant Americans. Clearly it served as the opening for African Americans to enter the space of the American university over the last forty years. Sport has emerged as a cultural strategy which, although clearly racialized, is not exclusive to African-American communities. It represents the reconfiguration of opportunity, identity, style, and achievement. Although overly simplistic, for the black male youth sport has represented an ostensibly sensible alternative to gangs (see Cole & King, 1998). Success in sport generates a great deal of cultural capital among male students; indeed, in the social script of the athlete, and of those students of marginal or racialized backgrounds, academic success can actually generate a debt in prestige. It is likely even that in particular spaces, a young male's masculinity can be compromised by a reputation of academic achievement.

Given this, it seems clear that a number of contingencies exist that render urban black communities particularly vulnerable to the inflation of so-called "hoop dreams." Rather than suggest, as Hoberman intimates, that this preoccupation is somehow the fault of the black community, we instead view it as the outcome of a nexus of "tendential forces" that conspires to offer highly constrained avenues of expression and achievement. Importantly, for students of all racial backgrounds, these collegiate athletic avenues are too often defined by a set of identities, values, practices, and subjectivities that run directly counter to what we believe is the agenda of the American university. Indeed, in an effort to reconcile its mission with its pivotal role in the racialized political economy of sport, the American university has emerged as a greatly conflicted institution.

RECLAMATION

At this particular moment in the history of the United States, an analysis of sport reveals an array of odd racial juxtapositions, alliances, and contradictions. For example, how can any school reconcile its continued, even robust, support for a racialized mascot broadly challenged by Native American students and faculty (and others) and the weak graduation rates of both its black and white student athletes who wear these images with its ostensible philosophy of a humane education? How could a prominent Southern university for so many years ignore the means and meanings of enacting Ole Miss football pride, Rebel style?

What kinds of racialized meanings and experiences are constituted by the predominance of African-American athletes on the fields and courts where so many of these collegiate Indian and other mascots prevail? Those occasions in which African-American students have allied themselves with Native American, Euro-American, and Latino students to protest these mascots and other issues confronting minority students assume monumental significance when contextualized by the plight of African-American athletes whose opportunities have been created and whose bodies have been exploited by the very same structures of imperial power that produce mascots. Given the location of black athletes within this system, we have little confidence that possibilities exist for them, or for student athletes of any color, to voice opinions, especially of dissent, in regard to the controversies discussed in this book.

The political economy of college sports and its favorite signs and symbols work to discourage engagement with social and national issues. In fact, as sport has become increasingly significant to the university in terms of revenue, and as playing sport as a Division I athlete has become increasingly important to those aspiring to lucrative, professional careers, the risks assumed by student athletes for speaking up and speaking out have increased. In the 1960s, reflective of a national trend, athletes more often took the opportunity to publicly express their convictions, especially those relating to issues of social justice. For example, at the Mexico City Olympics in 1968, African-American track athletes Tommie Smith and John Carlos held their clenched fists high, symbolizing black power, and they bowed their heads while on the medal stand, in protest of the Olympic participation of the apartheid nation of South Africa. And Mohammed Ali refused to be drafted into military service to fight the war in Vietnam and was convicted for draft evasion in 1968. The ability to voice such dissent on collegiate athletic teams was likely even more compromised because of the pressure of (all too often white) coaches, peers, and fans. Still, many student athletes ventured to be heard (Edwards, 1969; Lapchick, 1996, pp. 11–12; Wiggins, 1997).

At the University of Texas at El Paso (formerly Texas Western, winner of the 1966 basketball championship), in the autumn of 1967, several African-American football players staged a sit-in in the athletic dormitories to protest racist treatment from then-coach Bobby Dobbs and other coaching staff. They were angered over efforts to monitor their dating practices, their unequal living arrangements, and their being stacked into certain playing positions. Although Dobbs said that he would investigate these issues, nothing ever happened (see Wiggins, 1997, pp. 111-112). At the same school, the following year, nine track and field stars were kicked off the team because they protested the Mormon Church's treatment of blacks. David Wiggins (1997, p. 112) explains:

> Just a week after King's tragic death in Memphis, black trackmen at El Paso made plans to boycott the Easter weekend track meet with Brigham Young University. The athletes chose not to travel to Utah, both as a gesture of reverence to King and as a protest against Mormon ideology, which proclaimed the superiority of whites over blacks. The boycotters paid for their actions. Coach Wayne Vandenberg dismissed the nine . . . from the team and revoked their scholarships.

Two years later, fourteen African-American football players at the University of Wyoming met a similar fate after they announced their desire to wear black protest armbands during a future contest against Brigham Young (see Chapter 2).[3]

Perhaps in circumstances yet more constraining, a number of black students (non-athletes) at the University of Mississippi performed their own public defiance at the very center of a sporting spectacle. In Chapter 6 we addressed the insensitive atmosphere of racist humor and insults common in the Ole Miss football stands, and as a result, most black students did not attend the events. During the 1960s, however, one group made its presence conspicuous through defiance. Nadine Cohodas, in her book *The Band Played Dixie: Race and the Liberal Conscience at Ole Miss* (1997), wrote about these students:

> They sat together in the end zone and blatantly cheered for the opposing team, ever more lustily when a black player made an outstanding play. They refused to stand for the Alma Mater or "Dixie." Occasionally someone in the group would hold up a homemade banner: "Racist Athletic Department" or "Ole Miss Racism."

Such events underscore that students, even in the most circumscribed spaces, will not fail to reflect upon their immediate and even more distant circumstances.

Intercollegiate athletics contradicts the ideals of higher education, including (1) its efforts to engender in students a commitment to responsible citizenship, a deeper understanding of the democratic process, and an appreciation of the global community; (2) its aspirations to liberate students from complacency; and (3) its intention to allow them to fully realize cultural and ethnic diversity. Indeed, especially for student athletes (of color), the constraints of big-time college sports so compromise their opportunity to participate in progressive, social, and intellectual movements on campus that something is clearly lost by the athletes themselves, the broader university community, and public culture in general.

In the spring of 1986, as a junior at Purdue University, author Springwood became involved in the campus's South Africa anti-apartheid protest. The movement centered on efforts to make universities divest their monies from companies that did business in South Africa, such as Coca-Cola and IBM. At Purdue, the Free South Africa initiative grew to include demands for increased recruitment and retention of black faculty, better facilities and support for African-American students, and a public discussion with the university administration about all of these issues. In concert with the anti-apartheid movement across the country, at Purdue the public symbol of the protest became small, wooden shanties erected on the quadrangle, representing the shantytowns that were home to numerous black South Africans.

Originally, the Free South Africa movement at Purdue was started by a group of white, middle-class progressive students (both graduate and undergraduate), with a handful of black students also participating. The group constructed the first shanty on the quad during the first week of April, and various members spent nights there. Throughout the week, demonstrations and the distribution of leaflets were planned to attract attention to and support for the issue. By midweek, the Black Students Association (BSA) had formally joined the effort, followed a few days later by the Iranian Students Association and a number of campus churches. When members of the BSA attempted to erect an additional shanty, the university denied them a permit—a decision that appeared to be racial discrimination. In defiance of the administration, the BSA built its shanty, escalating the political stakes. In response, the administration greatly increased its security and demanded that by Friday evening all shanties be removed from the quad.

Friday night, by the time the sun went down, the members of the movement, which now included well over 200 highly committed students, as well as 300 additional involved supporters, had made the decision to defy the demand to take down the shanties. At this point, a confrontation was imminent, and to the movement, support in numbers was critical. A giddy, expectant, albeit tense, atmosphere dominated the quad, as students and media camped out, along with a number of professors and campus clergy. By the time a large number of buses and both marked and unmarked police cars began parking on nearby side streets, several hundred people were gathered around the shanties, singing, talking, planning, and even playing.

One image in particular stands out in Springwood's memory. Cheryl Lockwood, who would later become Springwood's life partner, participated in several races with other protesters, including many black football players who had come to support the group. James Medlock, known as "Meddy," was a power fullback who had turned out that night, and he and Cheryl teamed up for piggyback competitions (Cheryl rode atop Medlock's shoulders, not vice versa) that continued, beyond the shanties, until well after dark. By midnight, however, the players had to return to their dormitories. They could not spend the night with the group; they could not be present when a confrontation occurred; and they absolutely could not be arrested. But at dawn on Saturday, twenty-two students were in fact arrested while forming a protective circle around the shanties. Members of a Special Weapons and Tactics (SWAT) team escorted them into buses. Later, a football player lamented that he very much would have liked to be there, even to be arrested with the others, but that, most certainly, football coach Leon Burtnett would have removed him from the team and revoked his scholarship, which he had worked so many years to earn.

These events in 1986 highlight the limitations on student athletes' capacity to express themselves politically. If a large number of football players had spent that evening at the shanties and had been arrested, surely the incident would have attracted greater attention from the media and the community. College athletes actually possess a significant, largely unrealized source of political power in terms of what they might do to express their convictions. But the risks are high. The purpose here is not to evaluate those players for the way in which they showed their support but merely to underscore the constraints on expression, both direct and indirect, that obviously modulated their participation in an activity that clearly embodied the liberal idealism of the university as a site of debate, contention, and activism.

Where are the athletes? Where are their voices? Where are their minds? Universities must aim to resurrect the voices of student athletes in terms of something other than shoe contracts, sportsmanship, draft aspirations, graduation rates, and honor rolls. Universities must resist the passion with which communities and alumni so often defend clearly incongruous, intellectually bankrupt images and signs. Two recent counter-hegemonic interventions illustrate the promise of change.

In 1998, a movement addressing these issues emerged at Rutgers University. Various alumni, faculty, and students formed a group known as Rutgers 1000, whose purpose was to critique and challenge "big-time" revenue collegiate athletics at Rutgers University. Led by English Professor William C. Dowling, the group conveyed its message through a series of local and national op-ed essays, a site on the World Wide Web, and paid advertisements. As highlighted on its Web page, the aim of the organization is to rectify what is, in the view of its membership, an overemphasis on revenue sports at Rutgers. The following message, taken from an on-line petition, clarifies the position of Rutgers 1000:

> We . . . believe that among the various measures currently underway to transform Rutgers from a premier institution of higher learning into an average or below-average state university, one of the most ominous is the steadily increasing emphasis on "professionalized" college athletics.
>
> At the same time, we believe that, given concerted action by those who care about the quality of intellectual and academic life at Rutgers, there is yet time to reverse this threat to the integrity of the university.
>
> We therefore ask the Board of Governors to do the following:
>
> (1) Withdraw Rutgers immediately from the "Big East" conference in football and basketball;
>
> (2) Within a period of no longer than three years, remove Rutgers teams from NCAA Division IA;
>
> (3) During the same period, apply for membership in the Patriot League or other Division I-AA non-athletic scholarship conference whose level of athletic participation is commensurate with the intellectual and academic standing of Rutgers as an institution of higher learning.

In this statement, one can easily recognize the presence of an elitist longing to recuperate the high status once enjoyed by the Rutgers University of a seemingly lost era. While we are not concerned with the relative reputations of institutions of higher learning, we recognize that a number of the critiques of NCAA Division I sport advanced by Rutgers 1000 are similar to some of those in this book. For example, the organization notes that in the interest of winning, Rutgers has followed the course of many schools in stretching and even reconfiguring the academic standards by which students are chosen and evaluated. Further, it complains that college sport receives a conspicuous, favorably skewed budget for recruitment, training, performance, and facility, and even for enhancing spectacles. It believes that the relationship between athletics and academics is hopelessly complicated by a series of contradictions and concessions, therefore, it wants such a system dismantled and indeed extricated from its own political economy.

Their Web site cites a number of scholarly critiques of college sport, including Sperber (1990) and Sack and Staurowsky (1998), as it carefully attempts to counter any arguments that insist that revenue sport and academics do not have to be at odds (Rutgers 1000). The discourse on the Web page conveys a personal attack as well. Statements by an outspoken supporter of Rutgers athletics, University President Francis Lawrence (see Chapter 1), frequently appear, only to be followed by a deconstruction of his remarks. Ultimately, we agree with the solution proposed by Rutgers 1000, which essentially is to eliminate all of those contours and contradictions of university athletics that unite college sport with professional sport. Significantly, this book foregrounds an aspect of this political economy that Rutgers 1000 fails to address, at least directly. The organization does not confront race, or racial signs, in any fashion. It does not discuss mascots or other athletic traditions. Of course, its purpose is not to author a semiotic analysis of college sport, as we have endeavored to do. The Web site chronicles case after case of collegiate athletic scandal and foregrounds instances where the university pursued an athlete who clearly was not academically prepared. Some of the cases addressed deal with student athletes of color, but any indication of this is avoided. Such a move is likely strategic to avoid criticisms of racism.

We do not believe that Rutgers 1000 is racist. We understand its own political constraints. Our study, however, extends the arguments it conveys about mere academic standards and budgeting. We believe that the contradictions run much deeper and are supported in untold ways by systems of racial difference, superiority, and mimicry. NCAA Division I sport *has* become largely professionalized (Zimbalist, 1999) in the context of an embodied (post)national carnival of sport, history, race, and gender. It is a system that can only be understood in the context of hegemony and relations of power, for it is clearly a system that *exploits* the bodies and cultural memories of both Euro-American and non-white Americans. Collegiate sport and the NCAA ruling body that governs it have a tremendous investment in reproducing the *ideology* of amateurism that ostensibly marks its athletic programs and athletes (Sage, 1990). NCAA Division I basketball and football, at the very least, are clearly integrated into the political economy of their professional counterparts, if nothing more than serving as de facto minor leagues. But society continually endeavors to recuperate the amateur and scholastic status of this multibillion-dollar spectacle, in part, we believe, because in so doing a unique, discursive stage is set where prevailing constructions of race—and consequent opportunities and configurations of power—can be more easily reconciled. That is, if one acknowledges perhaps that "some traces" of racism, exploitation, misappropriation, or awkward and inaccurate symbolism characterize collegiate sport, then at least it serves a good purpose, education, in the long run. The ideology of amateurism and scholasticism, highlighted by paternalistic heroes such as Bobby Knight or Joe Paterno, fails to adequately meet student athletes' personal, social, and intellectual needs for education and physical recreation.

More recently, a disparate collection of scholars and students has challenged college sports, precisely for the political economy of racial signs animating it. In the summer of 1999, the Society for the Study of Indigenous Languages of the Americas (SSILA) held a conference at the University of Illinois in conjunction with a language institute sponsored by the Linguistic Society of America. Many of the participants learned—much to their horror—only after arriving on campus that Chief Illiniwek was the symbol of the university. After devoting much of the conference to discussing the matter, the members of the SSILA approved the following resolution:

> We, the members of the Society for the Study of the Indigenous Languages of the Americas, urge the administration and trustees of the University of Illinois to replace their "Chief Illiniwek" symbol with one that does not promote inaccurate, anachronistic, and damaging stereotypes of Native American people, or indeed members of any minority group.

Sally Thomason, president-elect of the organization, moreover indicated that the SSILA would not only boycott the University of Illinois but would not hold meetings in the state until the mascot was removed. An exchange between Greg Brown, a graduate student at the University of California at Santa Barbara, in attendance at the SSILA meeting, and Richard Herman, the provost of the University of Illinois, poignantly captures the shape and tensions of many universities' investments in the racial economy of college sport (Brown, personal communication).

Brown: Is it the goal of this university to pursue knowledge, truth, and accuracy of information in all areas?

Herman: Yes it is.

Brown: Do you believe that the Chief Illiniwek symbol is an accurate representation of the Native American peoples of this country?

Herman: Well . . . in *some* aspects, yes.

Brown (and others): Oh, really? . . . Like in what aspects, for example?

Herman: Well, he wears some actual items and uh . . .

Others: Nothing he wears represents the people of this area, and he has a mishmash of things from all over the place, most of which are not authentic at all from any band or tribe.

Herman: Oh. Well, I am not an expert about these things . . . you are the experts. I recognize that, which is why I am waiting to hear what you have to say. What can we do to try to resolve this conflict since people feel strongly on both sides?

Brown: Many people here are experts. The chief's dress and actions are *not* an accurate representation of any Native American group.

Herman: Okay, what can we do to more accurately represent Native Americans?

Brown: Well, for starters, no real chief would *ever* dress up and dance around on the field at a sports event . . . this would *never* happen.

Herman: Okay.

Brown: Talk to Native American people to find out who they are. Talk to Native American people to find out how they would like to be honored and perceived.

Herman: Okay.

Brown: Thank you.

The awkward, fumbling discourse of dominance and the polite refusal to listen mark postcolonial reformulations of whiteness as much as the continuing appropriation and staging of cultural difference. Listening to others, formerly marginalized, colonized, and mimicked, is the only hope for meaningful change at the University of Illinois (and beyond).

CONCLUSION

We conclude by emphasizing that the regime of sporting spectacles of race and other similar sign commodities are the result of *productive* power, in the sense articulated by Foucault (1979, p. 119), when he wrote:

> If power were never anything but repressive, if it never did anything but say no, do you really think one would be bought to obey it? What makes power hold good, what makes it accepted, is simply the fact that it doesn't only weigh on us as a force that says no, but that it traverses and produces things, it induces pleasure, forms of knowledge, produces discourse.

These mascots produce forms of subjectivity, (post)colonial forms that systematically enjoy broader spaces of empowerment than do the subjectivities of those peoples who have experienced histories of colonization. They are creations, and as such, they are practices which, phantasmagorically, *require* destruction. Indeed, their productivity ascends on a platform of cultural terror. As Taussig (1993, p. 136) wrote, "Why make images anyway? Why embody?—so now we see that making requires unmaking, embodiment its disembodiment."

These performances of redness, whiteness, and blackness are effective as practices of postcolonial American empire, precisely because they fashion identities by appropriating the lives and works of others, incorporating and reinscribing alterity within the daily lives of citizens. It is through the body that Native Americans, African Americans, Latinos, Asian Americans, and white Americans have been unmade, only to be continually re-made. The systems of representation analyzed in this book *work* because they are emptied representations of the social histories that they pretend to incorporate that elide, even dislocate, the terror of imperial whiteness in the United States. The desire for mascots and "hard bodies" locates the American self within a space of impossibility, wherein spectators fail to recognize the uneven, historical significance of the convergence and then slippage of professional sports, the American university, scholastic athletics, the embodiment of the Indian, the predominance of the black body of African-American athletes, and the absence of Native American students and faculty. The resilience of these overly simplistic, too-tired icons of redness, whiteness, and blackness reveals how individuals and institutions reimagine, reconstruct, and recuperate imperial identities, imagined communities, invented histories, and (im)possible worlds.

Notes

CHAPTER 1

1. Native Americans are virtually absent from contemporary intercollegiate athletics. Of the 13,439 scholarship athletes in 1997, forty (or roughly 1%) were classified as American Indians. In revenue sports, they have an even smaller presence. In 1997, only 1 out of 844 male basketball scholarships and 4 out of 860 female basketball scholarships went to American Indians. Consequently, we exclude them from our discussion here.

CHAPTER 3

1. Two decades after graduating, arguing for the fair and equitable treatment of Native Americans in public culture and federal policy, Montezuma remarked (1907, p. 214), "The gentleman with whom I lived at Urbana, while attending the University of Illinois, was told 'that he had better look out for that Indian; that he was liable to be killed by him at anytime; that he must not forget that an Indian was an Indian and could never be trusted.' "

2. NASSFP members report that such information came personally from Peoria Don Giles, who will neither confirm nor deny this. In correspondence with the Peoria, however, NASSFP makes a corroborating reference to such a transaction. The president's office at the University of Illinois has refused an invitation to comment on this issue.

CHAPTER 5

1. In contrast with Duke's assertion, in actuality, African Americans comprise much closer to 50 percent of all football players.

2. We view attempts to demonstrate or prove the inherent superiority of the black athlete, or the disproportionate athletic success of any "racial" group, to be

misguided. Such scholarship often is based on a misunderstanding of the complexity of human biophysical variation (see Marks, 1995) as well as an oversimplified understanding of relative success in athletics. We direct readers to an overview of studies of sports, race, and genetics: Davis (1990), Harpalani (1998), Hoberman (1998), and Hunter (1998).

3. Elsewhere (King & Springwood, 2000; Springwood & King, 2000), we have discussed nineteenth-century efforts by the U.S. government to control, suppress, and even eliminate various forms of Native American expression, such as the Sun Dance, war dances, the Ghost Dance, and potlatch celebrations. We claimed that such efforts were driven, in part, by a colonial worldview in which the colonists feared non-Christian forms of bodily performance as dangerously sexual and transgressive.

CHAPTER 6

1. It is important to note that Colonel Reb at that time remained more of a visual logo than an embodied mascot who stood on the field. It is somewhat difficult to chronologically trace the precise existence of the mascot, played, since at least the mid-1970s, by a student wearing, atop his head, an oversized representation of Colonel Reb's face.

2. Meredith had returned to campus to give a public talk in the campus chapel. The audience, comprised of black and white students, faculty, and local residents, applauded at the conclusion of his remarks. However, a group of approximately 100 white people walked out and assembled outside to chant the Ole Miss "Hotty Totty" song, symbolic of the Jim Crow era of the Old South (Stuart, 1982).

3. Letter to Porter Fortune by John C. McLaurin, dated September 3, 1982, contained in the Fortune Papers. See also Cohodas (1997, p. 201).

4. Lawrence Lucas, a black Catholic priest who chronicles racism in the Church in his book, *Black Priest, White Church* (1970), illustrates the degree to which Irishness has become a kind of generic space of ethnic Otherness, ostensibly open to all willing to wear green, drink green beer, or wear a shamrock. He was educated in Catholic schools and recalls the awkwardness of celebrating the St. Patrick's Day holiday:

> The school kids would put on a show before their parents got stoned in
> honor of the saint. I remember how cute everybody thought I was when
> I got out on the stage with my classmates singing my fool head off about
> being proud of all Irish that was in me. And you know, after a while I
> did begin to be proud of all the Irish that was in me, or all that I would
> have liked to have been in me. . . . I was a hit on the stage in All Saints
> on Irish night. And I was proud of the attention. The little darkie with

his green tie and green carnation singing with all his might, "I'm proud of all the Irish that is in me," was quite a success. . . . The following year I asked my mother if I had to take part in Irish night—not because I saw things clearly then but out of plain embarrassment. All Mom said was, "I'm glad you asked me. I don't think it's a necessary part of going to school." That was my last star performance as the cutest little Negro Irishman or Irish Negro in All Saints history. (1970, pp. 26–28)

CHAPTER 7

1. This scene, repeated annually, is made even more ironic and poignant, be-cause the department has formally declared its opposition to Chief Illiniwek (see Farnell, 1998; King & Springwood, 2000).

2. Bernard Lefkowitz, in his book *Our Guys: The Glen Ridge Rape and the Secret Life of the Perfect Suburb* (1997), details events leading up to the gang rape of a young, mentally retarded girl by several members of the Glen Ridge (New Jersey) high school's football team. His account is important because of the way in which it clarifies the extent to which local valorization of athletic heroes can create distorted, even criminal, experiences of masculinity and general infallibility in any community, regardless of race or class.

3. Importantly, although much too late to rescue their athletic careers or scholarships, on September 24, 1993, Wyoming University held a ceremony to honor these very players (see Lapchick, 1995).

Bibliography

Addonizio, Shari. (1998). Osceola's public life: Two images of the Seminole hero. In Jehanne Teilhet-Fisk ^ Robin Franklin Nigh (Ed.), *Dimensions of Native America: The contact zone* (pp. 90–95). Tallahassee: Museum of Fine Arts, Florida State University.

Adler, Patricia, & Adler, Peter. (1990). *Backboards and blackboards: College athletics and role engulfment*. New York: Columbia University Press.

Alvord, Clarence Walworth. (Ed.). (1920). *The centennial history of Illinois*. Springfield: Illinois Centennial Commission.

Anderson, Benedict. (1983). *Imagined communities: Reflections on the origin and spread of nationalism*. London: Thetford Press Limited.

Andrews, David. (1996). The fact(s) of Michael Jordan's blackness: Excavating a floating racial signifier. *Sociology of Sport Journal, 13* (2), 125–158.

Andrews, David. (forthcoming). Just what is it that makes today's lives so different, so appealing? Commodity-sign culture, Michael Jordan, and the cybernetic postmodern body. In C. Cole, J. Loy, & M. Messner (Eds.), *Exercising power: The making and remaking of the body*. Albany: State University of New York Press.

Andrews, Vernon. (1991). *Race, culture, situation and the touchdown dance*. Master's thesis, University of Wisconsin, Madison.

Andrews, Vernon. (1996). Black bodies—White control: The contested terrain of sportsmanlike conduct. *Journal of African American Men, 2* (1), 33–59.

Andrews, Vernon. (1998.) African American player codes on celebration, taunting, and sportsmanlike conduct. In G. Sailes (Ed.), *African Americans in sport* (pp. 145–180). New Brunswick: Transaction Press.

Arnold, Oren. (1951). *Savage son*. Albuquerque: University of New Mexico Press.

Ashe, Arthur R., Jr. (1988). *A hard road to glory: A history the African-American athlete* (3 vols.) New York: Warner Books.

Bamberger, Michael. (1996, May 6). School's out. *Sports Illustrated*, 50–57.

Banks, Dennis. (1993). Tribal names and mscots in sports. *Journal of Sport and Social Issues, 17* (1), 5–8.

Bataille, Gretchen M., & Silet, Charles L. P. (1980). *The pretend Indians: Images of Native Americans in the movies.* Ames: Iowa State University Press.

Baudrillard, Jean. (1983). *Simulations.* New York: Semiotexte.

Bauxar, Joseph J. (1978). History of the Illinois area. In Bruce Trigger (Ed.), *Handbook of North American Indians, volume 15: The Northeast* (pp. 594–601). Washington, DC: Smithsonian University Press.

Berkhofer, Robert. (1979). *White man's Indian: Images of the American Indian from Columbus to the present.* New York: Vintage Books.

Bhabba, Homi. (1994). *The location of culture.* New York: Routledge.

Boling, Emily, & Gregoire, Natasha. (1997, September 27). Tuberville asks fans to think about Rebel flag. *The Daily Mississippian.*

Borchers, A. Webber. (1959). Untitled letter, University of Illinois Archives.

Bourdieu, Pierre. (1990/1980). *The logic of practice.* Stanford: Stanford University Press.

Bourdieu, Pierre, & Passeron, Jean C. (1977). *Reproduction in education, society, and culture.* Beverly Hills: Sage.

Bridges, Tyler. (1994). *The rise of David Duke.* Jackson: University Press of Mississippi.

Brooks, Dana, & Althouse, Ronald. (Eds.). (1993). *Racism in college sports: The African American experience.* Morgantown, VA: Fitness Information Technology.

Brown, Michael F. (1996). On resisting resistance. *American Anthropologist, 98* (4), 729–749.

Burford, Cary Clive. (1952). *"We're Loyal to You, Illinois": The Story of the University of Illinois Bands under Albert Austin Harding for 43 Years.* Danville, IL: The Interstate.

Butler, Mike. (1997). Confederate flags, class conflict, a golden egg, and castrated bulls: A historical examination of the Ole Miss–Mississippi State football rivalry. *The Journal of Mississippi History, 59* (2), 123–139.

Byrd, Elizabeth. (Ed.). (1996). *Dressed in feathers: The construction of the Indian in American popular culture.* Boulder: Westview.

Callender, Charles. (1978). Illinois. In Bruce Trigger (Ed.), *Handbook of North American Indians, volume 15: The Northeast* (pp. 673–680). Washington, DC: Smithsonian University Press.

Chideya, Farari. (1995). *Don't believe the hype: Fighting cultural misinformation about African Americans.* New York: Plume.

Chief Illiniwek tradition. Undated document, University of Illinois Archives.

Chief Osceola and Renegade. (1999). On-line. Available: <www.fansonly.com/cgi-bin/cframe.cgi?/fsu/trads/fsu-trads.html>

Chowder, Ken. (1993). Fight to win. Fight to live. Fight to win win, win! *Smithsonian, 24* (8), 164–177.

Churchill, Ward. (1994). Let's spread the fun around. In *Indians are us? Culture and genocide in Native North America* (pp. 65–72). Monroe, ME: Common Courage Press.

Churchill, Ward, Hill, Norbert S., & Barlow, Mary Jo. (1979). An historical overview of twentieth century Native American athletics. *The Indian Historian, 12* (4), 22–32.

Coale, Phil. (1996, November 26). FSU sports enduring symbol in Renegade and Chief Osceola. *Tallahassee Democrat*, 1B.

Cohodas, Nadine. (1997). *The band played Dixie: Race and the liberal conscience at Ole Miss*. New York: Free Press.

Cole, Cheryl L. (1996). American Jordan: P.L.A.Y., consensus, & punishment. *Sociology of Sport Journal, 13*, 366–397.

Cole, Cheryl L., & Andrews, David. (1996). Look—It's NBA show time!: Visions of race in the popular imaginary. *Cultural Studies: A Research Annual, 1*, 141–181.

Cole, Cheryl L., & Denny, H. (1995). Visualizing deviance in the post–Reagan America: Magic Johnson, AIDS, and the promiscuous world of professional sport. *Critical Sociology, 20* (3), 123–147.

Cole, Cheryl L., & King, Samantha. (1998). Representing black masculinity and urban possibilities: Racism, realism, and *Hoop Dreams*. In Genevieve Rail (Ed.), *Sport and postmodern times* (pp. 49–86). Albany: State University of New York Press.

Comaroff, John, & Comaroff, Jean. (1991). *From revelation to revolution*. Chicago: University of Chicago Press.

Confederate Underground. On-line. Available: <http://members.tripod/~cupub>

Coombe, R. J. (1999). Sports trademarks and somatic politics: Locating the law in a critical cultural studies. In R. Martin & T. Miller (Eds.), *SportCult* (pp. 262–288). Minneapolis: University of Minnesota Press.

Curtis, Russel L. Jr. (1998). Racism and rationales: A frame analysis of John Hoberman's *Darwin's athletes. Social Science Quarterly, 79* (4), 885–891.

D'Alemberte, Talbot. (1995). We honor the Seminole legend. On-line. Available: <www.fsu.edu/~fstime/FS-Times/Volume1/Issue5/legend.html>

Davis, Laurel. (1990). The articulation of difference: White preoccupation with questions of racially linked genetic differences among athletes. *Sociology of Sport Journal, 7*, 179–187.

Davis, Laurel. (1993). Protest against the use of Native American mascots: A challenge to traditional, American identity. *Journal of Sport and Social Issues, 17* (1), 9–22.

Davis, Laurel, & Harris, Othello. (1998). Race and ethnicity in U.S. sports media. In Lawrence A. Wenner (Ed.), *MediaSport* (pp. 154–169). London: Routledge.

Davis, Mike. (1992). *City of quartz: Excavating the future of Los Angeles*. New York: Random House.

Debord, Guy. (1970/1967). *Society of the spectacle*. Detroit: Black and Red.

Deloria, Phillip. (1996). I am of the body: Thoughts on my grandfather, culture, and sports. *South Atlantic Quarterly, 95* (2), 321–338.

Deloria, Phillip. (1998). *Playing Indian*. New Haven, CT: Yale University Press.

Delsohn, Steve. (1998). *Talking Irish: The oral history of Notre Dame football*. New York: Avon Books.

Denzin, Norman. (1996). More rare air: Michael Jordan on Michael Jordan. *Sociology of Sport Journal, 13*, 319–324.

Dippie, Brian W. (1982). *The vanishing American: White attitudes and U.S. Indian policy*. Wesleyan University Press.

Dixon, Joseph K. (1972/1913). *The vanishing race: The last great Indian council*. New York: Popular Library.

Donaldson, Thomas. (1886). The George Catlin Indian gallery in the U.S. National Museum. *Annual report of the Board of Regents of the Smithsonian Institution* (pp. 1–93). Washington, DC: Smithsonian Institution Press.

Doyle, Andrew. (1996). Bear Bryant: Symbol for an embattled South. *Colby Quarterly, 2* (1), 72–86.

Duke, David. (2000). Tiger Woods, race, and professional sports. [essay posted on Web site, 2/14/00]: <http://www.Duke.org/writings/tigerwoods.html>

Duke, David, with Whitney, Glayde. (1998). *My awakening: A path to racial understanding*. Louisiana: Free Speech Books.

Dyson, M. Eric. (1993). Be like Mike: Michael Jordan and the pedagogy of desire. *Cultural Studies, 7* (1), 64–72.

Dyson, M. Eric. (1998). Giving whiteness a black eye. In Joe L. Kincheloe, Shirley R. Steinberg, Nelson M. Rodriguez, & Ronald E. Chennault (Eds.), *White reign: Deploying whiteness in America* (pp. 299–328). New York: St. Martin's Press.

Early, Gerald. (1994). Collecting the artificial nigger: Race and American material culture. In *The culture of bruising* (pp. 155–162). Hopewell, NJ: Ecco Press.

Edwards, Harry. (1969). *The revolt of the black athlete*. New York: Free Press.

Edwards, Harry. (1984). The collegiate athletic arms race: Origins and implications of the rule 48 controversy. *Journal of Sport and Social Issues, 8*, 4–22.

Eitzen, D. Stanley. (1999). *Fair and foul: Beyond the myths and paradoxes of sport*. Lanham, MD: Rowman and Littlefield.

Ensley, Gerald. (1997, November 1). Sammy Seminole: A step closer to Osceola. *Tallahassee Democrat*, 11E.

Entine, Jon. (2000). *Taboo: Why black athletes dominate sports and why we're afraid to talk about it*. New York: PublicAffairs.

Everybody plays, 1997–1998 visitor program. (no date). South Bend, College Football Hall of Fame.

Ewers, John. (1965). The emergence of the Plains Indian as the symbol of the North American Indian. *Annual report of the Board of Regents of the Smithsonian Institution* (pp. 531–544). Washington, DC: Smithsonian Institution Press.

Fanon, Frantz. (1968/1952). *Black skin, white masks*. New York: Grove Press.

Farnell, Brenda. (1998). Retire the chief. *Anthropology Newsletter, 39* (4), 1, 4.

Feinstein, John. (1998). *A march to madness: The view from the floor in the Atlantic Coast conference*. New York: Little Brown and Company.

Feldman, Allen. (1994). On cultural anesthesia: From Desert Storm to Rodney King. *American Ethnologist, 21* (2), 404–418.

The final four. (1989, March 20). [Special advertising section]. *Sports Illustrated*.

Fiske, John. (1993). *Power plays, power works*. London: Verso.

Fitzpatrick, Frank. (1999). *And the walls came tumbling down: Kentucky, Texas Western, and the game that changed American sports*. New York: Simon & Schuster.

Foucault, Michel. (1979). *Discipline and punish: The birth of the prison*. New York: Vintage.

Foucault, Michel. (1981). *The history of sexuality: Introduction*. Harmondsworth, England: Penguin Books.

Foucault, Michel. (1987). *The uses of pleasure*. Harmondsworth, England: Penguin Books.

Frankenberg, Ruth, & Mani, Lata. (1993). Crosscurrents, crosstalk: Race, postcoloniality, and the politics of location. *Cultural Studies, 7*, 292–310.

Franks, Ray. (1982). *What's in a nickname? Exploring the jungle of college athletic mascots*. Amarillo: Ray Franks Publishing Ranch.

Frazier, J. (1997). Tomahawkin' the Redskins: Indian images in sports and commerce. In D. Morrison (Ed.), *American Indian studies: An interdisciplinary approach to contemporary issues* (pp. 337–346). New York: Peter Lang.

Funk, Gary D. (1991). *Major violation: The unbalanced priorities in athletics and academics*. Champaign, IL: Leisure Press.

Gay, Geneva, & Baber, Williw L. (Eds.). (1987). *Expressively black: The cultural basis of ethnic identity*. New York: Praeger.

Gems, Gerald R. (1998). The construction, negotiation, and transformation of racial identity in American football: A study of Native and African Americans. *American Indian Culture and Research Journal, 22* (2), 131–150.

George, Nelson. (1998). *Hip-hop America*. New York: Penguin Books.

Giroux, Henry. (1992). *Reading ads critically*. London: Routledge.

Giroux, Henry. (1997). White squall: Resistance and the pedagogy of whiteness. *Cultural Studies, 11* (3), 376–389.

Goldman, Robert, & Popson, Stephen. (1998). *Nike culture*. Thousand Oaks, CA: Sage.

Gone, Joseph P. (1994). The contextual evaluation of a symbol. In *Media information packet: Native American students, staff and faculty for progress*. Urbana, IL.

Gone, Joseph P. (1995). Chief Illiniwek: Dignified or damaging? In *Media information packet: Native American students, staff and faculty for progress*. Urbana, IL.

Gould, Stephen Jay. (1996/1981). *The mismeasure of man* (2nd ed.). New York: W. W. Norton and Company.

Gramsci, Antonio. (1971). *Selections from the prison notebooks of Antonio Gramsci*. New York: International Publishers.

Gray, H. (1989). Television, black Americans, and the American dream. *Critical Studies in Mass Communication, 6,* 376–386.

Green, Michael K. (1993). Images of Native Americans in advertising: Some moral issues. *Journal of Business Ethics, 12,* 323–330.

Green, Rayna. (1988). The tribe called Wannabee: Playing Indian in America and Europe. *Folklore, 99,* 30–55.

Grossberg, Lawrence. (1992). *We gotta get out of this place: Popular conservatism and postmodern culture*. New York: Routledge.

Hale, Grace Elizabeth. (1998). *Making whiteness: The culture of segregation in the South, 1890–1940*. New York: Pantheon.

Hall, Stuart. (1981). Notes on deconstructing the popular. In R. Samuel (Ed.), *People's history and socialist theory* (pp. 227–240). London: Routledge and Kegan Paul.

Hall, Stuart. (1985). Gramsci's relevance for the study of race and ethnicity. *Journal of Communication Inquiry, 10* (2), 5–27.

Hall, Stuart. (1980). Race, articulation and societies structured in dominance. In *UNESCO, sociological theories: Race and colonialism*. Paris: UNESCO, pp. 305–345.

Hall, Stuart. (1991). Old and new identities, old and new ethnicities. In Anthony D. King (Ed.), *Culture, globalization, and the world system* (pgs. 41–68). London: Macmillan.

Harpalani, Vinay. (1998). The athletic dominance of African Americans—Is there a genetic basis? In G. Sailes (Ed.), *African Americans in sport* (pp. 103–120). New Brunswick, NJ: Transaction Press.

Hartung, Ron. (1998, October 15). Welcome back, men of '46, and please note. *Tallahassee Democrat*, 1C.

Hauser, Raymond. (1973). *An ethnohistory of the Illinois Indian Tribe, 1673–1832*. Microfiche, University of Illinois.

Hawkins, Billy. (1995/1996). The black student athlete: The colonized black body. *Journal of African American Men, 1* (3), 23–35.

Haworth, Karla. (1998, November 20). Graduation rates fall for athletes. *Chronicle for Higher Education*, A41–A43.

Hesburgh, Theodore M. (1990). *God, country, Notre Dame*. New York: Doubleday.

Hill, Lance. (1992). Nazi race doctrine in the political thought of David Duke. In Douglas D. Rose (Ed.), *The emergence of David Duke and the politics of race* (pp. 94–111). Chapel Hill: University of North Carolina Press.

Hoberman, John. (1997). *Darwin's athletes: How sport has damaged black America and preserved the myth of race*. Boston: Houghton Mifflin Co.

Hofer, Susan. (1994). Group formation in the marching Illini. Unpublished manuscript.

hooks, bell. (1995). Dreams of conquest. *Sight and Sound, 5* (4), 22–23.

Horsman, Reginald. (1981). *Race and manifest destiny: The origins of American racial Anglo-Saxonism*. Cambridge: Harvard University Press.

Hoxie, Frederick E. (1979). Red man's burden. *Antioch Review, 37*, 326–342.

Huhndorf, Shari. (1997). Playing Indian, past and present. In William S. Penn (Ed.), *As we are now: Mixed blood essays on race and identity* (pp. 181–198). Berkeley: University of California Press.

Hunter, David W. (1998). Race and athletic performance: A physiological review. In G. Sailes (Ed.), *African Americans in sport* (pp. 103–120). New Brunswick, NJ: Transaction Press.

Hurd, Michael. (1992, March 31). Knight needs to apologize. *USA Today*, 6C.

Ignatiev, Noel. (1995). *How the Irish became white*. New York: Routledge.

An Illinois illustrated newsfeature. Undated press release, University of Illinois Archives.

Iverson, Peter. (1982). *Carlos Montezuma and the changing world of American Indians*. Albuquerque: University of New Mexico Press.

Jackson, Eileen M. (1993). Whiting-out difference: Why nursing research fails black families. *Medical Anthropology Quarterly, 7* (4), 363–385.

Jameson, Fredric. (1991). *Postmodernism, or, the logic of late capitalism*. Durham, NC: Duke University Press.

Jones, James M. (1986). Racism: A cultural analysis of the problem. In John Dovidio & Samuel Gaertner (Eds.), *Prejudice, discrimination, and racism*. San Diego: Academic Press.

Kaplan, Amy. (1993). Black and blue on San Jaun Hill. In A. Kaplan & D. E. Pease (Eds.), *Cultures of United States imperialism* (pp. 219–236). Durham, NC: Duke University Press.

Kellner, Douglas. (1995). *Media culture: Cultural studies, identity and politics between modern and postmodern.* New York: Routledge.

Kellner, Douglas. (1996). Sports, media culture, and race—Some reflections on Michael Jordan. *Sociology of Sport Journal, 13,* 458–467.

Kimmel, Michael. (1996). *Manhood in America: A cultural history.* New York: Free Press.

King, C. Richard. (1998). *Colonial discourses, collective memories and the exhibition of Native American cultures and histories in the contemporary United States.* New York: Garland Press.

King, C. Richard. (Ed.) (2000). *Postcolonial America.* Urbana: University of Illinois Press.

King, C. Richard. (2001). Uneasy Indians: Creating and contesting Native American mascots at Marquette University. In C. R. King & C. F. Springwood (Eds.), *Team spirits: The history and significance of Native American mascots.* Lincoln: University of Nebraska Press.

King, C. Richard, & Springwood, Charles Fruehling. (1999). Playing Indian, power, and racial identity in American sport: Gerald R. Gems The construction, negotiation, and transformation of racial identity in American football. *American Indian Culture and Research Journal, 23* (2), 127–132.

King, C. Richard, & Springwood, Charles Fruehling. (2000). Choreographing colonialism: Athletic mascots, (dis)embodied Indians, and Euro-American subjectivities. *Cultural studies: A research annual.* Stamford, CT: JAI Press.

King, C. Richard, & Springwood, Charles Fruehling. (Eds.). (2001). Norman Denzin, ed. *Team spirits: Essays on the history and significance of Native American mascots.* Lincoln: University of Nebraska Press.

Kornbluth, J. (1995, April 22). Here comes Mr. Jordan. *TV Guide,* 22–26.

LaFeber, Walter. (1999). *Michael Jordan and the new global capitalism.* New York: W. W. Norton & Company.

Lapchick, Richard. (1991). *Five minutes to midnight: Race and sport in the 1990s.* Lanham, MD: Madison Books.

Lapchick, Richard. (1995). Race and college sport: A long way to go. *Race & Class, 36* (4), 87–94.

Ledbetter, James. (1992, September 1). Imitation of life. *Vibe,* 112–114.

Lefkowitz, Bernard. (1997). *Our guys: The Glen Ridge rape and the secret life of the perfect suburb.* New York: Vintage Books.

Legislature: Senate votes to put Seminole name into law. (1999, May 1). *Naples Daily News,* 1A.

Levin, Michael. (1997). *Why race matters*. Westport, CT: Praeger.

Lévi-Strauss, Claude. (1963). *Totemism*. Boston: Beacon Press.

Lewis, Richard Jr. (1995). Racial position segregation: A case study of Southwest Conference Football, 1978 and 1989. *Journal of Black Studies, 25* (4), 431–446.

Lick, Dale W. (1993). Seminoles—Heroic Symbol of Florida State University. On-line. Available: <www.fansonly.com/cgi-bin/cframe.cgi?/fsu/trads/fsu-trads-seminoles.html>

Lindstrom, Andy. (1982, September 19). Artist, FSU boosters at peace after savage same war. *Tallahassee Democrat*, 1A.

Lipsitz, George. (1998). *The possessive investment in whiteness: How white people profit from identity politics*. Philadelphia: Temple University Press.

Lott, Eric. (1993). *Love and theft: Blackface minstrelsy and the American working class*. New York: Oxford University Press

Lott, Tommy. (1999). *The invention of race: Black culture and the politics of representation*. Malden, MA: Blackwell Publishers.

Lubiano, Wahneema. (1992). Black ladies, welfare queens, and state minstrels: Ideological war by narrative means. In Toni Morrison (Ed.), *Race-ing justice, en-gendering power: Essays on Anita Hill, Clarence Thomas, and the construction of social reality* (pp. 323–363). New York: Random House.

Lucas, Lawrence. (1970). *Black priest, white church*. New York: Random House.

Lyotard, Jean-Francois. (1984/1979). *The postmodern condition: A report on knowledge*. Minneapolis: University of Minnesota Press.

Majors, Richard. (1998). Cool pose: Black masculinity and sports. In G. Sailes (Ed.), *African Americans in sport* (pp. 15–22). New Brunswick, NJ: Transaction.

Manring, M. M. (1998). *Slave in a box: The strange career of Aunt Jemima*. Charlottesville: University Press of Virginia.

Marcello, Ronald E. (1996). The integration intercollegiate athletics in Texas: North Texas State College as a test case, 1956. *Southwestern Historical Quarterly, 100* (4), 153–186.

Marks, Jonathan. (1995). *Human biodiversity: Genes, racism and history*. New York: Aldine de Gruyter.

Martin, Joel. (1996). My grandmother was a Cherokee princess: Representations of Indians in Southern history. In S. Elizabeth Bird (Ed.), *Dressing in feathers: The construction of the Indian in American popular culture* (pp. 129–147). Boulder: Westview Press.

Massa, Mark S. (1999). *Catholics and American culture: Fulton Sheen, Dorothy Day, and the Notre Dame football team*. New York: Crossroad Publishing Company.

McCarthy, Cameron. (1993). After the canon: Knowledge and ideological representation in the multicultural discourse on curriculum reform. In C. McCarthy

& W. Crichlow (Eds.), *Race, identity, and representation in education* (pp. 289–305). New York: Routledge.

McCarthy, Cameron. (1998). Living with anxiety: Race and the renarration of public life. In J. L. Kincheloe, S. Steinberg, N. Rodriguez, & R. Chennault (Eds.), *White reign: Deploying whiteness in America* (pp. 329–341). New York: St. Martin's Press.

McGrotha, Bill. (1987). *Seminoles!: The first forty years.* Tallahassee: Tallahassee Democrat.

McLaren, Peter. (1998). Whiteness is . . . the struggle for postcolonial hybridity. In J. L. Kincheloe, S. Steinberg, N. Rodriguez, & R. Chennault (Eds.), *White reign: Deploying whiteness in America* (pp. 63–75). New York: St. Martin's Press.

McReynolds, Edwin C. (1957). *The Seminoles.* Norman: University of Oklahoma Press.

Mechling, Jay. (1980). Playing Indian and the search for authenticity in modern white America. *Prospects, 5,* 17–33.

Mechling, Jay. (1996). Florida Seminoles and the marketing of the last frontier. In S. Elizabeth Bird (Ed.), *Dressing in feathers: The construction of the Indian in American popular culture* (pp. 149–166). Boulder: Westview Press.

Mellinger, Wayne, & Beaulieu, Rodney. (1997). White fantasies, black bodies: Racial power, disgust and desire in American popular culture. *Visual Anthropology, 9,* 117–147.

Mercer, Kobena. (1994). *Welcome to the jungle: New positions in black cultural studies.* London: Routledge.

Messner, Michael, & Don Sabo. (Eds.). (1990). *Sport, men, and the gender order: Critical feminist perspectives.* Champaign, IL: Human Kinetics Publishers.

Messner, Michael, & Sabo, Don. (1994). *Sex, violence, and power in sports: Rethinking masculinity.* Freedom, CA: The Crossing Press.

Michelson, Truman. (1916). Report on the Peoria Indians. Unpublished field report, Illinois State Archives.

Michener, James. (1976). *Sports in America.* New York: Random House.

Midol, Nancy. (1998). Rap and dialectical relations: Culture, subculture, power, and counter-power. In Genevieve Rail (Ed.), *Sport and postmodern times* (pp. 333–343). Albany: State University of New York Press.

Milanich, Jerald T. (1998). *Florida's Indians from ancient times to the present.* Gainesville: University Press of Florida.

Montville, Leigh. (1998, August 3). Golden boy. *Sports Illustrated.*

Montezuma, Carlos. (1888). The Indian of yesterday: The early life of Dr. Carlos Montezuma as written by himself. In John William Larner, Jr. (Ed.), *The papers of Carlos Montezuma* (Reel 5). Wilmington: Scholarly Resources.

Montezuma, Carlos. (1907). The government, the public, and the American Indian. *Alumni Quarterly of the University of Illinois, 1* (4), 213–222.

Montezuma, Carlos. (1921). Indian impostors. *Wassaja, 5* (10), 3–4.

Moore, Sally, & Myerhoff, Barbara G. (Eds.). (1977). *Secular ritual.* Amsterdam, Netherlands: Van Gorcum.

Moore, William V. (1992). David Duke: The white knight. In Douglas D. Rose (Ed.), *The emergence of David Duke and the politics of race* (pp. 41–58). Chapel Hill: University of North Carolina Press.

(NASSFP) Native American students, staff and faculty for progress. (1994). Media information packet. Urbana, IL.

NCAA Hall of Champions. (No date). Brochure.

Nelson, George. (1997). *Hip hop America.* New York: Penguin Books.

O'Connell, Daniel E. (1971, January 28). Unpublished letter to *The Milwaukee Journal.*

Ole Miss. (1927). University Yearbook, University of Mississippi Archives.

Ole Miss refuses to denounce the symbols of slavery and Jim Crow. (1997/1998). *The Journal of Blacks in Higher Education, 18,* 62–64.

Olsen, Jack. (1968, July 15). In an alien world. *Sports Illustrated,* 28–37.

Omi, Michael. (1997). In living color: Race and American culture. In Sonia Maasik & Jack Solomon (Eds.), *Signs of life in the U.S.A.: Readings on popular culture for writers* (2nd ed.) (pp. 491–503). Boston: Bedford Books.

O'Neill, William. (1995, February 13–27). In the name of diversity: Political correctness at Rutgers. *The New Leader,* 11–14.

Oriard, Michael. (1993). *Reading football.* Chapel Hill: University of North Carolina Press.

Oxendine, Joseph B. (1995). *American Indian sports heritage* (2nd ed.). Lincoln: University of Nebraska Press.

Palcic, James Louis. (1979). *The history of the Black Student Union at Florida State University, 1968–1978.* Unpublished doctoral dissertation, Florida State University, Tallahassee.

Palumbo-Liu, David (1997). Introduction: Unhabituted habituses. In D. Palumbo-Liu & H. U. Gumbrecht (Eds.), *Streams of cultural capital: Transnational cultural studies* (pp. 1–21). Stanford: Stanford University Press.

Perdue, Theda. (1992). Osceola: The white man's Indian. *Florida Historical Quarterly, 70* (4), 475–488.

Pewewardy, Cornel D. (1991). Native American mascots and imagery: The struggle of unlearning Indian stereotypes. *Journal of Navaho Education, 9* (1), 19–23.

Phillip, Mary-Christine. (1992). Rev. Theodore M. Hesburgh: Notre Dame's elder statesman speaks out on religion, racism, and education. *Black Issues in Higher Education, 9* (19), 8–12.

Pieterse, Jan Nederveen. (1992). *White on black: Images of Africa and blacks in western popular culture.* New Haven, CT: Yale University Press.

Pratt, Richard H. (1964). *Battlefield and classroom: Four decades with the American Indian, 1867–1904.* New Haven, CT: Yale University Press.

Price, S. L. (1997, August 12). Whatever happened to the white athlete. *Sports Illustrated*, 30–46.

Prochaska, David. (2001). At home in Illinois: Presence of Chief Illiniwek, absence of Native Americans. In C. R. King & C. F. Springwood (Eds.), *Team spirits: Essays on the history and significance of Native American mascots.* Lincoln: University of Nebraska Press.

Rail, Genevieve. (1998). Seismography of the postmodern condition: Three theses on the implosion of sport. In Genevieve Rail (Ed.), *Sport and postmodern times* (pp. 143–161). Albany: State University of New York Press.

Reeves, J. L., & Campbell, R. (1994). *Cracked coverage: Television news, the anti-cocaine crusade, and the Reagan legacy.* Durham, NC: Duke University Press.

Riess, Steve A. (1990). Professional sports as an avenue of social mobility in America: Some myths and realities. In Donald G. Kirk & Gary D. Stark (Eds.), *Essays on sports history and sports mythology* (pp. 83–117). College Station: Texas A&M Press.

Rinehart, Robert E. (1998). *Players all: Performances in contemporary sport.* Bloomington: Indiana University Press.

Robbins, Bruce. (1997). Mentorship and mobility in *Hoop Dreams. Social Text, 50*, 111–120.

Roediger, David. (1991). *Wages of whiteness: Race and the making of the American working class.* London: Verso.

Roediger, David. (1995). *Guineas, wiggers*, and the dramas of racialized culture. *American Literary History, 7*, 654–668.

Rogin, Michael. (1993). Make my day! Spectacle as amnesia in imperial politics. In Amy Kaplan & Donald E. Pease (Eds.), *Cultures or United States imperialism* (pp. 499–534). Durham, NC: Duke University Press.

Root, Deborah. (1996). *Cannibal culture: Art, appropriation, and the commodification of difference.* Boulder: Westview.

Rosaldo, Renato. (1989). *Culture and truth.* Boston: Beacon Press.

Rosenstein, Jay. (2000). In whose honor? Mascots and the media. In C. R. King & C. F. Springwood (Eds.), *Team spirits: Essays on the history and significance of Native American mascots.* Lincoln: University of Nebraska Press.

Rutgers 1000. Organizational Web site: <http://members.aol.com/rutg1000/colonial.htm>

Rutland, Jannetta. (1970, October 12). Indians upset over name of spirit chief. *The Florida Flambeau*, 1.

Sack, Allen J., & Staurowsky, Ellen J. (1998). *College athletes for hire: The evolution of the NCAA's amateur myth*. Westport, CT: Praeger.

Sack, Kevin. (1997, March 11). Old South's symbols stir a campus. *The New York Times*, 14A.

Sage, George H. (1990). *Power and sport in American sport: A critical perspective*. Champaign, IL: Human Kinetics Publishers.

Sandell, Jillian. (1995). Out of the ghetto and into the marketplace: *Hoop Dreams* and the commodification of marginality. *Socialist Review, 25* (2), 57–82.

Sansing, David G. (1999). *The University of Mississippi: A sesquicentennial history*. Jackson: University of Mississippi Press.

Sattler, Richard A. (1996). Remnants, renegades, and runaways: Seminole ethnogenesis reconsidered. In Jonathan D. Hill (Ed.), *History, power, and identity: Ethnogenesis in the Americas, 1492–1992* (pp. 36–69). Iowa City: University of Iowa Press.

Segal, Charles M., & Stineback, David C. (1977). *Puritans, Indians, and manifest destiny*. New York: G. P. Putnam's Sons.

Seton, Ernest Thompson. (1926). *The book of woodcraft and Indian lore*. Garden City, NY: Doubleday, Page & Co.

Shropshire, Kenneth L. (1996). *In black and white: Race and sports in America*. New York: New York University Press.

Slowikowski, Synthia Sydnor. (1993) Cultural performances and sports mascots. *Journal of Sport and Social Issues, 17* (1), 23–33.

Smedley, Audrey. (1993). *Race in North America: Origin and evolution of a worldview*. Boulder: Westview.

Smith, Earl. (1993). Race, sport, and the American university. *Journal of Sport and Social Issues, 17* (3), 206–212.

Smith, Earl. (1995). Hope via basketball: The ticket out of the ghetto. *Journal of Sport and Social Issues, 19* (3), 312–329.

Smith, Earl, & Harrison, C. Keith. (1998). Stacking in major league baseball. In Gary A. Sailes (Ed.), *African Americans in sport* (pp. 199–216). New Brunswick, NJ: Transaction.

The sound, the fury. (1996, December 16). *Sports Illustrated*, 22.

Sperber, Murray. (1990). *College sports, inc.: The athletic department vs. the university*. New York: Henry Holt.

Sperber, Murray. (1993). *Bring down the thunder: The creation of Notre Dame football*. New York: Henry Holt.

Spindel, Carol. (1997). We honor your memory: Chief Illiniwek of the halftime Illini. *Crab Orchard Review, 3* (1), 217–238.

Spivey, Donald. (1988). End Jim Crow in sports: The protest at New York University, 1940–1941. *Journal of Sport History, 15* (3), 282–303.

Spivey, Donald, & Jones, Thomas A. (1983). Intercollegiate athletic servitude: A case study of the black Illini student athletes, 1931–1967. *Social Science Quarterly, 55,* 939–947.

Springwood, Charles Fruehling. (1996). *Cooperstown to Dyersville: A geography of baseball*. Boulder: Westview.

Springwood, Charles Fruehling. (2001). Playing Indian and fighting (for) mascots: Reading the complications of Native American and Euro-American alliances. In C. R. King & C. F. Springwood (Eds.), *Team spirits: Essays on the history and significance of Native American mascots*. Lincoln: University of Nebraska Press.

Springwood, Charles Fruehling, & King, C. Richard. (2000). Race, power, and representation in contemporary American sport. In P. Kivisto & G. Rundblad (Eds.), *The color line at the dawn of the 21st century*. Thousand Oaks, CA: Pine Valley Press.

Springwood, Charles Fruehling, & King, C. Richard. (forthcoming). Race, ritual, and remembrance embodied: Manifest destiny and the symbolic sacrifice of Chief Illiniwek. In C. Cole, J. Loy, & M. Messner (Eds.), *Exercising power: The making and re-making of the body*. Albany: State University of New York Press.

Stacey, Jack. (1970, October 14). Basketball chief chooses Yahola as Indian name. *The Florida Flambeau*, 1.

Staurowsky, E. J. (1998). An act of honor or exploitation? The Cleveland Indians' use of the Louis Francis Sockalexis story. *Sociology of Sport Journal, 15* (4), 299–316.

Stick the ban. On-line. Available: <http://www.nationalist.org/docs/history/stick.html>

Stratton, Jon. (2000). Postcoloniality, race, and the land of new promise. In C. Richard King (Ed.), *Postcolonial America*. Urbana: University of Illinois Press.

Stuart, Reginald. (1982, October 3). 20 years after admitting Meredith, Ole Miss merges with its old and new images. *The New York Times*, 28A.

Sturtevant, William C. (1971). Creek into Seminole. In Eleanor B. Leacock & Nancy O. Lurie (Eds.), *North American Indians in historical perspective* (pp. 92–128). New York: Random House.

Suggs, Welch. (1999, May 14). A color line for the grid iron? *Chronicle of Higher Education*, A59–A60.

Takaki, Ronald. (1993). *A different mirror: A history of multicultural America.* Boston: Little, Brown and Company.

Tate, Greg. (1992, September 1). The sound and the fury. *Vibe*, 15.

Taussig, Michael. (1993). *Mimesis and alterity: A particular history of the senses.* New York: Routledge.

Testerman, Jeff. (1998, October 13). Chief speaks on tribe's past, future. *St. Petersburg Times*, 1B.

There was a time. On-line. Available: <www.southerninitiative.com/olemiss.htm>

Tibbetts, Dennis. (1993). Minstrel show. In *Media information packet: Native American students, staff and faculty for progress.* Urbana, IL.

Turner, Patricia. (1993). *I heard it through the grapevine: Rumor in African-American culture.* Berkeley: University of California Press.

Turner, Patricia A. (1994). *Ceramic uncles and celluloid mammies: Black images and their influence on culture.* New York: Anchor Books.

Turner, Victor W. (1978). *The ritual process.* Harmondsworth, England: Penguin.

Vanderford, H. (1996). What's in a name? Heritage or hatred: The school mascot controversy. *Journal of Law and Education, 25*, 381–388.

Vescey, George. (1970). *Harlem Globetrotters.* New York: Scholastic Book Services.

Wenner, L. (1993). The real red face of sports. *The Journal of Sport and Social Issues, 17* (1), 1–4.

West, Patsy. (1981). The Miami Indian attractions: A history and analysis of a transitional Mikasuli Seminole environment. *Florida Anthropologist, 34* (4), 200–224.

Wheat, Jack. (1993, December 19). Graduate is Seminole by birth—and by FSU diploma. *Tallahassee Democrat*, 1B.

White, Shane, & White, Graham. (1998). *Stylin': African American expressive culture from its beginnings to the zoot suit.* Ithaca, NY: Cornell University Press.

Whitley, David. (1999, April 21). Noles facing politically correct times. *The Tampa Tribune* [sports section] 1.

Wickman, Patricia R. (1991). *Osceola's legacy.* Tuscaloosa: University of Alabama Press.

Wideman, J. E. (1990, November). Michael Jordan leaps the great divide. *Esquire*, 140–145, 210–216.

Wieberg, Steve. (1992, April 2). Stage set for knight's act in final four. *USA Today*, 10C.

Wiegman, Robin. (1995). *American anatomies: Theorizing race and gender.* Durham, NC: Duke University Press.

Wiggins, David. (1997). *Glory bound: Black athletes in a white America*. Syracuse: Syracuse University Press.

Wojcieszak, Doug. (1995, July 31). Controversy over Chief Illiniwek gets better by the minute. *Daily Illini*, 3.

Wonsek, Pamela L. (1992). College basketball on television: A study of racism in the media. *Media, Culture, and Society, 14*, 449–461.

Workman, Bill. (1997, October 15). Third apology for Stanford band antics. *The San Francisco Chronicle*, A13.

Wright, J. Leitch, Jr. (1986). *Creeks and Seminoles: The destruction and regeneration of the Muscogulge people*. Lincoln: University of Nebraska Press.

Yaeger, Don, & Looney, Douglas S. (1993). *Under the tarnished dome: How Notre Dame betrayed its ideals for football glory*. New York: Simon and Schuster.

Yetman, Norman R., & Berghorn, Forrest J. (1993). Racial participation and integration in intercollegiate basketball: A longitudinal perspective. *Sociology of Sport Journal, 10*, 301–314.

Young, Robert C. (1995). *Colonial desire: Hybridity in theory, culture and race*. New York: Routledge.

Zimbalist, Andrew. (1999). Unpaid professionals: Commercialism and conflict in big-time college sports. Princeton: Princeton University Press.

Index

Adams, George, 46
Addonizio, Shari, 76, 81, 82
Adler, Patricia, 5
Adler, Peter, 5
Affirmative action, 99
African Americans: absence as mascots, 4; as animalistic, 115, 116; athletic scholarships and, 9–10; as center of sports industry, 103, 181*n1*; commodification of, 111, 159; confinement to playing field, 93; criminality and, 107, 116; dehumanization of, 103, 114, 115, 119; as deviant, 117, 119; discourse on, 104; disempowerment of, 128; domination of sports by, 29, 181*n1*; entry into college sports, 17; Euro-American idioms and, 101; exaggerations of, 104; exploitation of, 31, 36, 159; former exclusion from sport, 4; graduation rates, 10, 170; hypersexualization of bodies of, 104, 107, 117, 118; idealized images of, 92; interracial dating and, 117, 118; lack of progress beyond athlete role, 31; marginalization of, 29; media representations of, 116–117, 120, 121; mimicry of, 102, 104; need for discipline, 122; Negro-ape metaphor and, 115, 116; as object of longing, 104; perceived athletic superiority of, 112, 181*n2*; perseverance and cre-
ation of universities, 26; physiological features of, 10, 11; policing of style of, 122–125, 161; positions of authority and, 10, 29, 96; predominance as athletes, 101; as professional athletes, 10; racialization of, 111; recruitment by universities, 103; in revenue sports, 10; romantic readings of, 102; "stacking" and, 10–11; stereotypes of, 11, 13, 96, 104, 106, 107; in student body, 10; supposed inferiority of, 99
Agee, Arthur, 35–39, 167
Agency, 164–169
Alligator (Seminole), 79
American Dream, 34, 35, 37
American Indian Fellowship, 82
American Indian Movement, 62, 68
Anderson, Benedict, 54
Andrews, David, 12, 103, 109, 114, 116, 161, 162
Andrews, Gail, 95
Andrews, Vernon, 5, 103, 114, 123, 125
Apalachi Tribe, 78
Ashe, Arthur, 18
Auburn University, 86
Aunt Jemima, 16, 105

Bamberger, Michael, 121
Banks, Dennis, 45
Barkley, Charles, 112–114
Barrett, Richard, 140